THE LITERARY FUNCTION OF
POSSESSIONS IN LUKE-ACTS

by

Luke Timothy Johnson

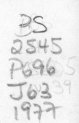
Published by
SCHOLARS PRESS
for
The Society of Biblical Literature

Distributed by

SCHOLARS PRESS
Missoula, Montana 59806

THE LITERARY FUNCTION OF POSSESSIONS IN LUKE-ACTS

by
Luke Timothy Johnson

Library of Congress Cataloging in Publication Data
Johnson, Luke Timothy.
    The literary function of possessions in Luke-Acts.

    (Society of Biblical Literature dissertation series ;
no. 39 ISSN 0145-2770)
    Originally presented as the author's thesis, Yale,
1976.
    Bibliography: p.
    1. Property—Biblical teaching. 2. Bible, N.T. Luke
and Acts—Criticism, interpretation. etc. I. Title. II.
Series: Society of Biblical Literature. Dissertation
series ; no. 39.
BS2545.P696J63   226'.4'06   77-21055
ISBN 0-89130-200-X

Printed in the United States of America
1 2 3 4 5

5562 UM Printing Services

TABLE OF CONTENTS

ABBREVIATIONS

Beginnings
F. J. Foakes-Jackson and K. Lake, eds. The Beginnings of Christianity Part I The Acts of the Apostles.
  Vol. I Prolegomena I: The Jewish, Gentile and Christian Backgrounds (London: Macmillan and Co., 1920).
  Vol. II Prolegomena II: Criticism (London: Macmillan and Co., 1922).

Ropes
  Vol. III The Text of Acts. Ed. by James Ropes (London: Macmillan and Co., 1926).

Lake-Cadbury
  Vol. IV English Translation and Commentary. Ed. by Kirsopp Lake and Henry J. Cadbury (London: Macmillan and Co., 1933).
  Vol. V Additional Notes to the Commentary. Ed. by Kirsopp Lake and Henry J. Cadbury (London: Macmillan and Co., 1933).

Dibelius
Martin Dibelius, Studies in the Acts of the Apostles. Trans. by Mary Ling (London: SCM, 1956).

Dupont, Beatitudes
Jacques Dupont, Les Béatitudes.
  Vol. I Le problème littéraire--les deux versions du Sermon sur la montagne et des Béatitudes. 2nd ed. (Louvain: E. Nauwelaerts, 1958).
  Vol. II La Bonne Nouvelle (Paris: J. Gabalda, 1969).
  Vol. III Les Evangelistes (Paris: J. Gabalda, 1973).

Dupont, Etudes
Jacques Dupont, Etudes sur les Actes des Apôtres (Lectio Divina 45; Paris: Editions du Cerf, 1967).

Haenchen
Ernst Haenchen, The Acts of the Apostles. Trans. by B. Noble et al. from Die Apostelgeschichte. 14th ed. [Meyer; Göttingen: Vandenhoeck and Ruprecht, 1965], (Philadelphia: Westminster, 1971).

Recueil
Recueil Lucien Cerfaux. 2 vols. (Biblioteca Ephemeridum Theologicarum Lovaniensium VI-VII; Gembloux: J. Duculot, 1954).

SLA   Leander Keck and J. Louis Martyn, eds.
            Studies in Luke-Acts (Nashville:
            Abingdon, 1966).

Bibliographic references will be given fully for other works in
their first citation; thereafter, works will be referred to by
author's name and (when author is represented by more than one
work and when clarity seems to require it) by an abbreviated
title. For other abbreviations we follow the listing in the
JBL 90 (1971) 513-519.

TO JOY WITH LOVE.

INTRODUCTION

Acts 4:32ff, which describes the first believers in Jerusalem holding their possessions in common and laying the profits from their sold lands and houses at the feet of the Apostles, has received considerable attention in the history of New Testament interpretation.[1] For Patristic and Monastic commentators the passage provided a model of the "Angelic Life," a moral example for all Christians[2] and a literal model for the perfect Christians, the Monks.[3] Reformed commentators

---

[1]In addition to the older surveys of A. McGiffert and J. Hunkin in Beginnings II 363-433, the history of research on Acts can be found in E. Trocmé, Le "Livre des Actes" et l'Histoire (Paris: Presses Universitaires de France, 1957) 1-19; Haenchen, 14-49; Dupont Etudes 11-224; C. K. Barrett, Luke the Historian in Recent Study (London: Epworth Press, 1961). Recent work is discussed by W. Van Unnik, "Luke-Acts, a Storm Center in Contemporary Scholarship," SLA 15-32 and I. H. Marshall, "Recent Study of the Acts of the Apostles," ExpT 80 (1968-9) 292-296.

[2]Apart from the Homiliae in Acta Apostolorum of Chrysostom (PG LX 13ff) there is no full patristic commentary on Acts. Some fathers use 4:32 as a proof text in polemic, for example Origen, Contra Celsum VIII 12 (PG XI 1534); Ambrose, De Fide I, 2, 18 (CSEL 78, 10); Hilary of Poitiers, De Trinitate I, 28 and VIII, 5 (PL X 40 and 240). Frequently 4:32 was used paraenetically, as in Augustine, De Trinitate XIII, 2, 5 (PL XLII 1017), De Catech. Rud. XXIII, 42 (PL XL 340); Cyprian, Ep. VII, 3 (PL IV 248), De Unit. Eccl. 25 (PL IV 534), De Opere et Eleem. 25 (PL IV 644); and often in Chrysostom, e.g., In Ep. Prim. ad Cor. VI 4 ("the angelic life") and XXI 7 (PG LXI 54 and 179), In Matt. XXI 1, XXXII 6 (PG LVII 295 and 385), In Joh. LXXV 5 (PG LIX 410). To legitimate the holding of Christians' property by Bishops, Acts 4:35 was used by Urban I, Ep. ad Omnes Christ. (PG X 135f); the same text was used to justify believers giving alms to Bishops rather than directly to the poor in Basil, Ep. 150:3 (PG XXXII 606).

[3]That monks were successors to the primitive community finds classic expression in Cassian, Institutes II 5 and Conferences XVIII 5 (PL XLIX 85, 1094-6). Cf. also Augustine, De Sanct. Virg. 45, De Op. Monach. 25 (PL XL 423, 572), Enn. in Ps. 132 2-3 (PL XXXVII 1750), Ep. 211:5 (PL XXXIII 960); Athanasius, Vita S. Anton. 2 (PG XXVI 842); Jerome, Epp. 58:4, 130:14 (PL XXII, 582, 1118); Reg. Benedicti 33, 34: Pachomius, Lib. S. Ors. 27:50; Reg. Magistri 82:20-21; 87:14f; Caesarius of Arles, Stat. Sanct. Virg. 20:21; Basil, Long Rule Q. 7, 19,

rejected any monastic implications in the passage, but saw in
the practice of the first Christians an example of the authentic unity of heart and charity which flowed from the gift of
the Spirit.[1] Critical scholarship moved from a spiritual
interpretation of the text to an analysis of its linguistic
and literary characteristics. J. Wettstein discerned that in
the language of the passage was to be found a clear expression
of the hellenistic topos concerning friendship.[2] By speaking
of the first believers as being ψυχὴ μία, the author in effect
recalled the classic definition of friendship, regarded
already by Aristotle as proverbial;[3] and by continuing ἦν
αὐτοῖς πάντα κοινά, he resonated the equally proverbial saying
τοῖς φιλοῖς πάντα κοινά, an expression which enjoyed the

32, 34, 35; Short Rule Q. 85, 93, 131, 135, 148, 187, 252.
Monks were not alone in tracing their ancestry to Acts.
According to Epiphanius' Panarion I, II, 30:17 the Ebionites
derived their name and practice from the apostolic community
(PG XLI 434); on this, cf. L. Keck, "The Poor among the Saints
in Jewish Christianity and Qumran," ZNW 57 (1966) 59. H. von
Schubert has shown that the sectarians of Münster inherited
this tradition, in Der Kommunismus der Wiedertäufer im Münster
und seine Quellen (Sitzungsberichte der Heidelberger Akademie
der Wissenschaften; Phil. Hist. Klasse, 11, 1919).

[1]Luther used Acts 4:32f in attacking monks and mendicants,
in Deut. Mos. cum Ann. (Weimar XIV 657) and De Vot. Mon. Mart.
Luth. Iud. (Weimar VIII 642), and used the passage to rebut
the claim of the peasants that all things were common to all,
in Wider die räuberischen und mörderischen Rotten der Bauern
(Weimar XVIII 359). Calvin castigates the "fanatic spirit" of
the Anabaptists who would use this text to overthrow "omnis
politia," and the "ridicula impudentia monachorum" who considered themselves to be following the "regulam apostolicam."
Against these deviations, Calvin declares the text "est autem
singulare exemplum caritatis . . . ut sciamus nostra
abundantia sublevandum esse fratrum inopiam," In Acta
Apostolorum ed. A. Tholuck (Berlin: Gustave Eichler, 1833)
50-51, 81-82.

[2]J. Wettstein, Novum Testamentum Graecum II (Amsterdam:
Dommerian, 1752) 470. Calvin (In Act. Apost., 51) had already
associated the expression omnia amicorum communia with the
Pythagoreans. H. Grotius, Annotationes in Novum Testamentum V
Ad Acta Apostolorum (Groningae: W. Zuidema, 1828) 21-22, 33,
knew of the expression ψυχὴ μία from Aristotle and Plutarch
and of the language used about possessions by Philo, Josephus
and Iamblichus.

[3]Nichomachean Ethics IX, 8, 2. The earliest extant
expression of it appears to be in Euripides' Orestes 1046.

widest currency, particularly among hellenistic philosophical
schools.[1] Since the time of Wettstein the hellenistic provenance of the language in this passage has been repeatedly
affirmed[2] and can be said to have the nearly unanimous approval
of scholars.[3] The discovery of the Dead Sea Scrolls, and in
particular the Community Rule (1QS) which legislated a strict

---

[1]The proverb is found frequently in places where friendship or the ideal state is discussed. For a guide to the
location of the topos, cf. F. Hauck, "κοινός," TDNT 3 (1965)
789-809; L. Dugas, L'Amitié Antique (Paris: Félix Alcan, 1914)
1-68; R. Eglinger, Der Begriff der Freundschaft in der
Philosophie (Basel: Inaug. Diss., 1916); G. Bohnenblust,
Beiträge zum Topos περί φιλίας (Berlin: Universitäts-
Buchdruckerei von Gustav Schade, 1905).

[2]Cf. A. Loisy, Les Actes des Apôtres (Paris: Emile
Nourry, 1920) 259-261; O. Bauernfeind, Die Apostelgeschichte
(Theologischer Handkommentar zum Neuen Testament V; Leipzig:
A. Deichertsche, 1939) 87-88; A. Wikenhauser, Die Apostel-
geschichte (RNT 5; Regensburg: Friedrich Pustet, 1961) 69; H.
Conzelmann, Die Apostelgeschichte 2nd ed. (HNT 7; Tübingen:
J. C. B. Mohr [Paul Siebeck], 1972) 37, 44; H. Zimmermann,
"Die Sammelberichte der Apostelgeschichte," BZ n.f. 5 (1961)
81-82; E. Plümacher, Lukas als hellenistischer Schriftsteller
(Studien zur Umwelt des Neuen Testaments 9; Göttingen:
Vandenhoeck & Ruprecht, 1972) 16-17; J. Dupont, "L'Union
entre les premières Chrétiens dans les Actes des Apôtres,"
NRT 91 (1969) 902; Etudes 508-513; H. J. Cadbury, "The Sum-
maries of Acts," Beginnings V 399, n. 2; H.-J. Degenhardt,
Lukas Evangelist der Armen (Stuttgart: Kath. Bibelwerk, 1965)
165; H. Seesemann, Der Begriff ΚΟΙΝΩΝΙΑ im Neuen Testament
(BZNW 14; Giessen: Alfred Töpelmann, 1933) 88-89; L. Cerfaux
(Recueil 2, 150-152) was so impressed by the similarities
between Acts 4:32ff and Plato's Republic V 462C, and
Iamblichus' Life of Pythagoras 167-169 that he suggested the
possibility of a literary dependence.

[3]B. Gerhardsson, "Einige Bemerkungen zu Apg. 4:32," ST 24
(1970) 142-149 has objected to the view that the language of
the passage comes from the hellenistic language about friendship, arguing (p. 144) that Qumran shows the ideal of community
property to have been present within Israel. This is true, but
the question concerns the language used to express the ideal,
and in the sectarian documents we do not find anything like the
language here employed by Luke. Gerhardsson further argues
that the "Houses" of Hillel and Shammai practised a "Güter-
gemeinschaft" though he does not support this with any references and must admit (p. 144), "Zu Zeit des N.T. haben wir
allzugeringe Informationen." We shall see below that the
evidence is indeed scanty, and there is nowhere any language
similar to that used by Luke. Gerhardsson's positive argument
(pp. 145-146) is no more convincing.

community of property among members of the sect,[1] stimulated
many efforts to discover linguistic or institutional links
between the Lukan passage and the Scrolls.[2] The quest appeared
encouraging, for the Dead Sea Community provided a contemporary
and geographically plausible source for the phenomenon described in Acts. The result of all these efforts, however, has
been largely negative, and it can be said with some certainty
that whatever the historical connections may have been between
Qumran and the first Christian community in Jerusalem, it
remains unlikely that the author of Acts depended on the
language or ideas of Qumran.[3] The hellenistic provenance of
the language seems certain, and it appears equally likely that
the hellenistic _topos_ on friendship was consciously employed
by the author.

The language of 4:32ff, however, also suggests that the
author may have intentionally colored the hellenistic _topos_
with phraseology typical of the Septuagint. Thus by placing
καρδία in the phrase ἦν καρδία καὶ ψυχὴ μία, he amplified the
Greek proverb by means of the traditional biblical expression
for the inner man, the heart.[4] More conclusively, the phrase

---

[1]Because they seem to deal with considerably different
social settings, the evidence of the Community Rule and the
Damascus Rule must be distinguished. Among the important
passages are 1QS 1:11, 3:2, 5:1-3, 5:14-20, 6:17-24, 7:6,
7:24-25; and CD 13:11, 14:12.

[2]Cf. the review of some thirty-two authors in H. Braun,
Qumran und das Neue Testament I (Tübingen: J. C. B. Mohr [Paul
Siebeck], 1966) 143-149; also the well-balanced presentation of
J. Fitzmyer, "Jewish Christianity in Acts in Light of the
Qumran Scrolls," SLA 233-257, and P. Benoit, "Qumran et le
Nouveau Testament," NTS 7 (1967) 276-296.

[3]The more obvious differences have been frequently noted.
Comparisons are not made easier by the divergent literary
types of the documents, or by the fact that the two Qumran
documents appear to be dealing with different settings, not
only from Acts but also from each other; cf. Braun, 148-149.

[4]ψυχὴ μία occurs as a translation of lb 'ḥd at I Chr.
12:39. Cf. J. Weiss, Die Apostelgeschichte (Leipzig: J. C.
Hinrichs'sche, 1893) 100. "Heart and soul" is a common enough
combination in the LXX, as in Deut. 6:5 and related passages;
cf. Haenchen, 231; Degenhardt, 170; Dupont Etudes, 513. But
the connection of "one soul" to "holding all things in common"
is so obviously in accord with the hellenistic _topos_ that
Dupont (Etudes, 513; "L'Union," 904) suggests Luke used καρδία

in 4:34 οὐδὲ γὰρ ἐνδεής τις ἦν ἐν αὐτοῖς is a clear reminiscence of Deut. 15:4, which promised that in the days when the
commandments of God were perfectly observed there would be no
more need in the land.[1]

The language of the passage already indicates that whatever the historical basis or tradition underlying the
description,[2] Luke has moved in the direction of idealizing
it, implying by his choice of words that this first community
of believers fulfilled both the Greek ideal of friendship and
the Jewish longing for a land free from need.[3] It is not clear
from the language alone whether Luke meant this idealization to
express something about the nature of the first community
alone, or whether he intended the first community to be seen
as a model for the Christian communities of his own day.[4]

Attention has also been paid to the literary form of this
passage.[5] Out of the long and frustrating search for sources

---

to give the expression "une coloration plus biblique."

[1]Weiss, 101; Lake-Cadbury, 48; Loisy, 260; Bauernfeind,
83; Cerfaux, Recueil 2, 153; Degenhardt, 170-171; Haenchen,
231; Dupont, "L'Union," 903; Beatitudes III 42, n. 2; in the
earlier Etudes 510, Dupont was cautious about seeing a reference to Deut. 15:4 here.

[2]The possibility that an historical practice underlay
Luke's account can scarcely be dismissed on the grounds that
Luke has not described any "Organisation der Produktion";
Conzelmann, Apg. 37.

[3]Haenchen, 233; Cerfaux Recueil 2, 152; Degenhardt, 170-
171, 222; Plümacher, 18; Dupont, Etudes 519; "L'Union," 903.

[4]Gerhardsson, 148 and Degenhardt, 19 claim that the description is intended as a model for other churches. This
position is rejected by H. Conzelmann, The Theology of St.
Luke trans. by G. Buswell (New York: Harper and Row, 1961)
14-15, 233; cf. also Conzelmann Apg., 37.

[5]Sherman Johnson, "A proposed Form-Critical Treatment of
Acts," ATR 21 (1939) 22-31, attempted a classification of forms
in Acts along the lines established by Dibelius for the Gospels.
While not mentioning 2:41ff or 4:32ff explicitly, he regarded
the stories about Barnabas, Ananias and Sapphira as Novellen,
"aetiological in their explanation of the economic situation
of Judean Christianity," (23). Johnson was unaware of
Dibelius' own skepticism about the applicability of form-
critical methods to Acts, as expressed in his 1923 essay
"Stilkritisches zur Apostelgeschichte," now found in Dibelius,
1-25.

beneath the narrative of the first part of Acts,[1] there has
slowly emerged a conviction shared by most scholars that the
apparent repetition and paralleling found in the passages 2:41-
47, 4:32-35 and 5:12-16 are not due to the influence of different and parallel sources, but represent the editorial work of
the author, who advanced his narrative in these places by
means of the literary device which has come to be called the
Summary.[2] The Summary generalizes and universalizes particular

---

[1]For our passage two kinds of hypotheses have been
advanced; those holding 4:32ff to be part of one source
spanning the whole first portion of Acts, and those holding
that 4:32ff represents, in an inferior or superior source, a
doublet of 2:41ff. C. Torrey's The Composition and Date of
Acts (HTS I; Cambridge: Harvard University Press, 1916)
advanced the theory that a single Aramaic source underlay all
of Acts 1-15. Though not finding great acceptance (among the
many rebuttals, cf. H. Sparks, "The Semitisms of Acts," JTS
n.s. 1 [1950] 16-28, and H. Cadbury, "Luke--Translator or
Author?" American Journal of Theology 24 [1924] 436-455), his
argument stimulated research into the semitic coloration of
Luke's language, the best result of which to date is M.
Wilcox's The Semitisms of Acts (Oxford: Clarendon Press, 1965).
A more persuasive hypothesis was advanced without much reaction
by L. Cerfaux (Recueil 2, 63-103 and 125-156), who saw in the
first part of Acts a source coming from hellenistic Jewish
Christians of Jerusalem. The various two-source theories proposed by F. Spitta, Die Apostelgeschichte, ihre Quellen und
deren geschichtlicher Wert (Halle: Waisenhause, 1891) 61-95;
A. Harnack, Die Apostelgeschichte (Beiträge zur Einleitung in
das N.T. III; Leipzig: J. C. Hinrichs'sche, 1908) 143ff; and
more recently B. Reicke, Glaube und Leben der Urgemeinde (ATANT
32; Zürich: Zwingli-Verlag, 1957) 55-57, have proved less than
convincing. The best treatment of this complex history is J.
Dupont, The Sources of the Acts trans. by K. Pond (New York:
Herder and Herder, 1964).

[2]Most of the attention centered on 4:32ff in recent years
has been as a "major summary" together with 2:41ff and 5:12ff.
The definition of these passages as redactional summaries
arose in part out of the search for sources in the first part
of Acts; thus L. Dieu, "Marc, source des Actes? ch. I-XV," RB
29 (1920) 555-569 and RB 30 (1921) 86-96; and L. Cerfaux, "La
Composition de la première partie du Livre des Actes," Recueil
2, 63-103. The influential article of J. Jeremias, "Untersuchungen zum Quellenproblem der Apostelgeschichte," ZNW 36
(1937) 205-221 was a response to the two-source theory of
Harnack. The work of Jeremias and P. Benoit, "Remarques sûr
les 'Sommaires' de Actes 2:42 à 5," Aux Sources de la Tradition
Chrétienne (Bibliotheque Théologique; Mélanges Maurice Goguel;
Neuchatel: Delachaux & Niestle, 1950) 1-10, emphasized trans-
positions between summaries and moved toward the hypothesis of
a later redactor. Benoit's conclusions appear to be accepted
by Dupont, Etudes, 40. Already in The Style and Literary

incidents received from tradition.[1] In the case of 4:32-35,
it has been suggested that the extraordinary generosity of
Barnabas (4:36-37) and the fraudulent gift of Ananias and
Sapphira (5:1-11) were isolated instances of giving of which
the author was aware from the tradition, and that by means of
the Summary he elevated these instances to the level of a
universal practice.[2]

The form-analysis complements the linguistic analysis and
points in the same direction: by form and by language, the
author was idealizing the practice of the community. Despite
a considerable amount of divergence concerning details,[3] the

---

Method of Luke (HTS VI; Cambridge: Harvard University Press,
1920) 111, 115-118, H. J. Cadbury had spoken of generalization
by means of summaries as a literary habit of Luke. This view
he amplified in The Making of Luke-Acts (New York: The
Macmillan Co., 1927) 58-59, 324-329, and in "The Summaries of
Acts," Beginnings V 392-402. Without finally committing himself, Cadbury inclined to the view that the summaries came
entirely from Luke's hand (cf. Beginnings V 393, 399, n. 2).
Meanwhile M. Dibelius (Dibelius 9, 127-128) took the position
that the summaries were entirely Luke's work, a technique by
which he "formed a mosaic" out of the fragments of tradition.
H. Zimmermann, "Die Sammelberichte," 71-82 also gives relatively more credit to the author. The position of Dibelius is
followed by Haenchen, 195: "To us the summaries appear to
flow entirely from the pen of Luke." A review of these positions can be found in Haenchen, 193-196; Degenhardt, 160-163,
and H. Zimmermann, Neutestamentliche Methodenlehre (Stuttgart:
Katholisches Bibelwerk, 1968) 243-257.

[1]Dibelius 9, 127f; Cadbury, Making, 58; Beginnings V 393;
Zimmermann, "Die Sammelberichte," 71; Cerfaux, Recueil 2, 75;
Trocmé, 195.

[2]Conzelmann, Apg., 45; Haenchen, 233; Dibelius 9;
Beginnings V 399-400; Zimmermann, Methodenlehre 254; Dupont,
Etudes, 511-512.

[3]The attempt to discern the relationship of tradition to
redaction in these passages is obviously of less concern to
those (Cadbury, Dibelius, Haenchen) who regard the summaries
as completely Lukan. Cerfaux (Recueil 2, 74-78) finds that:
a) v. 43a breaks the continuity of discussion of community
goods, but fits at 5:13; 4:33b is not discussed. b) The core
of the first summary is 2:46-47a; the rest is taken over from
other summaries, with the exception of 2:42 which comes from
Luke. c) 5:12-16 was originally attached directly to 4:32ff.
Jeremias ("Untersuchungen," 206-208), finds: a) 4:33 intrusive. 4:33a comes from 5:42 and 4:33b from 2:47. b) 5:15f is
a later addition to 5:12-14, and fits better at 8:6f and
19:11f. c) 2:41-42 is an older summary; 2:43-47 a later

8

hypothesis that 4:32ff, 2:41ff and 5:12ff are distinguishable
literary units and represent (at least at some stage of the
writing) a creative interpretation of the tradition by the
author enjoys virtually universal acceptance.

This conclusion, it might be thought, would lead exegetes
to pay closer attention to these passages within their context,
and to focus on the thought of the author revealed by the
placement of these reflective summaries within that context.
But in fact, the tendency has been to isolate the passages
called Summaries, to develop editorial theories on the basis of
supposed borrowings and anticipations occurring within the
Summaries,[1] and to interpret the meaning of the passages simply
from within themselves, with only a casual attention paid to

elaboration constructed on the basis of the other two summaries.
d) There are therefore an earlier (2:41-42; 4:32, 34ff; 5:11-
14) and a later (2:43-47; 4:33; 5:15f) stage of redaction.
Benoit ("Sommaires," 1-10) regards as primitive 2:42, 46-47;
4:32, 34-35; 5:12a, 15-16. Inserted "si maladroitment" into
these summaries by a later redactor were 2:43-45; 4:33; 5:12b-
14. The latest examination by H. Zimmermann (Methodenlehre
250-254) is too complex to summarize briefly.

[1]These studies appear to move logically to one of two
positions, either that Luke had an earlier source which he
parcelled out through chapters 2-5 in order to flesh out his
narrative, or that Luke wrote a part of the present summaries
and a later redactor clumsily expanded them. That Luke both
wrote the summaries and then proved incapable of amplifying his
own summaries goes against our knowledge of Luke's skill. We
should however ask these questions to the above cited recon-
structions: 1) Has the question of 'appropriateness' been
perhaps too quickly answered? Doesn't 4:33, for example,
perform an important literary function in the flow of verses
from 4:31 to 4:34? 2) Isn't it possible that the repetition of
certain expressions (like "signs and wonders") may represent
less of a mechanical transposition between summaries and more
the pulse of literary motif? 3) Has focussing upon the similarities between the first and second summaries hindered our
ability to acknowledge their even more striking differences?
4) Is it possible to relate the content of the summaries to
structural and thematic elements throughout the work, so that
the summaries appear less as make-shift fillers in the narrative? The divergent conclusions of the three careful scholars
outlined above should perhaps prompt us to move past the
question concerning the technical relationship of tradition
to redaction in these passages, and start to ask the exegetical
question: even if part of the passages are traditional, how
was the author using them to express his own thought?

their literary placement.[1]

We must ask therefore if after the linguistic and form analysis of the passage, there still remain serious exegetical questions. If such questions remain, then we must move beyond the analysis of language and form and seek a way of approaching the text which will yield satisfactory answers.

The questions which still emerge from the text as it comes to us in its present form do not arise from the possible historical phenomenon Luke was describing, but from the shape of the text itself. The questions come down to the basic one of understanding not simply the language but the thought of the author. What is happening at this place in Luke-Acts which has led the author to put words together in this fashion? This general question can be broken down into at least the following particular ones:

1) Why are there two passages describing the community of goods in Luke-Acts, and only two? Why do they occur where they do? It does not follow that because each description comes after a bestowal of the Spirit (2:1-4, 4:31), it was an automatic reflex of the author to describe the inner life of a community, for he mentions explicitly other outpourings of the Spirit (8:17, 10:44, 19:6) which are followed by no such descriptions. Indeed, we should not too quickly assume that the outpourings in chs. 2 and 4 are to be considered alike.

2) More significantly, why does the community's practice in regard to possessions receive such attention in these descriptions of the inner life of the community in the first place? If the Summary of ch. 4 depends on 4:36-5:11, we might ask why these stories were told where they were, and not after the Summary of ch. 2.

3) Can there be found an intelligible relationship between this description of a community of goods, with its universal and radical implications ("no one called anything

---

[1]Cf. Dupont, "L'Union," 898: "De nombreux points de contact et une parenté évidente unissent ces passages, qui posent des problèmes littéraires à peu près identiques et soulignent les même traits dans les formules parallèles ou complémentaires. Il est donc tout indiqué de les éclairer l'un par l'autre." Cf. also Benoit, "Sommaires," 1, and Cerfaux, Recueil 2, 126.

10

that he had his own" 4:32), and the author's presentation elsewhere concerning the ideal attitude towards possessions, or
must we be content to regard this description as the alien
presence of another tradition within the text? We are faced
here not simply with the frequently noted inconsistencies in
the narrative itself,[1] but a possible conflict of ideology.
It can be said with fair certainty that Luke elsewhere presents
almsgiving as the ideal way of handling possessions.[2] Yet the
ideal of community possessions is in tension with, if not
actually contradictory to, the ideal or practice of almsgiving.[3] The suggestion that Luke intended the community of
goods to be seen as the perfect expression of the spirit of
almsgiving resolves the difficulty, but may be too facile.[4]
This question becomes like the first, why here and nowhere
else? Does the imagery of community possessions fulfill a
function in the text which is uniquely demanded by the context
and the impression the author wished to make here and only
here?[5]

4) There are obvious similarities between the two passages
which describe community goods, but what are we to make of the

---

[1] Some of the inconsistencies are small and probably demand
of the author a concern he did not have, but for the record:
Peter and John in 3:6 have no money, a strange fact if they
held the community purse; 8:3 and 12:12 indicate that some
believers did not sell their houses; in 11:30 the collection
from Antioch comes not to the Twelve or the Seven but to the
Presbyters; 4:34 would suggest a universal practice, 5:4 a
voluntary practice. These and other small problems are discussed in W. Franklin, Die Kollekte des Paulus (Scottsdale:
Mennonite Publishing House, 1938) 42ff. The inconsistencies
emphasize what the form and language already make clear: that
Luke was idealizing.

[2] Lk 11:41; 12:33; 16:9; 18:22; 19:8; Acts 9:36; 10:2, 4,
31; 20:35.

[3] An absolute community of goods would make the giving of
alms impossible, a perception found in the Exodus Rabbah,
Mishpatim, Par. 31:5: "David said, 'Lord of the Universe,
make Thy world be evenly balanced (yšb 'wlmk) as it says,
Let the world be made equal (yšb) before God.'" God replied,
'If I balance my world (''šb 't 'wlmy šwh) then "Love and
Truth, who will practice them?"'"

[4] Degenhardt, 183.

[5] Cf. above, p. 8, n. 1.

differences? The most striking difference lies in the role of
the Apostles. In the first description, the power and teaching
of the Apostles is stressed, but we would have no inkling from
that description alone that the Apostles had anything to do
with possessions. In fact, when in 3:6 Peter and John say
they have no money to give in alms, this would be strange if
they were already pictured as heading up the distribution of
goods; but if we are reading along continuously in the story
(and were reading it for the first time), Peter's remark would
not sound strange; the Apostles were not yet involved in the
handling of the community's possessions. In 4:32ff, however,
the Apostles are placed emphatically at the center of the
community's shared goods. Three times the ritual of laying
possessions at the feet of the Apostles is repeated (4:35, 37;
5:2). Then, suddenly, in 6:2ff, the Apostles abandon their
role in the community distribution, and we hear nothing more
about their handling of the community's goods. Why, then, are
the Apostles so dominantly featured in 4:32ff? We have already
seen that the author was generalizing and idealizing. Was he
also using the language about possessions to say something
about the Apostles as well? If so, what?

5) Finally, what is the relation of 4:32ff to its immediate and broader contexts? Immediate: Is the description of
4:32ff simply inserted in this place for convenience, or to
fill a lacuna in the tradition,[1] or does it represent a new
development in the narrative? In particular, how does 4:32ff
fit between the account of the bestowal of the Spirit (4:31)
and the story of Ananias and Sapphira?[2] Broader: Can this
immediate context be grasped at all without an understanding
of the place and role of the Jerusalem narrative in the whole

---

[1] Dibelius, 127.

[2] Even if the summary is a filler, adding no new information, does it establish a new or different perspective than
that contained in the elements of the tradition, and thereby
color what is found in the tradition? We can ask this about
the expression "at the feet of the Apostles" for example. Did
this expression originate in the Barnabas account, the Ananias
account, or both? Or did the author place the expression in
each? In either case, what emphasis is given to the expression
by using it again within the summary statement?

of Luke-Acts?

These questions, it will be noted, are not of a historical
or explicitly theological nature but rather of a literary
character. They are questions which pertain immediately and
exclusively to the working of the passage within the work,
seeking the meaning of the passage not as it relates to some
other body of knowledge, but as it relates to the literary
coherence of the work Luke-Acts. The answers to these questions, therefore, are not to be found in any other discipline
than that of a careful, attentive and independent reading of
the author's own words, that is, in a literary analysis of
Luke-Acts. Before beginning such a reading, however, it is
proper to outline some of the general attitudes which motivate
and shape the enterprise.

The first presupposition to which an interpreter beginning
a literary analysis of Luke-Acts is committed is that it is as
a whole and in each of its parts the work of a single author.
There is no disputing the author had previous sources which he
employed, a fact obvious for the Gospel. Source theories for
Acts, however, have not shed any significant light on the meaning of the work as a whole;[1] and for the Gospel, Redaction-

---

[1]Cadbury (Making, 69) has noted, "The attempt to establish
and distinguish written Greek sources for the passages recorded
only by Luke seems doomed to prove unsatisfactory and largely
subjective," and in another place ("Four Features of Lukan
Style," SLA, 88), "Whatever the underlying sources and development -- the present text is compatible with authorship by a
single author." The reason for this is, as Dupont (Sources,
166-167) has well noted, "The information is not only reported
in his own style, in its very substance it generally reflects
his personality. Everything is done as if Luke were at the
origin not only of the edited version, but even of the sources
on which this version is based." Even while noting the caveat
issued by R. Bultmann, "Zur Frage nach den Quellen der
Apostelgeschichte," New Testament Essays ed. by A. J. B.
Higgins (Studies in Honor of T. W. Manson; Manchester: University Press, 1959), the position which makes most sense for a
literary analysis of Acts is that associated with Haenchen.
In addition to his commentary, 81-90, cf. "Tradition und
Komposition in der Apostelgeschichte," ZTK 52 (1955) 205-225,
and "The Book of Acts as Source-Material for the History of
Early Christianity," SLA 261-262. That we cannot definitely
find such sources and that a literary analysis does not depend
on such a determination, however, does not imply that the
possible description of such sources would not be of value for
an historical reconstruction. Nor need we follow the lead of

Criticism has revealed the extent Luke (as the other evangelists) shaped traditional materials to his own ends.[1] Neither
have arguments against a unity of authorship for the work Luke-
Acts as a whole proved convincing.[2] But a literary analysis
presumes more than the simple recognition that the work as a
whole bears a uniformity of style; it presumes that the writer
was more than a collector and collator of sources,[3] was in fact

---

Dibelius, 4, and Haenchen, 82, in excluding on principle the
possibility of traditions springing up around the Apostles from
the earliest days. Cf. the incisive remarks on this issue by
J. Jervell, Luke and the People of God (Minneapolis: Augsburg
Publishing House, 1972) 19-39.

[1]While it is true that in the Gospel our knowledge of
Luke's sources helps us discover the distinctiveness of Luke's
position over against those sources, it is equally true that if
we did not have those sources, we would never be able to guess
where they underlay his text, and more significantly, the story
of Luke's Gospel would emerge with the same prima facie coherence as Acts. It is altogether too facile to claim that the
Gospel gives us insight into the way Luke treats his sources.
It tells us something about the way Luke has handled one of his
sources, Mark. The difficulties of establishing a Q text (not
to mention its order) behind the material shared by Matt and Lk
is evidence enough of our ignorance of Luke's treatment of that
and possible other sources in the Gospel. I. H. Marshall,
Luke: Historian and Theologian (Exeter: Paternoster Press,
1970) 19-20, has rightly emphasized that the tendency of redaction critics to define Luke's teaching by means of contrast to
the parallels should be balanced by the common sense appreciation that Luke included traditions because to at least some
degree they reflected his own viewpoint and should therefore be
considered as fully a part of his teaching as his alterations.

[2]The theory of Loisy, 89ff and 105ff, has deservedly found
no adherents. Cf. the remarks of Dupont, Sources, 19ff, and
Trocmé, 28-29. The linguistic arguments against the unity of
authorship for the Gospel and Acts of A. C. Clark, The Acts of
the Apostles (Oxford: Clarendon Press, 1933) 393-408 have been
rebutted by W. L. Knox, The Acts of the Apostles (Cambridge:
University Press, 1948) 3-15, 100-109. Trocmé, 34, concludes:
"rien ne s'oppose à la reconnaissance de l'unité complète de
l'oeuvre à Théophile."

[3]The reductio ad absurdum of the "scissors and paste"
approach to Lukan authorship is represented by A. Q. Morton
and G. H. MacGregor, The Structure of Luke and Acts (New York:
Harper and Row, 1964). M. Goguel, "Quelque Observations sur
L'oeuvre de Luc," RHPR 33 (1953) 47, had a low opinion of Luke
as a writer and historian: "Le redacteur des Actes est
beaucoup plus dominé par ses sources qu'il ne les domine . . .
c'est un compilateur, pas très adroit . . .". Quite another
view is held by P. Schubert, "The Structure and Significance

an author in the fullest sense. The more one reads Luke-Acts,
the more intricate and subtle appear the traces of the author's
creativity in every phase of the narrative, and the more the
impression grows that the thought, imagination and art of one
man were responsible. This unity of authorship begins as a
presumption, but it cannot remain simply that; the present
study will focus on certain of the traces of Lukan thought
which substantiate it.

An obvious, overwhelming, but too long overlooked fact
impelling the reader to see in the work of Luke the hand of a
literary artist and not merely an editor is the very existence
of Luke-Acts as a single if two-volumed narrative.[1] The story
of the first Christians could have been told in any number of
ways. It is Luke's art that has convinced us the story of the
Church is really the continuation of the story about Jesus, and
he has made this connection not arbitrarily[2] but with such
naturalness that until very recently we accepted without much
question that the way Luke told the story was the way it
happened, indeed had to have happened.[3] Luke has grasped the
story about Jesus and the story of the early Church in a single
vision, and has communicated that vision so effectively that at
every point Jesus' story anticipates that of the Church, and
the story of the Apostles and first Christians is inexplicable
apart from what Luke has said about Jesus.[4]

---

of Luke 24," Neutestamentliche Studien für Rudolf Bultmann
(BZNW 21; Berlin: A. Töpelmann, 1954) 185: "Luke is a
littérateur of considerable skill and technique. His literary
methods serve his theology as his theology serves them."

[1]Cadbury, Making, 8-9, "They are not merely two independent writings from the same pen; they are a single continuous
work."

[2]Few today would agree with the remark of Torrey (Composition, 68) that "In relation to the Third Gospel the Book of
Acts was plainly an afterthought" [emphasis his].

[3]The originality of Luke's enterprise is stressed by
Dibelius, 103, 192; Haenchen, SLA 258; U. Wilckens, "Interpreting Luke-Acts in a Period of Existentialist Theology," SLA 61;
and W. Van Unnik, "The 'Book of Acts' the Confirmation of the
Gospel," NovT 4 (1960) 26.

[4]"Luke had to write this book in such a way as to show
that the story of the Church was not an independent or

We are not in this study attempting to account for all of
Luke's literary method, but the literary function of a particular aspect of the narrative. But one element of Luke's
literary procedure should be discussed here because of its
importance for this study, and that is Luke's literary use of
prophecy. "Proof from Prophecy," or the apologetic argument
that what happened to Jesus (particularly his death and resurrection) was a fulfillment of the prophecies of the O.T., is of
course an essential component in the very self-understanding of
the first Christians, and manifests itself variously throughout
the writings of the New Testament. But Luke has expanded and
refined this understanding to a marked degree, and has made the
prophetic mode a literary method.[1]

Luke has first of all expanded the idea of the fulfillment
of Prophecy so that the sayings of the Prophets are fulfilled
not only in the events of Jesus' ministry, death and resurrection, but events in the life of the Church as well, the various
stages of the apostolic mission being authenticated by the
prophecies which foretold them (cf. e.g., Acts 3:24, 13:40,
15:15, 28:25ff). Secondly, Luke has refined the notion of
prophetic fulfillment. He does not follow Matthew's somewhat
mechanical alignment of specific texts with occurrences in the
life of Jesus, introduced by the typical ἵνα πληρωθῇ. It is,
rather, characteristic of Luke to understand the whole story of
Jesus and the early Church globally as fulfilling the Prophets.
Illuminating in this respect is the characteristic Lukan use of
δεῖ, whether it refers to the suffering and rising of Jesus
(Lk 9:22, 17:25, 24:7, 26, 44; Acts 3:21, 17:3), or the apostasy of Judas and election of Matthias (Acts 1:16-21), or the

---

spontaneous movement, but the outcome of the life of Jesus,"
Barrett, 60. Cf. also U. Wilckens, Die Missionsreden der
Apostelgeschichte (WMANT 5; Neukirchen: Neukirchener Verlag,
1961) 94: "Die Epoche der Kirchengeschichte gründet in der
Epoche der Jesuszeit und muss deshalb konsequent aus ihr
verstanden werden."

[1]"Luke did not invent the Christian 'proof-from-prophecy'
but in a special way he made it a principle for the composition
of a continuous historical work," N. A. Dahl, "The Story of
Abraham in Luke-Acts," SLA 152. The orientation of the following remarks is similar to, though arrived at independently,
that of Schubert, "Structure and Significance."

sufferings of Paul (Acts 9:16) and all Christians (Acts 14:22).
The δεῖ expresses for Luke the working of the Divine Will to
bring to fulfillment all that Moses and the Prophets have said,
even when he does not mention specific texts.[1]

More significant for the present study is the way in which
Luke has employed prophecy and the fulfillment of prophecy as a
literary pattern. There are at least two ways in which he does
this. In both, the prophecy and its fulfillment are to be
found in the narrative itself. The prophecy is not spoken by
one of the Prophets of old, but by one of the characters in the
story, and the prophecy finds its fulfillment in the subsequent
development of the story.

A. The first and most obvious way in which Luke does this
is by explicit prophetic statements which color and to a certain extent govern the subsequent course of the narrative.[2]
Luke of course shares with the other synoptics the three pre-
dictions of the death of Jesus (Lk 9:21, 9:44, 18:32) which are
fulfilled in the passion narrative; but he also makes the
prophecy about the suffering and witness of Jesus' disciples
find explicit fulfillment in Acts 4 and 5,[3] the prophecy about

_____

[1]W. Grundmann, "δεῖ" TDNT 2 (1964) 23, is correct in
stating, "The whole of God's will for Christ and for man is
thus comprehended in the δεῖ as Luke conceives it," but is less
than accurate when he concludes from the usage of the term in
eschatological contexts that in itself it is "an eschatological
term in the N.T." Cf. the remarks of Conzelmann, Theology,
153-154 and Marshall, Luke, 107-109; cf. also E. Fascher,
"Theologische Beobachtungen zu δεῖ," Neutestamentliche Studien,
228-254. It is especially characteristic of Luke to attach the
δεῖ to the fulfillment of the Scriptures explicitly: he does
it six times (Lk 22:37; 24:26, 44; Acts 1:16, 21; 17:3), Matt
once (26:54), John once directly (29:9) and by allusion in
3:14; 12:34.

[2]Referring to programmatic statements like Acts 1:8,
Dibelius, 193-194, says, "We should observe here that references such as these, which give a literary significance to
events within the book itself, are to be found several times
in Acts and are a clear indication of the author's literary
purpose."

[3]

Lk 21:12-15	Acts 4:3ff
12a ἐπιβαλοῦσιν ἐφ' ὑμᾶς τὰς χεῖρας αὐτῶν	3a ἐπέβαλον αὐτοῖς τὰς χεῖρας
12b παραδιδόντες εἰς τὰς συναγωγὰς καὶ φυλακάς	3b καὶ ἔθεντο εἰς τήρησιν
	5a συναχθῆναι αὐτῶν

the proper response to an unbelieving city (Lk 9:5, 10:11) find
fulfillment in Acts 13:51,[1] the prophecy about the place of the
Twelve as judges over Israel (Lk 22:30) find fulfillment in the
first chapters of Acts,[2] and the prophecy of Agabus about
Paul's sufferings in Jerusalem (Acts 21:11) find fulfillment in
the subsequent narrative.[3]

Of special significance for the interpretation of Luke-
Acts, however, is Luke's manner of placing such prophetic
statements at key junctures in the narrative, statements which
function programmatically for the events which follow. The
clearest example is certainly the prophecy of Jesus in Acts
1:8 that the mission of His witnesses will move from Jerusalem
through Judea and Samaria to the ends of the earth. There is
no doubt that the geographical movement of the Acts narrative
functions as a fulfillment of this prophecy.[4] Jesus' prophecy
at the end of the Gospel (24:46ff) clearly functions in the
same way.[5] There is good probability, therefore, that the

12c ἐπὶ βασιλεῖς καὶ ἡγεμόνας		ἄρχοντες, κτλ . . .	
12d ἕνεκεν τοῦ ὀνόματός μου	7	ἐν ποίᾳ δυνάμει ἢ ἐν ποίῳ ὀνόματι	
13 ἀποβήσεται ὑμῖν εἰς μαρτύριον		[5:32 καὶ ἡμεῖς ἐσμεν μάρτυρες]	
15 οὐ δυνήσονται ἀντιστῆναι ἢ ἀντειπεῖν		4:14 οὐδὲν εἶχον ἀντειπεῖν	

[1]For the significance of the gesture, cf. H. J. Cadbury,
"Dust and Garments," Beginnings V, 269ff.

[2]The justification for this position will be discussed
later in the study.

[3]παραδώσουσιν εἰς χεῖρας ἐθνῶν (21:11) recalls the
language of the third passion prediction in Lk 18:32:
παραδοθήσεται γὰρ τοῖς ἔθνεσιν. It has frequently been noted
that the final journey of Paul to Jerusalem has been written
to reflect the passion of Jesus. Cf. Haenchen, 602-605;
Johnson, 27; Dibelius, 201; J. C. O'Neill, The Theology of
Luke in its Historical Setting 2nd ed. (London: S.P.C.K.,
1970) 67-69.

[4]The programmatic character of this verse is generally
recognized. Cf. e.g., Ph.-H. Menoud, "Le Plan des Actes des
Apôtres," NTS 1 (1954-5) 46; E. Lohse, "Lukas als Theologe der
Heilsgeschichte," EvT 14 (1954) 260-261; Haenchen, 144;
Conzelmann, Apg. 22; Dupont, Etudes, 396; Trocmé, 84; R. Zehnle,
Peter's Pentecost Discourse (SBLMS 15; Nashville: Abingdon,
1971) 99.

[5]Schubert, "Structure and Significance," 169.

prophetic statements which conclude the work as a whole (Acts
28) and begin it (the infancy narratives) deserve particular
attention.

It is necessary for the interpreter, therefore, to pay the
closest attention to such programmatic (prophetic) statements
and to seek to discover the way in which they find their fulfillment in the narrative. In Luke-Acts, it is frequently not
the immediate context alone which provides the key to understanding a passage, but the way in which a series of passages
may be organized to follow one of these prophetic statements.
By means of the explicit prophecies within the narrative, Luke
gives the reader a perspective from which to understand the
rest of the story.

B. Luke has also used prophecy as a literary pattern by
the way he has established the most intimate relation between
speech and action in the story. The formal speeches of Acts
have long been recognized as having (at least) the function of
speeches in Greek histories, that is of presenting an interpretation of the events found in the narrative.[1] But the pattern

----

[1]As so frequently in the study of Acts the basic insights
have come from Cadbury (Making, 184-193, and "The Speeches in
Acts," Beginnings V, 402-427) and M. Dibelius, "The Speeches in
Acts and Ancient Historiography," Dibelius, 138-185. That Luke
uses the speeches within his narrative in much the same way
that hellenistic historians did is not questioned; controversy
enters in when the further significance of the speeches is considered. Are we, as Dibelius suggested, to see these speeches
as models for preaching? Are we to see in the speeches
examples of primitive preaching, or the archaizing style of
the author? The majority of recent studies on the speeches
have concerned themselves with these issues and have focussed
primarily on the so-called "missionary speeches," with a range
of positions falling between C. H. Dodd, The Apostolic Preaching and its Development (London: Hodder and Stoughton, 1936),
who sees the speeches as containing the core of the primitive
kerygma, and U. Wilckens, Die Missionsreden, who regards the
entire speeches as Lukan compositions reflecting a distinctive
Lukan theology. For a review of opinions, cf. Wilckens, 7-31
and Dupont, Etudes, 41-56. For an interesting hypothesis
regarding the archaizing element, cf. Plümacher, 32-79. If we
move beyond the missionary sermons and look at all the speeches
in Acts (not only Paul's defense speeches, but also Peter's
address on the election of Matthias and his short replies
before the Council), we must recognize that whatever their
other possible functions, the speeches in these cases serve to
advance and interpret the narrative.

we speak of here applies as much to the Gospel as to Acts, and
reveals itself as a distinctive literary trait. The pattern is
simply that Luke makes the action immediately following a saying or speech fulfill or exemplify the point of the saying or
speech, often with a considerable degree of irony. The speech
or saying thus becomes within the narrative a kind of "self-
fulfilling" prophecy. Luke uses this pattern so frequently and
subtly that at this point we can only mention the following
examples; most of them will be examined more closely in the
course of the study: the rejection of Jesus at Nazareth (Lk
4:16-30);[1] John the Baptist and the Sinful Woman (7:18-50);[2]
the Ten Pounds and the entry into Jerusalem (19:11-40);[3] Peter
and the Council (Acts 5:29ff);[4] Stephen and the Council
(7:1-60);[5] Paul in Pisidia and the Jews (13:16-52).[6] In each
case, the speech and action are so closely intertwined that the
significance of both is to be discovered in their mutual
dependence.

If we are to approach Luke-Acts as a literary work, it is
natural to ask what kind of work it is, that is, to what

---

[1] The Prophet is not accepted by his own country, 4:24;
Jesus' townspeople reject Him, 4:28. Cf. below, pp. 91ff.

[2] The people and the tax-collectors accept the Prophet John,
while the Pharisees and Scribes do not (7:29); Jesus the
Prophet is rejected by Simon the Pharisee but accepted by the
sinful woman (7:36-50). Cf. below, pp. 99ff.

[3] The king is not accepted by his citizens (19:14); Jesus
is proclaimed as king by his disciples (19:38) but rejected by
the Pharisees (19:39). Cf. below, pp. 168ff.

[4] God must be obeyed rather than men (Acts 5:29); God
raised up Jesus who was rejected by you (5:30); we are witnesses together with the Spirit given to those who obey God
(5:32); the leaders seek to kill the Apostles (5:33). Cf.
below, pp. 49f.

[5] Stephen, filled with the Holy Spirit and working signs
and wonders (6:8) attacks those who rejected Moses (who worked
signs and wonders) and Jesus (powerful in word and deed) and
have thereby rejected God (7:51ff). They kill Stephen. Cf.
below, pp. 75-76.

[6] Paul's speech closes with warning (13:41); the Jews
reject Paul (13:45); Paul speaks explicit words of rejection
(13:46-47); Gentiles rejoice (13:48); Jews reject (13:50);
Barnabas and Paul reject them (13:51). Cf. below, pp. 54ff.

literary genre does it belong?[1] For the purposes of this
study, however, a technical definition of genre is of less
significance than a firm grasp of the character of the narrative. It can be argued that Luke has moved in the direction of
making the Gospel (whether or not we can appropriately refer to
"Gospel" itself as a genre) a biography of Jesus.[2] Acts has
been variously described as a Romance,[3] a History[4] and an
Apology.[5] These (and perhaps other) genres can be applied with

[1]The difficulty of classifying N.T. writings according to
the genres of the ancient world is exemplified by Bultmann's
attempt to define "Gospel" according to genre in The History of
the Synoptic Tradition rev. ed. trans. by J. Marsh (New York:
Harper and Row, 1968) 368-374. The fact that Luke's work has a
preface and thereby presents itself as a form of literature (at
least in the sense that it would be on the open market and not
read only by a Christian community, cf. Dibelius, 146-147;
Cadbury, Beginnings II, 490ff) makes the attempt more inviting
but none the less elusive. The variety of conclusions reached
by scholars in this matter should caution against too precipitous a decision.

[2]Cadbury, Making, 127-132, discusses the reasons for
calling Luke's Gospel a biography, but concludes that "If we
take Luke's work as a whole, as we should do, and not by
halves, biography is not the word for it." (132).

[3]E. Goodenough, "The Perspective of Acts," SLA 57; Barrett,
15; cf. also H. J. Cadbury, The Book of Acts in History (New
York: Harper and Brothers, 1955), 8: "Sometimes the ficti-
tious romances offer the best parallel. I do not know where
one can get so many illustrations of the idiom and ideas of the
author of Acts in 150 pages as the love story of his near
contemporary, Chariton of Aphrodisias."

[4]Wilckens, 92; Barrett, 12-14; Cadbury, Making, 133;
Marshall, Luke, 21-76; E. Ehrhardt, "The Construction and
Purpose of the Acts of the Apostles," ST 12 (1958) 45-46.

[5]Classifying Acts as an Apology usually results in an
emphasis on the defense of all of Christianity over against the
Jews and the State (Cadbury, Making, 306-316; Conzelmann,
Theology, 137-149; B. S. Easton, The Purpose of Acts [London:
S.P.C.K., 1936]; further references in Dupont, Etudes, 394), or
on the defense of Paul from one direction or another (cf.
Goodenough, 54; Jervell, 153-207; Trocmé, 59). C. H. Talbert,
Luke and the Gnostics (New York: Abingdon, 1966), saw Acts as
an Apology or defense of orthodoxy against the threat of
Gnosticism. More recently, Talbert has classified Luke-Acts
among the hellenistic philosophic biographies, suggesting that
Luke's purpose in using this genre was again to fight Gnosticism; cf. Literary Patterns, Theological Themes and the Genre
of Luke-Acts (Missoula: Scholars Press, 1974) 125-134.

a fair degree of accuracy to either Luke or Acts. But the
tendency has been to focus on one or the other part of the work
in trying to define its genre.[1] What are we to call Luke-Acts
as a whole? If Luke has created one unified narrative, is
there a pre-existing genre within which it fits?[2] One problem
with beginning an analysis of Luke-Acts from the point of view
of a specific genre is that elements which fit that particular
genre may be emphasized at the expense of others which do not.
It may be better to begin with a general category which will
facilitate the reading of the text without unduly limiting or
biasing the data.

The general category which will be employed in this study
is that of the Story.[3] Such a category may at first appear to

---

[1]"Recent studies of Acts have shown that it is almost
always unsatisfactory to isolate any one theme as representing
Luke's total purpose, because to do so fails to do justice to
the whole book . . . each of these claims may contain some, but
none contains all of the truth," S. G. Wilson, The Gentiles and
the Gentile Mission in Luke-Acts (NTSMS 23; Cambridge: University Press, 1973) 265-266.

[2]The contemporary attention to Luke-Acts as a single work
has led many writers to speak less of genre and more about the
character of the narrative. Thus Trocmé, 49-50, speaks of the
whole work as a "Gospel," and Marshall, 218ff, as a work of
evangelism; Van Unnik, 59, as the "confirmation of the Gospel,"
and O'Neill, xi, 138f, as an apologetic written for purposes of
conversion.

[3]This classification would at first sight appear to agree
with the approach of Haenchen (as in "Tradition und Komposition," 209): "Er hat nicht -- oder jedenfalls nicht nur --
Quellenschriften übernommen und miteinander verbunden, sondern
er hat ganze Szenen und . . . Szenenfolge auf grund sehr
verschiedenartigen Traditionen selbst frei gestaltet." But
even though in his commentary Haenchen stresses the Lukan composition of individual narratives and does emphasize certain
elements of continuity (notably in the Cornelius sequence), his
treatment remains largely atomistic. That this is not entirely
due to the limitations of a commentary format is shown by this
statement: "He writes History by telling stories; short,
impressive, and dramatic scenes in relatively independent
succession . . . he uses a peculiar technique; he joins short,
compact, picturesque stories together like the stones of a
mosaic," SLA 259-260 [emphasis added]. The mosaic imagery we
met already in Dibelius, 127. But Acts does not present itself
to the reader as anything so static as a mosaic; it presents a
highly dramatic sweep of events ranging over an astonishing
(consider the shortness of the work!) area of space and time;
cf. Van Unnik, "Confirmation," 35.

be so broad as to be useless, but it is not. The category of
Story effectively distinguishes Luke-Acts from what it is not:
a theological tract, for example, or a rule of discipline, or
a liturgical formulary. What we would expect from those sorts
of documents we do not, or should not, seek from Luke-Acts.
Positively, seeing Luke-Acts at the level of the Story
provides us with important clues for its interpretation.[1]

Every story has characters, and a plot. The portrayal of
the characters[2] and the descriptions of their actions (or more
precisely, inter-actions) are the force which moves the plot to
a satisfactory conclusion. A story, in other words, is
inherently dramatic, possesses a dramatic structure. The word
structure, however, can be misleading if it is understood
statically, for the dramatic nature of a story is found precisely in movement, change and conflict. A story can of course
accommodate within itself other kinds of structures.[3] Luke-

---

[1]Concerning the neglect of the story-line in the analysis
of Luke-Acts, W. A. Beardslee, Literary Criticism of the New
Testament (Philadelphia: Fortress, 1970) 52, notes, "In all the
recent intense study of Acts, not much attention has been paid
to the narrative pattern in these terms . . . Cadbury is the
only recent scholar who has taken the dramatic structure of the
human side of the narrative seriously." Cf. also the critical
remarks of Van Unnik, "Eléments artistiques dans l'Evangile de
Luc," L'Evangile de Luc ed. by F. Neirynck (Bibliotheca
Ephemeridum Theologicarum Lovaniensium XXXII; Gembloux: J.
Duculot, 1973) 129-131, concerning the tendency of recent
scholarship to so emphasize Luke the theologian as to neglect
the medium through which that theology appears.

[2]By "portrayal of character" we do not suggest that in
this ancient document we find the sort of attention paid to
individual consciousness which characterizes contemporary
literature. The characters of Luke are described exteriorly,
and indeed by means of stereotype. But the stereotypes themselves are important for the dramatic tension in the story.
The characters of folklore are also stereotyped (the Handsome
Prince, the Wicked Stepmother, the Innocent Child, the Kindly
Fairy), but precisely by means of these stereotypes the folk-
tales of every language dredge the terror and delight of the
reader's unconscious, and thereby exercise a lasting charm.

[3]The abundance of parallels in Luke-Acts have been often
noted, as in Cadbury, Making, 231, and G. W. H. Lampe, "The
Holy Spirit in the Writings of St. Luke," Studies in the
Gospels ed. by D. E. Nineham (Essays in Memory of R. H. Lightfoot; Oxford: Basil Blackwell, 1955) 195ff. They have however
exercised a fatal attraction for those studies of Luke-Acts

Acts, for example, clearly contains a definite and important
geographic structure.[1] But if the story is well constructed,
these structures serve to advance the dramatic movement of the
plot.

What are some of the clues for interpretation which come
from regarding Luke-Acts at the level of the story? First, our
attention is centered on the characters of the story, for they
are the ones who make the plot move. In Luke-Acts, it is Jesus
and the Apostles who are the main characters.[2] To an extraordinary degree, everything that happens in Luke-Acts happens

---

which have set out to be literary studies, e.g. R. Morgenthaler, Die lukanische Geschichtsschreibung als Zeugnis 2 Vols.
(Zürich: Zwingli-Verlag, 1949), M. D. Goulder, Type and History
in Acts (London: S.P.C.K., 1964), and Talbert, Literary
Patterns. It cannot be denied either that there are patterns
of parallelism in the work, or that they have a certain
literary importance. But when the "law of duality" (Morgenthaler [II, 5] speaks of 'Zweiheitsgesetz') is elevated to the
level of a totally dominating literary pattern, it falls apart.
See for example Morgenthaler's struggle (Vol. I, passim) to fit
triadic structures into structures of two or four or six, or
Goulder's (36-39) long argument that the shipwreck of Paul was
intended by Luke to parallel the death and resurrection of
Jesus. Talbert's tables appear more sober. But a careful
analysis of his many lists of parallels reveal that frequently
the similarity between passages is more apparent than real,
that often they are due to the paraphrase of the author, and
that there is little consistency of norm between parallelism of
structure or content (cf. e.g. 26-27, 57). More distressing is
that the significance of the parallels is only unlocked by the
key of an extrinsic theological principle. Thus Morgenthaler
(Vol. II, 8) finds the key to the law of duality in a text from
Deut 19:15. Goulder (34) depends on the principle of the Body
of Christ, and Talbert (103) on "the Early Catholic concept of
an ideal Apostolic Age followed by the emergence of Heresy."
Finally, such one-sided emphasis upon the cyclic tends to
obscure what is the most impressive aspect of Luke's work, that
of progress, growth and change.

[1]Conzelmann, Theology, 18-94; also "Zur Lukasanalyze,"
ZTK 49 (1952) 16-33; Menoud, "Le Plan," 44-51.

[2]It may with some justification be objected that in Luke-
Acts, God is really the main actor, who by his intervention
makes the story move. This is emphasized by Haenchen in regard
to the spread of the mission. Yet it is through the human
characters that God's action is made present. However powerful
or abrupt the manifestation of his power or will (by Angel to
Mary and Zachary, visions to Peter and Paul, by the outpouring
of the Spirit on the Apostles, indeed by the resurrection of
Jesus), it is the change wrought in the human characters and
their actions which translate these divine interventions. Dahl

as a result of the action of these characters or in response to
them. Part of their description, therefore, is the response
they engender. Our attention is drawn thereby to those who do
the responding to these main characters. In Luke-Acts, there
are really no sub-plots; the secondary characters do not lead
lives of their own, or have their own stories, but are important solely as they are drawn into contact with the central
characters. Whatever the small and enlivening touches of
individuality given them by the author, it is in their response
to the main characters, and as representatives of particular
modes of response that their importance for the story is found.

Another clue for interpretation offered by seeing Luke-
Acts as a story is that the narrative, if well constructed,
possesses a dramatic logic. There is movement and development
from one incident or speech to another, and a fittingness to
this progression. The degree to which Luke's story has convinced us for so long of its correctness is testimony enough to
his skill in constructing the story; he is a master story-
teller.[1] If we take this seriously, we will also take seriously

---

("Story of Abraham," 152-3) is right when he says, "Whatever
the Greek, Hellenistic and Roman components of Luke's historiography may have been, his own conscious intention was to write
history in biblical style, or rather, to write the continuation
of the biblical history." If we look to the biblical histories
we must agree that the overt and powerful interventions of God
make Moses no less the hero of the Exodus or David of the Court
History. Similarly, the theological influence of Tyche and
Isis in the Golden Ass do not detract from Lucius' place as the
main character of the Romance.

[1] It is this skill which frustrates attempts to discover
sources behind the narrative. Luke's account at first seems
plausible; then closer examination reveals inconsistencies,
loose threads -- perhaps a source! -- but the thread leads
nowhere. Let us suppose an Antiochean source, and try to
relate that to the evidence given concerning Paul and Barnabas.
We see how Luke introduces each very discreetly into the narrative (4:36-37, 8:1-3) with just enough information to be por-
tentous for the future; then amplifies the role of Paul (9:1-
26); then brings Paul and Barnabas together briefly (9:27);
then separates them (9:30); then amplifies the role of Barnabas
alone (11:22ff); then reunites him to Paul (11:25-26) and sends
them to Jerusalem together (11:30), bringing them back (12:25)
in time for their commission by the Church of Antioch (13:2);
then when Barnabas' role is completed, finally separating them
for good (15:36). And all through this complex progression,
Luke has interwoven the accounts concerning Peter in Jerusalem
and Judea! If it is difficult to spot a source behind such

the influence of the story-line as a clue to understanding a
particular passage. It is not enough to establish a spatial
context of before and after; we must seek to place a passage
precisely within the dramatic flow of the narrative, recognizing that there is in all probability a good literary reason
for the passage occurring in this place and none other, and
that the author has offered us in the story itself the possibility of grasping that reason.

We have suggested that a literary interpretation of Luke-
Acts must take seriously prophecy as a literary pattern, and
the shape of the narrative as story. How do these points
relate to our approach to the passage which has served as our
starting point, Acts 4:32ff? If we see this passage as part of
a story, we pay the closest attention to the way the story
moves to and from the passage; we must note especially the role
of the main characters before, during and after this passage;
we must attend to the way in which minor characters are seen as
responding to these main figures. Finally we must discover
whether the placement and significance of the passage may be
related to the presence of a literary prophecy within the story.

Both the questions we have put to the text and the
approach to these questions we have suggested make it clear
that this study is resolutely literary in character.[1] This
deliberate limitation of the inquiry means that certain kinds
of questions will not be pursued. The first is the question of
historicity. Although there is supporting evidence that certain early Christians practiced some form of communal property[2]

---

masterful weaving, it is also hard to recognize the author who
accomplished it as one having only a casual interest in the
connection between short vivid stories.

[1]A literary analysis of any ancient document must of
course also to some extent be "historical," if only because
the historical setting places certain limits of meaning available to the author. The present study does not seek to de-
historicize the text by viewing it as a timeless structure of
meaning, but rather as an historically conditioned structure
of meaning.

[2]Didache 4:8: οὐκ ἀποστραφήσῃ τὸν ἐνδεόμενον
συγκοινωνήσεις δὲ πάντα τῷ ἀδελφῷ σοῦ καὶ οὐκ ἐρεῖς ἴδια εἶναι.
εἰ γὰρ ἐν τῷ ἀθανάτῳ κοινωνοί ἐστε πόσῳ μᾶλλον ἐν τοῖς θνητοῖς;
Barnabas 19:8: κοινωνήσεις ἐν πᾶσιν τῷ πλησίον σου καὶ οὐκ
ἐρεῖς ἴδια εἶναι. εἰ γὰρ ἐν τῷ ἀφθάρτῳ κοινωνοί ἐστε πόσῳ

and it is possible that Luke could have been idealizing an actual practice,[1] the significance of this possibility will not be examined, but only the significance of Luke's description of the practice in its literary function. The second set of questions excluded by this approach is what might be classified as religionsgeschichtliche questions, namely the various kinds of relations which may have existed between the descriptions of Luke and the examples of the ideal of community property found elsewhere in the world roughly contemporaneous to Luke, in the sectarian documents emerging from Qumran,[2] in the writings found within certain hellenistic philosophic schools,[3] and in

---

μᾶλλον ἐν τοῖς φθαρτοῖς; Haenchen, 6, denies any dependence here on Acts, which would of course render these independent witnesses to the practice. It is intriguing to find that the warrant for sharing goods comes closer to the argumentation of Paul (cf. I Cor 9:11; Rom 15:26) than of Acts. Cf. also Lucian of Samosata, Death of Peregrinus 13: καταφρονοῦσιν οὖν ἀπάντων ἐξ ἴσης καὶ κοινὰ ἡγοῦνται.

[1]The argument that the need for a collection to the saints in Jerusalem was caused by the straitened circumstances resulting from the sale of all the property, so that there was nothing more to be held in common, has some merit. Cf. Haenchen, 235; Franklin, 25-50; K. F. Nickle, The Collection (SBT 48; Naperville: Alec R. Allenson, 1966) 23-24.

[2]There is no ideological relationship in the Qumran texts between the practice of community goods and any ascetic ideal, or a community self-consciousness as "the poor," a designation which is used in Qumran not in reference to possessions, but in biblical fashion as a self-designation over against powerful foes. We take a position here against that of D. Flusser, "Blessed are the Poor in Spirit," IEJ 10 (1960) 5, and H. Kandler, "Die Bedeutung der Armut im Schriften von Chirbet Qumran," Jud 13 (1957) 193-209, and in agreement with L. Keck, "The Poor among the Saints in Jewish Christianity and Qumran," 54-78. The community of goods in Qumran is related to the separatist ideology of the sect; community of goods is a demand of purity. A possible historical root of this ideology may be found in the texts which speak of the struggle between the "poor" and the rapacious priests of Jerusalem; cf. 1QpHab 8:8-12; 9:4-5; 12:3-10; 4QpPs37 2:9-10; CD 4:15; 6:16. Degenhardt (188-207) correctly attaches the Qumran practice concerning possessions to the observance of purity, but does not go far enough.

[3]The relationship between the sharing of goods in Acts and the ideal of the philosophic schools still needs considerable examination, not only because of the similarity in language (cf. notes on pp. 2-3, above) but also because of: a) the way the Neo-Pythagorean writings attach the sharing of goods to a higher spiritual unity, e.g. friendship with all living things (cf.

the evidence offered by hellenistic Judaism.[1] The ideal was so
widespread that it is the more striking the Rabbinic tradition
retains so little trace of it.[2] A comparative study of these

Iamblichus, Life, 108); b) the way Luke colors his portrait of
the Apostles with the tones of the Philosopher (e.g. παρρησία
2:29, 4:13, 29, 31, etc.; the Socratic appeal to obeying God
rather than men, 5:29; Paul at Athens, etc. [cf. Plümacher,
1-31]); c) the way that early observers of the Christian sect
identified it as a philosophic school, and the way this designation was taken over by the Apologists of the second century.
What influence did Luke have in this development? Cf. R.
Wilkin, "Collegia, Philosophical Schools, and Theology," The
Catacombs and the Colosseum ed. by S. Benko and J. O'Rourke
(Valley Forge: Judson Press, 1971) 268-291.

[1]The descriptions of the common life of the Essenes/
Therapeutae (for the argument supporting the identification of
these with Qumran cf. G. Vermes, "Essenes -- Qumran --
Therapeutae," RQ 2 [1960] 427-433) by Josephus (JW II, 122;
Ant. XVIII, 20) and Philo (On the Contemplative Life, 13-16;
That Every Good Man is Free, 12; Hypothetica, 11:4ff) are
important for showing how hellenistic Jews would transform a
Judean phenomenon into the clothing of a philosophic school.
Of course the possibility that hellenization may have influenced the Jewish phenomenon in the first place cannot be
overlooked, either; cf. B. Dombrowski, "hy'd in 1QS and τὸ
κοινόν: An Instance of early Greek and Jewish Synthesis," HTR
59 (1966) 293-307. Like Luke, Philo had no problem with introducing the proverb on friendship into a biblical story, cf. On
Abraham, 40. On the other hand, the descriptions of Philo and
Josephus also show us the extent to which Luke's description
remains semitic, or better, biblical in tone.

[2]Contrary to the suggestion of C. A. Scott, "The 'Fellowship' or κοινωνία," ExpT 35 (1923-4) 567, that Acts 2:41 can be
explained in the light of the Pharisaic Haburah, we have no
evidence from the earliest Pharisaic sources (Mishnah Demai 2;
Tosephta Demai 2; BT Bekoroth 30a-31a) that would indicate such
a sharing of goods as an ideal. Cf. J. Neusner, "The Fellowship ('bwrh) in the Second Jewish Commonwealth," HTR 53 (1960)
125-142 and C. Rabin, Qumran Studies (London: Oxford University
Press, 1957) 22-36. Although the root 'rb figures prominently
in Qumran texts concerned with the mingling of property (cf.
1QS 6:22; 7:24-25; 8:22; 9:8), the Mishnah Erubin indicates
that outside Qumran any "partnership" formed according to its
regulations existed not to fulfill an ideal of community
sharing, but to extend mobility on the Sabbath. There may have
been, in fact, some sort of rabbinic attack on the idea of
holding goods in common. Cf. Pirke Aboth, 5:10, and the very
late Midrash Rabbah on Koheleth I, 8, 3, concerning the minim.
But these texts are so obscure, we cannot be sure. Acts 4:34
makes an allusion to Deut 15:4; a reading of the Sifre on that
passage will indicate how far removed the ideal of community
property was from the rabbinic commentators. For a guide to
the Rabbinic materials in this area, cf. G. F. Moore, Judaism
in the First Centuries of the Christian Era, 3 Vols. (Cambridge:

traditions needs to be done, by taking into full account the integrity of the ideal within each of its literary and institutional manifestations before making comparisons. As an attempt to grasp the significance of the motif of community possessions within the literary structure of Luke-Acts, the present study can be regarded as a first step towards the establishment of such a thorough structural comparison.

Harvard University Press, 1927-30) II, 162-179; Str-B IV, 536-558; and L. Frankel, "Charity and Charitable Institutions," Jewish Encyclopedia (1903) III 667-670.

CHAPTER ONE

In order to situate the passages about the community of goods in chs. 2 and 4, it is necessary to survey rapidly all the passages in Acts which speak about possessions. Immediately striking is the way in which the passages are distributed. In the first eight chapters of Acts there are seven passages in which possessions figure more or less prominently.[1] In marked contrast, the last twenty chapters contain very little about possessions. We will begin by looking first at these later chapters.

A. Possessions in Acts 9-28:

1. In chapters nine and ten, Luke twice mentions almsgiving in descriptions of pious persons. Tabitha or Dorcas is described in 9:36: αὕτη ἦν πλήρης ἔργων ἀγαθῶν καὶ ἐλεημοσυνῶν ὧν ἐποίει. The piety of Cornelius is more elaborately described. He was a man εὐσεβὴς καὶ φοβούμενος τὸν θεὸν σὺν παντὶ τῷ οἴκῳ αὐτοῦ ποιῶν ἐλεημοσύνας πολλὰς τῷ λαῷ καὶ δεόμενος τοῦ θεοῦ διὰ παντός (10:2). That Cornelius had the good fortune of hearing the word about Jesus is twice attributed to his prayer and almsgiving (10:4, 31). These descriptions are typical for pious persons in Judaism,[2] and are not related by the author to the practice of community goods.

2. On three occasions Luke describes a loss of possessions experienced by those who confront Paul. In the first, the slave girl of Philippi who possessed mantic powers is exorcized by Paul (16:18); her owners, realizing that with her loss of powers departed as well ἡ ἐλπὶς τῆς ἐργασίας αὐτῶν

---

[1]The election of Matthias (1:15-26); first community description (2:41-47); healing of the lame man (3:1-10); second community description (4:32-37); Ananias and Sapphira (5:1-11); the appointment of the Seven (6:1-7); Simon Magus (8:18-24).

[2]Among the many passages in praise of almsgiving, cf. Mishnah Peah 1:1; Pirke Aboth 1:2; Aboth de-Rabbi Nathan 4; BT Berakoth 5b, 8a; Shabbath 156b; Rosh Hashanah 16b; Gittin 7a,b; Sukkah 49b.

(16:19), dragged Paul and Silas before the magistrates. A second incident involved Demetrius and the silversmiths of Ephesus. The success of Paul's preaching threatened their livelihood (19:24-5), and they caused a riot. Both these passages speak of possessions in a way familiar to us from the polemics of hellenistic philosophers, in which the opponents of true teaching are invariably described as money-lovers who resist the truth because it hurts their pocket-book.[1] This convention is in fact used by Luke elsewhere, and the two incidents fit into a wider pattern used in the Gospel. But in these two cases, the possessions motif is certainly not central, and of course completely unrelated to community of goods. A third mention of loss of property occurs in the story immediately preceding that of the silversmiths. After the Jewish exorcists (the Sons of Sceva) were routed by the demon who recognized only the power of Jesus and Paul (19:15), a great fear came upon the city (19:17) and as a result a great number of those who had become believers (but who still, it seems, practiced magic) burned their magic books, at a considerable monetary loss (19:19). This passage presents certain intriguing echoes of chs. 2 and 4 (the role of the Spirit-filled Apostle, the fear aroused in the city, the shedding of possessions), but of course the believers here do not hold goods in common, but simply dispossess themselves of magic books.[2]

3. The previous passages spoke about possessions in terms of response to Paul. What does Luke say about Paul's own use of possessions? In 18:3, we are told that Paul worked for a living, practicing together with Aquila the trade of tent-maker at Corinth where he stayed for a considerable length of time

---

[1]Whether directed against Sophists or Philosophers, the charge of φιλαργυρία was part of the stereotyped topos of polemic against opponents. Cf. e.g., Julian the Apostate, Or. 6:181C, 198B, 200C; Dio Chrysostom, Or. 32:9, 11; 35:1; 77/8: 37; Epictetus, I, 29, 55-57; I, 9, 19-20; II, 16, 3; II, 17, 3; III, 24, 78; Lucian of Samosata, The Runaways 14 and 20; Nigrinus 25; Icaromenippus 5 and 30; Timon 56; Menippus 5; Death of Peregrinus 15-16; Hermotimus 9-10.

[2]The point of the incident is of course to be found in 19:20: οὕτως κατὰ κράτος τοῦ κυρίου ὁ λόγος ηὔξανεν καὶ ἴσχυεν. The power of the Gospel overcomes the power of magic. Cf. Haenchen, 567-568.

(18:18). Luke makes no attempt to relate this labor of Paul to
any community of goods which may have existed in Corinth.

In the farewell speech at Miletus (20:18-35) Paul concludes with passionate words in defense of his ministry, and
singles out his lack of greed (the true teacher does not have
φιλαργυρία) and his service to others: ἀργυρίου ἢ χρυσίου ἢ
ἱματισμοῦ οὐδενὸς ἐπεθύμησα. αὐτοὶ γινώσκετε ὅτι ταῖς χρείαις
μου καὶ τοῖς οὖσιν μετ᾽ ἐμοῦ ὑπηρέτησαν αἱ χεῖρες αὗται.
πάντα ὑπέδειξα ὑμῖν ὅτι οὕτως κοπιῶντας δεῖ ἀντιλαμβάνεσθαι
τῶν ἀσθενούντων . . . (20:33-35). The speech is a "pastoral"
sermon, in which Paul is explicitly presented as a model for
the presbyters to follow.[1] His remark about his lack of greed
(which echoes Samuel's farewell to Israel, I Sam 12:3), is
straightforward. But what is the point of Paul's positive
example?[2] It is that the leaders are so (οὕτως) to support
themselves by their labor that they might help the needs of the
weak. This picture of the leaders of a community working to
support the community is unlike the picture of the Apostles in
Jerusalem receiving the donations of the believers at their
feet. Nor is there any language in this passage which would
suggest a community of goods. Luke employs none of the distinctive imagery of chs. 2 and 4, even when this speech provided him with an excellent opportunity for doing so.

When Paul comes on his final and fateful visit to
Jerusalem, he is told by James and the presbyters to show a
sign of amity to those who thought he was preaching against the
Law by participating in a rite of purification. A striking
detail in this small scene is that Paul is asked to pay their
fee (δαπάνησον) for the rite (21:24). Paul is seen as having
his own funds to dispense, with no implication that he should
draw on a community store to perform this act. Again, in

---

[1]Cf. J. Dupont, Le Discours de Milet; Testament Pastoral
de Saint Paul (Lectio Divina 32; Paris: Editions du Cerf,
1962); J. Munck, "Discours d'adieu dans le Nouveau Testament
et dans la littérature biblique," Aux Sources de la Tradition
Chrétienne, 155-170; H. Schürmann, "Das Testament des Paulus
für die Kirche," Traditionsgeschichtliche Untersuchungen zu den
synoptischen Evangelien (Düsseldorf: Patmos-Verlag, 1967)
310-340.

[2]The picture of Paul supporting himself and others amplifies the presentation of 18:3.

24:26, it is said that Felix had hopes ὅτι χρήματα δοθήσεται
αὐτῷ ὅπο τοῦ Παύλου. At the very end of Acts we find Paul
dwelling ἐν ἰδίῳ μισθώματι (28:30). This is only a passing
reference and perhaps should not be pushed too strongly, but
the ἴδιος again supports the picture of Paul as one who lives
out of his own means and not, for example, supported by the
community of goods of the Roman congregation.

The details we have mentioned here are small and scarcely
present a full picture, but the Paul of Acts is a man who works
to support himself, has money to help those more needy than
himself, and funds of his own to dispense when needed. In this
regard, Luke is close to the picture Paul draws of himself.
Thus in his defense of his apostolic mode of life in I Cor 9,
Paul claims the right (and supports it from the Scriptures) to
share in the σάρκικα of the community to whom he has given τὰ
πνευμάτικα (9:11), but insists even more strongly that he and
Barnabas did not take advantage of this right (9:15), that no
stumbling block might be placed in the way of the Gospel
(9:12).[1]

4. The Collection in Paul and Acts: The agreement
between Luke and Paul on the general portrait of Paul's use of
possessions makes even more puzzling Luke's treatment of Paul's
final trip to Jerusalem. We are able to discuss the distinctiveness of Luke's presentation, because from Paul himself we
have ample evidence concerning the trip. According to Paul,
the reason he went to Jerusalem was to extend κοινωνία from the
communities he had established to the Jerusalem community by
means of a collection. Of this motivation we find nothing in
Acts.

Paul mentions the collection repeatedly in his genuine
letters. In his account of his meeting with the Jerusalem
leaders in Gal 2:10, he says that the only requirement imposed
on Barnabas and himself was μόνον τῶν πτωχῶν ἵνα μνημονεύωμεν ὃ
καὶ ἐσπούδασα αὐτὸ τοῦτο ποιῆσαι. In Luke's version of the
Jerusalem Council in Acts 15, no mention is made of this

---

[1]Cf. also I Cor 4:12; I Thess 2:9; II Thess 3:7. Haenchen
594, says that the picture of Paul in Acts 20:33 is a "pious
exaggeration," in the light of II Cor 11:9, but the overall
testimony from Paul would support at least the part of Luke's
presentation that Paul worked to support himself.

requirement.

Paul's Corinthian correspondence shows that Paul came to
regard the collection as an important if not critical element
in his ministry. In I Cor 16:1-4, he lays plans for the taking
up of the collection in Macedonia and Achaia, plans complex
enough to include the sending of emissaries and letters of
recommendation (16:3-4). If, as is quite possible, chapter
eight of Second Corinthians was originally a separate letter,
Paul considered the matter significant enough to warrant such
attention.[1]

The collection is again uppermost in Paul's mind at the
conclusion of Romans, which was written shortly before he left
for Jerusalem.[2] Again it is evident that Paul sought to
establish κοινωνία with the Jerusalem community precisely
through the gift of money, but was not at all certain of
success.[3] From Paul's own words, therefore, we are left in

---

[1]As II Cor comes to us, both chs. 8 and 9 deal with the
collection. The most fascinating aspect of Paul's language in
speaking about the collection is the way it approaches that of
Luke in Acts 2 and 4. He speaks of it as a κοινωνία τῆς
διακονίας τῆς εἰς τοὺς ἁγίους (II Cor 8:4), and employs the
concept of ἰσότης dear to hellenistic utopian writers: οὐ γὰρ
ἵνα ἄλλοις ἄνεσις ὑμῖν θλῖψις ἀλλ' ἐξ ἰσότητος . . . ὅπως
γένηται ἰσότης (II Cor 8:13-14). For the relationship of
κοινωνία to φιλία, cf. Aristotle, Nichomachean Ethics, VIII,
11, 12; IX, 12, 1. For ἰσότης and φιλία, cf. Iamblichus, Life
of Pythagoras, 162 and 180; Diogenes Laertius, Lives of Eminent
Philosophers, VIII, 1, 10; Plato, Laws, 741A, 744B, 757A, 837A;
Aristotle, Nichomachean Ethics, VIII, 5, 5; 6, 7; 7, 3-4. Cf.
also G. Stählin, "ἴσος," TDNT 3 (1965) 343-349. Paul also uses
language of cultic flavor in discussing the collection. He
calls it a λειτουργία in II Cor 9:12-13 (cf. also Rom 15:26).
On this aspect of his language, cf. A. J. Malherbe, "The
Corinthian Contribution," Restoration Quarterly 3 (1959) 230-
231. The emphasis Paul places on the collection winning the
favor not only of God but also of men (II Cor 8:20-21) and
convincing the Jerusalem Church not only of the generosity of
his communities but also the quality of their faith in the
Gospel (II Cor 9:13), shows that the motivation of charity was
qualified by the hope of healing breaches and affirming the
unity of the churches.

[2]νυνὶ δὲ πορεύομαι εἰς ʼΙερουσαλὴμ διακονῶν τοῖς ἁγίοις
(Rom 15:25). It is interesting that Paul (15:26) uses as a
motivation for generosity the same image of "fleshly-spiritual"
parity between communities as he has used in I Cor 9 as govern-
ing the relationship between the Corinthian community and
himself.

[3]He concludes (15:21) on a pessimistic note, asking the

34

no doubt why he went to Jerusalem. It was to perform a
λειτουργία, a public act of διακονία, which through the gift
of money would extend κοινωνία to the Jerusalem community from
the communities of Paul.

If we had only the Acts account, we would have no idea
that this is why Paul made his journey to Jerusalem. Luke
seems to be particularly well acquainted with Paul's movements
at this point. Indeed, the correlation of Acts and the letters
at this point enables us to establish a plausible chronology
for this period of Paul's life.[1] But Luke gives us not a clue
of Paul's real purpose. In Acts 19:21, Paul makes up his mind
to go to Jerusalem, and Luke knows that he sent emissaries
before him to Macedonia (19:22). In 20:16, Paul's eagerness
to reach Jerusalem before Pentecost is noted, but in neither
case is there mention of the collection.

In Jerusalem, Luke tells us only of the brief meeting
between Paul and the elders and their suggestion that he perform an act of reconciliation (!), with no mention of the
gesture of reconciliation Paul himself intended.[2] Indeed, if
it were not for one passing remark in Paul's defense before
Felix, Luke would have left us totally in the dark concerning
Paul's motivation. There, Paul says δι' ἐτῶν δὲ πλειόνων
ἐλεημοσύνας ποιήσων εἰς τὸ ἔθνος μου παρεγενόμην καὶ προσφοράς
(24:17). This at least tells us that Paul brought money with
him to Jerusalem, but the "alms and offerings to my nation"
sound little like the διακονία τοῖς ἁγίοις of which Paul has

_____

Roman community for prayer that ῥυσθῶ ἀπὸ τῶν ἀπειθούντων ἐν τῇ
Ἰουδαίᾳ καὶ ἡ διακονία μου ἡ εἰς Ἰερουσαλὴμ εὐπρόσδεκτος τοῖς
ἁγίοις γένηται.

[1]H. J. Cadbury, The Book of Acts in History, 123-124; E.
Trocmé, Le "Livre des Actes" et l'Histoire, 86; J. Knox,
Chapters in a Life of Paul (New York: Abingdon, 1950) 71.

[2]H. Wendt, Die Apostelgeschichte (Meyer; Göttingen:
Vandenhoeck & Ruprecht, 1913) 300, sees in the διακονία of
21:19 a reminiscence of the collection. Luke uses the term
elsewhere in this connection (11:29), but in the nearest context (20:24) it means Paul's ministry of preaching; the
possibility of its referring to the collection here is slight;
cf. Haenchen, 608. If it were such a reminiscence, it is all
the stranger that Luke has Paul's gesture of reconciliation
replaced by that of James.

spoken.[1]

We can only speculate about the reasons for this lacuna in Luke's presentation of Paul.[2] If Luke knew about Paul's collection even so little as he revealed in 24:17, we would have expected him to exploit it as an example of the κοινωνία he had himself described in chs. 2 and 4. Is it possible that Luke knew more than he wished to tell? Luke leaves the motivation for the Jerusalem trip mysterious, but he does portray Paul's way there as a path of suffering.[3] Did he know very well of the gift Paul brought, and know as well that the gift did not succeed in the way Paul wanted, that perhaps the leaders in Jerusalem did not establish κοινωνία with Paul, and did nothing perhaps to forestall his arrest and imprisonment?[4] The thought is suggestive, but must remain speculative. What is certain is that Luke was aware that Paul had brought alms with him to Jerusalem, yet failed to exploit this as an

---

[1]Haenchen (655) notes correctly, "It is only because we know about Paul's great collection from his letters that we recognize an allusion to it here; for Luke's readers that was not possible." Dupont ("L'Union entre les premières Chrétiens dans les Actes des Apôtres," 914) points out the strangeness of this presentation: ". . . après avoit décrit sous les plus vives couleurs la κοινωνία dans la première communauté de Jérusalem, Luc nous deçoit en ne nous donnant qu'une image incomplète et imparfaite de la pensée de Paul au sujet de la κοινωνία qui unit les Eglises Chrétiennes entre elles et avec leur centre, Jérusalem; il a laissé dans l'ombre, en particulier, le rôle de la grande collecte en relation avec cette κοινωνία."

[2]Knox, Chapters, 71; for two other suggestions concerning Luke's motivation, cf. Trocmé, 61 and K. Nickle, The Collection, 148-150.

[3]Dibelius, 201; J. C. O'Neill, The Theology of St. Luke in its Historical Setting, 67-69; C. H. Talbert, Literary Patterns, Theological Themes and the Genre of Luke-Acts, 16.

[4]"The conclusion is clear: either the author of Acts was ignorant of the offering brought to Jerusalem by Paul and of its importance to him, or he deliberately transformed his information for the sake of his portrait of Paul. In view of the terminology of 24:17, the latter alternative is to be preferred. Perhaps he treated the offering this way because he knew it failed to do what Paul hoped it would; at the same time, his concern to show the unity of Paul and the Jerusalem Church would prevent him from saying so," L. Keck, "The Poor among the Saints in the New Testament," ZNW 56 (1965) 107.

expression of a community of goods.

What is still stranger is that Luke does involve Paul in a collection to Jerusalem as a representative of the Antioch community in Acts 11:27-30, 12:25. This collection was engendered by the prophecy of Agabus that a great famine was to arrive. The disciples in Antioch each set aside as they were able money for the διακονία to the brothers in Judea, and the collection was sent to Jerusalem διὰ χειρὸς Βαρναβᾶ καὶ Σαύλου (11:30). We note at once that this collection takes place at the beginning of Paul's career rather than at the end, and immediately following his recruitment by Barnabas. This sequence of events will be analyzed more closely at the end of this study.

B. Possessions in Acts 1-8:

In the last twenty chapters of Acts we have been able to find only eleven passages which deal in any way with possessions, and most of them have been passing references. In the first eight chapters, however, the situation is strikingly different; here there are seven passages, only one of which (3:6) can be considered a passing reference. Moreover, when we examine these passages, we discover that they are found within certain patterns.

1. We note first of all that in every passage about possessions the Apostles are somehow involved. a) In the account of the death of Judas and the election of Matthias (1:12-26), Judas' use of money is intertwined with the abandonment of the apostolic office. b) In the first description of the community life, although the Apostles play no role in the community goods, their authority within the community is twice emphasized (2:42, 43). c) In the healing of the lame man (3:1-9), Peter contrasts the silver and gold which the Apostles do not possess to the power of healing which they do (3:6). d) In the second description of community life (4:32-37), the power and authority of the Apostles is not simply stressed in regard to preaching (4:33), but they are placed at the center of the community goods (4:35, 37). e) In the story of Ananias and Sapphira (5:1-11), the Apostle Peter receives the fraudulent gift of the couple (5:2), confronts them with their

deceit (5:3), and speaks the word which strikes them dead.
f) In the appointment of the Seven (6:1-7), the Apostles
abandon their place in the distribution of goods and appoint
others to take their place. g) In the story of Simon Magus
(8:9-24), there is a confrontation between the Apostle Peter
and a man who wishes to buy his way into the apostolic power.

Simply the coincidence of talk about possessions and talk
about the Apostles should lead us to wonder about the relation
between the two. Is the author intending in each of these
instances to say something simply about possessions, or something about the Apostles? Or to put it another way: in each
of these passages, does the incident recounted appear to center
around the possessions as such, or around the Apostles and
their authority?

2. It should also be noticed that this preponderance of
materials about possessions occurs within the limits of the
story about the Jerusalem community. Even in the Simon Magus
story set in Samaria, Peter and John are sent down from
Jerusalem to confirm the work of Philip.

3. Finally, these passages are set within a certain
dynamic pattern. In three of the passages (2:41ff, 4:32ff,
6:1ff), the talk about possessions figures in the context of
the life of the believers and Apostles within the community;
in three other passages the use or attitude toward possessions
figures in stories about rejection, either from the community
(Ananias and Sapphira) or the apostolate (Judas and Simon
Magus). The pattern comes together most clearly in 4:32-5:11,
where the juxtaposition of the account about the community of
goods and the death of the couple is joined literarily (cf.
4:35, 37 and 5:2) and thematically (by the power and authority
of the Apostles).

We see, then, that our beginning passage, 4:32-35, has a
certain paradoxical character. On the one hand, it is
(together with 2:41ff but more elaborately) unique in Acts in
speaking about a community of goods. On the other hand, it
shares with other passages in the first eight chapters of Acts
by being centered in the Jerusalem ministry, involving the
power and authority of the Apostles, and being part of a dynamic of inclusion/exclusion.

Having made these preliminary remarks about the motif of possessions in Acts as a whole, we can now begin to follow our program of interpretation, by placing them within the story. It was suggested above that it is the characters of the story which should receive our first attention since it is from them the story flows. We start then, by analyzing the literary description of the main characters of Acts.

C. The Men of the Spirit in Acts

We have already been puzzled by the way in which Luke seemed to have good knowledge of Paul's movements in his trip to Jerusalem, yet either did not know or, as is more likely, knew and chose to alter the purpose of that visit. Commentators have grappled with this paradox again and again; the movements of the Paul of Acts can be fitted so closely to the Paul of the letters,[1] yet he remains altogether such a different figure. Paul identifies himself as an Apostle,[2] yet Luke gives him this title only in passing (Acts 14:4, 14) and then together with Barnabas. Paul sees himself as the Apostle to the Gentiles,[3] and while deeply concerned about the fate of the Jews (Rom 9-11), sees his own role as that of stimulating them to emulation of the faith of the Gentiles. But Luke presents Paul, in spite of repeated threats to turn exclusively to the Gentiles (13:46, 18:6, 28:28), still at the very end addressing the Jews (28:17). One can argue whether the teaching on the Law and of justification by faith is the most essential pauline teaching, but it is certainly among his most distinctive: in Acts there is only the merest approach (explicitly) to this teaching in the words of Paul (13:38-9).[4]

---

[1]Cf. the many ingenious correlations brought forward by W. Paley, Horae Paulinae (London: J. Davis, 1790), and the still impressive exposition of W. Ramsay, St. Paul the Traveller and the Roman Citizen (New York: Putnam, 1904).

[2]Rom 1:1; 11:13; I Cor 1:1; 4:9; 15:9; II Cor 1:1; 12:12; Gal 1:1; 1:17; I Thess 2:7.

[3]Rom 1:5; 11:13; 15:16; 15:18; Gal 1:16; 2:2; 2:8; 2:9; I Thess 2:16.

[4]The frequently cited essay by Ph. Vielhauer, "Zum 'Paulinismus' der Apostelgeschichte," EvT 10 (1950-51) 1-15,

The most striking divergence is undoubtedly in the style
of Paul. Paul confesses himself to be a man of little
eloquence,[1] yet Acts presents him as the most masterful of
orators, at every turn fitting his words aptly to his audience
and occasion, so much the speaker that the pagans of Lystra
think him the very incarnation of Hermes (Acts 14:12). The
Paul of the letters is a man subject to rejection and humilia-
tion, forging out of his experiences a theology of the cross.[2]
The Paul of Acts moves from glory to glory, meeting no affront
without an appropriate response, suffering no setback which
does not turn to a still more impressive triumph. Luke paints
Paul's journey to Jerusalem in sombre colors, it is true; but
at the very point of his arrest, Paul is a figure of magnifi-
cence, and as he makes his slow way to Rome through endless
hearings, he continually proves himself the master both of
court oom rhetoric and the perils of shipwreck, so that at the
end of Acts we find the prisoner Paul not really confined, but
living in his own quarters, preaching the Word "unhindered."[3]

---

is important for having centered continental scholarship on
what is distinctively Luke's contribution to the New Testament.
Like Conzelmann's pioneering work, however, Vielhauer's influence has outstripped the merit of the essay. It suffers from
severe problems in method and presupposition. Using his
methods, it would be as easy to show I Thess unpauline as Acts.
For a helpful balancing presentation on justification outside
the pauline writings, cf. A. Descamps, Les Justes et la Justice
dans les évangiles et le christianisme primitive hormis la
doctrine proprement paulinienne (Gambloux: J. Duculot, 1950).
At least the catch-phrase "Early-Catholicism" should be dropped
from the lexicon of sober exegesis. Cf. also O'Neill,
Theology, 175.

[1]I Cor 2:1-3 and especially II Cor 11:6: ἰδιώτης τῷ λόγῳ.
Paul's view of himself was apparently shared by his community:
ἡ δὲ παρουσία τοῦ σώματος ἀσθενὴς καὶ ὁ λόγος ἐξουθενημένος
(II Cor 10:10).

[2]Cf. e.g., I Cor 2:1-3; II Cor 1:8-11; 4:7-11. But
neither should this picture be overdrawn, for Paul clearly
claimed to have the ability to work powerful deeds, precisely
in service to the Gospel; cf. I Cor 2:4; I Thess 1:5 and above
all II Cor 12:12: τὰ μὲν σημεῖα τοῦ ἀποστόλου κατειργάσθη ἐν
ὑμῖν ἐν πάσῃ ὑπομονῇ σημείοις τε καὶ τέρασιν καὶ δυνάμεσιν.
That is Lukan enough!

[3]Our description agrees in general with Haenchen, 112-115.
We would not agree, however, that Luke's solution to the Jew/
Gentile problem was so different from Paul's as Haenchen, 113,

The Paul of Acts does not only look different from the
Paul of the letters; he also looks very much like the Peter of
Acts. It has frequently been noted how much Peter and Paul
sound alike in their speeches, particularly when Paul is
preaching to Jews, as at Antioch in Pisidia (13:16ff). Peter
and Paul also perform remarkably similar miracles.[1] The resemblances are so marked that we must ask whether there might
underlie Luke's presentation some more basic understanding of
spiritual authority which has shaped his presentation of both
figures. Rather than speaking of a petrinizing of Paul, or a
judaizing, we may be able to speak of a model of understanding
which applies with some variation[2] to both figures. We might
also ask whether this same model of spiritual authority applies
as well to the other main characters in Acts. If such a model
exists, it will be revealed not by a theological comparison, or
a study of titles and offices, but through a literary analysis,
that is, as Luke presents them dramatically. We shall in fact
find that not only Peter and Paul but all the main characters
of Acts are described according to a particular model, and that
it does reveal a basic understanding of spiritual authority.[3]

Acts can rightly be called the Book of the Holy Spirit.[4]

---

thinks: "God willed the mission and that was sufficient." But
it is clear that Luke found the warrant for the Gentile mission
in the Scriptures (Acts 2:21; 3:24-26; 15:15-18), a position
not entirely foreign to Paul (cf. Rom 9-11 and 15:8-12).

[1]These parallels have often been pointed out, as by B. S.
Easton, The Purpose of Acts, 7; M. D. Goulder, Type and
History in Acts, 65ff, and Talbert, Literary Patterns, 23-24.

[2]W. Mundle, "Das Apostelbild der Apostelgeschichte," ZNW
27 (1928) 44-45, goes too far when he says, "Petrus und Paulus
sind nur die Namensträger eines farblosen Typus und nicht
Gestalten von Fleisch und Blut . . .". They may be presented
in typical terms, but the Peter who confronts the Council, who
hammers on the door of Mary's house, and the Paul who escapes
by basket over the walls of Jericho, who preaches so long
Eutyches falls asleep and out the window, who holds up his hand
and stills a mob, are scarcely "colorless."

[3]Cf. Dibelius, 132.

[4]Cf. G. W. H. Lampe, "The Holy Spirit in the Writings of
St. Luke," 159-200, especially 159 and 165; H. von Baer, Der
Heilige Geist in den Lukasschriften (BWANT 39; Stuttgart: W.
Kohlhammer, 1926), especially 85 and 108-109; R. Zehnle,

Not only does the Spirit actively intervene at every critical
stage of the mission (cf. e.g. 8:29, 39; 10:19; 11:12; 13:2, 4;
16:6, 7; 19:1; 20:22), but it is the gift of the Holy Spirit
which initiates the mission and gives it its shape. Luke
includes in his narrative five separate accounts of the bestowal of the Spirit (2:1-12; 4:28-31; 8:15; 10:44; 19:6). Yet
although it is clearly his understanding that all believers
have received the Spirit, he portrays certain characters as
possessing the Spirit in a special way, or with special power[1]
which manifests itself in the speaking of God's Word and the
performance of signs and wonders.

The citation from Joel 2:28-32 which opens Peter's Pentecost sermon (Acts 2:17ff) is offered by Luke as the Scriptural
interpretation of the outpouring of the Spirit, and, appearing
where it does, functions as a programmatic statement concerning
the nature of this outpouring, conditioning all the subsequent
references to the Spirit in Acts.[2] It therefore deserves our

---

Peter's Pentecost Discourse, 126-128. A. Ehrhardt ("The
Construction and Purpose of the Acts of the Apostles," 55)
calls Acts the "Gospel of the Holy Spirit," but then goes on
to claim (78), with what basis he does not say, that "the
whole doctrine of the Catholic Church concerning the Holy
Spirit rests upon the prominent place accorded to His coming
in the second chapter of Acts." (!) E. J. Epp, The Theological Tendency of Codex Bezae Cantabrigiensis in Acts (NTSMS 3;
Cambridge: University Press, 1966), 117, argues that the
emphasis upon the Holy Spirit is strengthened in the "western"
readings.

[1]W. B. Tatum, "The Epoch of Israel: Luke i-ii and the
Theological Plan of Luke-Acts," NTS 13 (1966-7) 191, argues
that the difference between the age of Israel and the age of
the Church can be seen by the fact that in the infancy narratives "only a few chosen individuals receive the Spirit.
Within the Church, everyone is a recipient . . . everyone is
a prophet" [emphasis his]. While we can agree that in Acts
all believers receive the Spirit, it is also evident that the
figures we are about to discuss are portrayed as prophets in a
way that other believers (the Ethiopian Eunuch, Cornelius,
Ananias of Damascus, Aeneas and Tabitha, Rhoda, Timothy, Lydia,
Priscilla and Aquila) are not. These believers, like the shep-
herds in the birth story, are not described as prophets.

[2]As we shall note later, the Nazareth pericope (Lk 4:16ff)
has the same function in defining for the whole Gospel the
Spirit-filled nature of Jesus' ministry.

closest attention.[1]

---

[1]We must acknowledge here the necessarily tentative nature of the judgments made on the text which follows. The textual problem of Acts in general is notorious, primarily because of the widely divergent readings offered respectively by the so-called "Egyptian" and "Western" traditions. Textual critics have argued for the superiority of one tradition over the other. For the Egyptian as the preferred text, cf. J. Ropes, Beginnings III ccl ff; for the Western (which he prefers to call Z), cf. A. C. Clark, The Acts of the Apostles, xxiiff. More recently, scholars have followed an eclectic approach to the text, as argued for by G. Kilpatrick, "An Eclectic Study of the Text of Acts," Biblical and Patristic Studies ed. by J. Birdsall and R. Thomson (In Memory of R. P. Casey; New York: Herder, 1963) 64-77. The eclectic approach demands many judgments, and since the criteria are not absolute, the result has been a great deal of disagreement about a great many readings. Cf. A. Klijn, "In Search of the Original Text of Acts," SLA 103-110. The situation in regard to Scripture citations is even worse, for although Luke generally follows the LXX with considerable exactness in his explicit citations (cf. Dupont, Etudes, 272) and in some cases his argument appears to rest upon the LXX reading (cf. Etudes, 257, Haenchen, 448), some of his citations vary considerably from the LXX we possess. Here the possible factors responsible for the variation multiply. Luke may have had a version of the LXX we do not; it is possible that his Greek text was influenced by a) the MT, b) a Targumic reading or series of readings, c) a text which had a prehistory in an apologetic or liturgical writing. For a discussion of these possibilities, cf. B. Lindars, New Testament Apologetic (Philadelphia: Westminster Press, 1961) 13-31, and M. Wilcox, The Semitisms of Acts, 180-185. On the other hand, variations could be due to NT copyists, who wanted to conform the citation to the LXX (but which version did they have?) or who made alterations with a tendentious interest (as Epp has tried to show for D). Finally, the variation may be due to the author himself, who emended the text in order to make a certain point, emphasize a certain nuance, or fit the text more closely to the context. The judgment that the variation is due to the author must rest on the cumulative probability established by the following factors: a) the reading in question is well attested by NT mss and can reasonably be accepted as the "correct" reading; b) the reading is not found in the mss of the LXX which we possess, or the reading there can be accounted for by assimilation; c) the reading can be seen as motivated by the literary or theological concerns of the author. Even when such a judgment is made, it remains at best probable. Our argument which follows does not rest exclusively on the position we take concerning the alterations in the Joel citation (though we are convinced of that position), for the alterations emphasize elements present in the citation as it is found in the LXX.

Luke has altered[1] the LXX text of Joel in three significant ways. a) In v. 17, he has changed μετὰ ταῦτα to ἐν ταῖς
ἐσχάταις ἡμέραις[2] λέγει ὁ θεός.[3] b) In v. 18, he has added to
the text the words καὶ προφητεύσουσιν.[4] c) In v. 19, he has

---

[1]The arguments of M. Rese, Alttestamentliche Motive in der
Christologie des Lukas (Studien zum Neuen Testament 1;
Gütersloh: Gerd Mohn, 1969) 48ff, that the variants in the Joel
citation are from Luke, appear more convincing than those of T.
Holtz, Untersuchungen über die Alttestamentliche Zitate bei
Lukas (TU 104; Berlin: Akademie-Verlag, 1968) 5-14, that Luke
was faithfully following the reading of a ms tradition of the
LXX. Cf. also Zehnle, 28ff.

[2]μετὰ ταῦτα is the reading of the LXX with no known variants (Zehnle, 28, n. 11). Of the NT mss, only B 076 Cyr. of
Jer. Catech. xvii, 19 and sah have this reading. On the other
hand, ἐν ταῖς ἐσχάταις ἡμέραις is witnessed to by Dℵ A and the
overwhelming majority of witnesses. The two readings are con-
flated by C 467 1319. Haenchen, 179, thinks B must be original
because, "In lukan theology the last days do not begin as soon
as the Spirit has been outpoured!" Cf. also Haenchen,
"Schriftzitate und Textüberlieferung in der Apostelgeschichte,"
ZTK 51 (1954) 162. Agreeing with Haenchen are Holtz, 7, and
Wilckens, Missionsreden, 33, n. 2. Ropes (16-17) considers the
D reading to have been a transposition from v. 18, and thinks B
must have been original. ἐν ταῖς ἐσχάταις ἡμέραις is held by
the majority of the editions, Kilpatrick, 65; Cerfaux, Recueil
2, 98; Conzelmann, Apg. 34; Zehnle, 29. On strictly textual
grounds, the reading of the majority against B would have to
be preferred.

[3]The LXX has neither ὁ θεός, the reading of most NT mss,
nor ὁ κύριος, which is read by D E 242, 467, Lat. Ir. Ropes
(17) finds ὁ θεός original and an adaptation to fit the context; cf. also Conzelmann, Apg. 32; Haenchen, 179; Rese, 48-49;
Zehnle, 32; Holtz, 6. For κύριος as correct (because of the
tendency to use θεός to avoid confusion between "lords") cf.
Kilpatrick, 66, Cerfaux, Recueil 2, 98. No substantive difference is at stake, but as the harder reading, θεός is to be
preferred. More interesting is the evidence it offers of
Luke's willingness to adapt for context.

[4]There are a few mss of the LXX which contain καὶ
προφητεύσουσιν (Zehnle, 33; Holtz, 11) but they are late and
probably harmonized with Acts, the great majority of whose mss
contain the reading. Ropes (17) regards the words as a "western non-interpolation" and would reject them, as would
Cerfaux, Recueil 2, 98. Haenchen (179) regards the reading
as coming from an early scribal error, Holtz (11-12) as deriv-
ing from a ms prior to Luke. Holding the reading as original
are Zehnle, 33; Conzelmann, Apg. 34; and Kilpatrick, 66. In
this case it is easier to suppose that the words would be
dropped in an attempt to harmonize with the LXX than that they
stemmed from a scribal error. The hand of the author seems
particularly evident here.

altered καὶ δώσω τέρατα ἐν τῷ οὐρανῷ καὶ ἐπὶ τῆς γῆς αἷμα καὶ πῦρ καὶ ἀτμίδα καπνοῦ to read καὶ δώσω τέρατα ἐν τῷ οὐρανῷ ἄνω καὶ σημεῖα ἐπὶ τῆς γῆς κάτω ktl.[1]

Each of these alterations is important for revealing Luke's understanding. By "in the last days" Luke emphasizes the eschatological nature of the Pentecost event. This out-pouring of the Spirit is the beginning of the "last days," which look forward to the singular ἡμέραν κυρίου (v. 20).[2] The addition of the words "and they shall prophesy" strengthens an element already present in v. 17, and makes clearer Luke's precise understanding of the nature of the Spirit; it is the Spirit of prophecy.[3]

The addition of "signs" in v. 19 is particularly interest-ing, for it renders the Scriptural citation in effect the first occurrence of the legitimation for the expression "signs and wonders" in Acts. It is important to note that the phrase functions precisely as a qualification of the prophetic

---

[1]Although in some mss of the LXX there occur individual words from this reading, it is probably due to the influence of Acts (Zehnle, 33; Holtz, 12-13). The NT ms evidence is secure. Once more, this intricate variation is most plausibly attribu-table to the author.

[2]As we have seen above, the difficulties with the reading "in the last days" stem from a view of Lukan eschatology characteristic of Conzelmann and Haenchen. This view is not the only available. Cf. e.g., Marshall, Luke: Historian and Theologian, 77-102. There is nothing in the Lukan presentation to prevent agreement with Cerfaux, Recueil 2, 98: "Les temps eschatologiques Chrétiens commencent a la Pentecôte" [emphasis added]. The tension here between "the last days" (v. 17) and the "great day of the Lord" (v. 20) agrees with that in 3:20-21 between the "times of refreshment" (realized in the gift of the Spirit) and the "restoration of all things," (which will occur when the Christ returns). In any case, the phrase used by Luke simply sharpens an eschatological note already present in the LXX version, as has been pointed out by F. Mussner, "In den letzten Tagen (Apg. 2:17a)," BZ n.f. 5 (1961) 263-265.

[3]The argument of Holtz (11-12) that the element of pro-phesying is not germane to Peter's speech and therefore this phrase would not have been added by the author, cannot be accepted. As we shall see, the verses immediately following establish a connection between the prophetic Spirit and the signs and wonders associated with the prophet Moses, and the description of Jesus in 2:22 is clearly related to the descrip-tion of the prophet Moses in 7:22.

Spirit.[1] Luke employs here a phrase which in the LXX became a
commonplace for describing the work of God in the Exodus. In
fact nearly every occurrence of "signs and wonders" in the LXX
refers to the Exodus story (cf. e.g., Ex 4:8, 9, 17, 28, 30;
7:3, 9; 10:1, 2; 11:9-10; Num 14:11-12; Deut 4:34; 6:22; 7:19;
11:3; 26:8; 29:3; Pss 77:43; 104:27; 134:9).[2] The agent
through whom God worked these signs and wonders in the Exodus
was Moses. In light of the development which will follow in
chs. 3 and 7, one passage from Deut 34:10-12 is of particular
importance: καὶ οὐκ ἀνέστη ἔτι προφήτης ἐν Ἰσραὴλ ὡς Μωυσῆς
ὃν ἔγνω κύριος αὐτὸν πρόσωπον κατὰ πρόσωπον ἐν πᾶσι τοῖς
σημείοις καὶ τέρασιν ὃν ἀπέστειλεν αὐτὸν κύριος ποιῆσαι αὐτὰ
ἐν γῇ Αἰγύπτῳ . . . ἔναντι παντὸς Ἰσραήλ.[3]

Luke's adaptation of the Joel citation, therefore,
emphasizes that the gift of the Spirit is an eschatological
gift, that it is prophetic, and that this Spirit of Prophecy
is manifested in the working of signs and wonders. It is not
surprising to find that "signs and wonders" becomes in Acts a
literary shorthand for identifying those figures who possess
the Spirit in a special way. Let us now consider each of the

---

[1]Ropes (17) sees the addition of ἄνω σημεῖα and κάτω as
simply rhetorical flourishes of the author. It is more correct
to see with Cerfaux, Recueil 2, 98, and Rese, 49, a deliberate
anticipation of the description of Jesus in 2:22, that is, as a
Christologically motivated alteration of the text. We would go
further, however, and note that as a programmatic prophecy it
also legitimates through the scriptural citation the picture of
the Apostles as prophetic workers of signs and wonders. K.
Rengstorf, "σημεῖον," TDNT 7 (1971) 242, correctly emphasizes
the connection here between the signs and wonders and the Moses
typology applied to Jesus and Stephen. To distinguish this
usage, however, from that of the Apostles, and to regard the
attribution of signs and wonders to them as unconnected to the
Moses typology is arbitrary. Can it not be that the use of the
expression itself acts as a Leit-Motif in establishing such a
connection?

[2]Rengstorf, "σημεῖον," TDNT 7 (1971) 216, 221.

[3]The text brings together a) the picture of Moses as the
Prophet who saw God face to face; b) the notion of the "raising
up" of a Prophet; c) in a formulation: οὐκ ἀνέστη ἔτι . . .
which would lend itself to the expectation of such a Prophet;
d) the sending (Ex 3:10, Acts 7:34) of the Prophet Moses by
God; e) to work signs and wonders; f) among the people, or
before Israel.

main characters as Luke has described them.[1]

    1. <u>Peter and the Apostles</u>: The Apostles (speaking here of the Twelve, since this is Luke's main referent for the term) are singled out in a special way as the recipients of the Spirit. The risen Jesus tells them to remain in Jerusalem to await τὴν ἐπαγγελίαν τοῦ πατρὸς (1:4). When the Apostles ask Jesus if at that time He would restore the kingdom to Israel, his response prophesies both their mission and the power they will receive to fulfill it: λήμψεσθε δύναμιν ἐπελθόντος τοῦ ἀγίου πνεύματος ἐφ' ὑμᾶς, and the result of this is that they are to be his μάρτυρες, beginning in Jerusalem, and reaching to the ends of the earth (1:8). The first part of this prophecy is fulfilled at Pentecost, the rest by the subsequent narrative of Acts.

    As a result of receiving the Holy Spirit, Peter can proclaim the Word about Jesus μετὰ παρρησίας (2:29),[2] and identify himself and his fellow Apostles as μάρτυρες to the resurrection of Jesus (2:32).[3] In 2:43, the Apostles are said to work πολλά τε τέρατα καὶ σημεῖα.

---

[1]Our development here could be shortened by listing key words or parallels in columns, but our purpose is the discovery of the way Luke structures his narrative by certain motifs. The fullness of our citations from the Greek text, it is hoped, will draw the reader's attention not simply to the repetition of certain words (for words by themselves are not the vehicles of meaning) but on the way the author uses those words and phrases to construct a literary pattern.

[2]H. Schlier, "παρρησία," <u>TDNT</u> 5 (1967) 875ff, has shown that the word is not associated with the prophets in the LXX. Its use by Luke is one example of the "Philosopher" model coloring the "Prophet" model. Schlier (882) suggests the term is found primarily in contexts of preaching. It would be more accurate to say contexts of witnessing, which, frequently occurring before hostile audiences, call forth the attitude of παρρησία.

[3]There is no disputing that "witnessing" plays an important role in Luke-Acts, but the precise content or significance of that witnessing is controverted. For the range of positions, cf. H. Strathmann, "μάρτυς," <u>TDNT</u> 4 (1967) 492ff; L. Cerfaux, <u>Recueil</u> 2, 157-174; A. Retif, "Témoignage et Predication Missionaire dans les Actes des Apôtres," <u>NRT</u> 73 (1951) 152-165; Marshall, <u>Luke</u>, 41-44; Jervell, <u>Luke and the People of God</u>, 96ff; Trocmé, 65-66; S. Brown, <u>Apostasy and Perseverence in the Theology of Luke</u> (AnBib 36; Rome: Pontifical Biblical Institute, 1969), 53ff. The following points can

When Peter and John are before the Council, Peter addresses them πλησθεὶς πνεύματος ἁγίου (4:8), and from the παρρησία of Peter and John, the leaders are able to recognize that they had been with Jesus (4:13). Immediately after this first skirmish with the authorities, the Apostles pray: δὸς τοῖς δούλοις σου μετὰ παρρησίας πάσης λαλεῖν τὸν λόγον σου ἐν τῷ τὴν χεῖρά σου ἐκτείνειν σε εἰς ἴασιν καὶ σημεῖα καὶ τέρατα γίνεσθαι διὰ τοῦ ὀνόματος τοῦ ἁγίου παιδός σου ᾿Ιησοῦ (4:29-30), and even as they pray, they are filled with the Holy Spirit, καὶ ἐλάλουν τὸν λόγον τοῦ θεοῦ μετὰ παρρησίας (4:31). The Apostles are then said in 4:33 to give μαρτύριον[1] to the resurrection of Jesus with δυνάμει μεγάλῃ. In 5:12, again, it is said that διὰ δὲ τῶν χειρῶν τῶν ἀποστόλων ἐγίνετο σημεῖα καὶ τέρατα πολλὰ ἐν τῷ λαῷ.

Once more before the Council, Peter says καὶ ἡμεῖς ἐσμεν μάρτυρες τῶν ῥημάτων τούτων καὶ τὸ πνεῦμα τὸ ἅγιον ὃ ἔδωκεν ὁ θεὸς τοῖς πειθαρχοῦσιν αὐτῷ (5:32). In this statement, the testimony of the Apostles and that of the Holy Spirit are

---

be made in passing: a) The primary referent of witnessing is the resurrection of Jesus (explicitly in 1:21; 4:33; together with the death of Jesus in 2:32; 3:15; 5:32; 10:39-42; 13:31). b) It is as witnesses to the resurrected Jesus that Stephen (22:20) and Paul (22:15; 26:16) can be given that title. c) The designation of Paul as witness is not accidental, but solemn and intentional; if the designation conflicts with a scholarly construction of what witnessing meant for Luke, it is the construction which must be altered. Strathmann and Cerfaux, for example, go too far in emphasizing the element of contrast in 13:31-32; a fair reading of the text indicates that καὶ ἡμεῖς stresses continuity as much as contrast. d) The role of the Holy Spirit in witnessing cannot be overemphasized. Cerfaux (164) is correct in stating: "Il faut donc assimiler le 'témoignage' prononcé dans l'Esprit avec la prophetie. Les Apôtres sont des prophètes, et c'est en tant que prophètes qu'ils annoncent la résurrection . . .".

[1]For the complicated textual problem of 4:33, cf. Ropes, 44-45. In spite of the "harder" B reading, it is probably better to accept the reading of p8 et al.: τῆς ἀναστάσεως τοῦ κυρίου ᾿Ιησοῦ. Although Wendt, Apg., 118, wants to read τοῦ κυρίου as modifying the Apostles, Haenchen, 231, and Conzelmann, Apg., 44, are correct in attaching it to τῆς ἀναστάσεως. For the use of μαρτύριον (elsewhere in Acts, at 7:44 with a different meaning; in Lk, taken from the source in 5:14 and 9:5; but cf. Lk 21:3), cf. Strathmann, 504.

48

brought into the closest possible connection.[1] The Apostles
are also called μάρτυρες in 10:39, 41 and (by Paul) in 13:31.
Cf. also the use of διαμαρτύρομαι in 2:40; 8:25; 10:42.

By witnessing to the resurrection of Jesus, the Apostles
speak God's Word (2:41; 4:4; 4:29, 31; 6:2, 4; 8:25). This is
elsewhere called evangelizing (5:42; 8:25), teaching (4:2, 18;
5:21, 25, 28, 42) and preaching (10:42).

The Apostles are men filled with the Holy Spirit, who
speak God's Word by witnessing boldly to the resurrection of
Jesus, and who demonstrate the power of their message by working signs and wonders.

An essential element in Luke's description of the Apostles,
however, is the response of their hearers. He designates the
sphere of their activity as "the people" (ὁ λαός),[2] expressing
in 10:41 his understanding of the relationship between the
Apostles and the people: God raised Jesus up on the third day
to be revealed οὐ παντὶ τῷ λαῷ ἀλλὰ μάρτυσιν τοῖς
προκεχειροτονημένοις ὑπὸ τοῦ θεοῦ ἡμῖν . . . . καὶ παρήγγειλεν
ἡμῖν κηρῦξαι τῷ λαῷ ktl. Paul also refers to the Apostles in
Jerusalem as τοῖς συναναβᾶσιν αὐτῷ ἀπὸ τῆς Γαλιλαίας εἰς
Ἰερουσαλήμ οἵτινες νῦν εἰσιν μάρτυρες αὐτοῦ πρὸς τὸν λαόν
(13:31). This relationship is manifested in the narrative.
Peter speaks πρὸς τὸν λαόν (3:12), and the Apostles work signs
and wonders ἐν τῷ λαῷ (5:12). They are told by the angel to
stand and speak to the people (5:20) and do so (5:25). The
leaders of the people, on the other hand, are angry because the
Apostles are teaching the people (4:2), and, in order that
their teaching may not spread further among the people (4:17),
forbid them doing so, but they cannot take more drastic action
for fear that they will be stoned by these same people (4:21,

---

[1]This assimilation of witnesses is important for our
understanding of the Ananias and Sapphira story.

[2]We are not attempting here to define "the People" in the
technical sense as "Israel," but only trying to analyze Luke's
usage in dramatic terms. Our own view of the place of "the
People" in Luke's thinking will emerge in the course of the
study, and does not stem from the analysis of a single term,
but the whole pattern of Luke's presentation. The view we will
present is substantially in accord with that of N. A. Dahl,
"'A People for His Name' (Acts 15:14)," NTS 4 (1957-8) 319-327.

5:26) who are in awe of the Apostles (2:47, 5:13).

These last references indicate that although the Apostles preached to all the people, they received a mixed response; of those who heard the word some accepted and some rejected it. It is most important to note that in the Jerusalem narrative, the Apostles met with unqualified success among the people as a whole. Rejection came not from the people as such, but from the leaders of the people. The one exception to this is the case of Ananias and Sapphira, which we will look at more closely later. We should also note that Luke has emphasized the division in the people generated by the Apostles' teaching by the way he has arranged his narrative, that is, by contrasting successively positive and negative responses. Thus after Peter's discourse of ch. 3, the leaders of the people are filled with fury and lay hands on the Apostles (4:2), while Luke notes immediately that many believed τῶν ἀκουσάντων τον λόγον (4:4). The questioning and threatening of the Apostles before the Sanhedrin (4:5-21) is followed by the return to the community, the establishment in power by the gift of the Spirit, and the description of the community's sharing (4:23-37). This is followed by the negative response of Ananias and Sapphira (5:1-11). Following Ananias and Sapphira is the account of the great power and prestige enjoyed by the Apostles among the people (5:12-16), which in turn is followed by the account of the second appearance before the Sanhedrin (5:17-41). This pattern of juxtaposition accentuates the dynamic of acceptance and rejection, and strengthens the impact made by the content of the individual stories.

If the Apostles are filled with the Spirit and in that Spirit speak God's Word, we are not surprised to find Luke describing the opposition to that Word as an opposition to the Holy Spirit. Ananias and Sapphira "falsify the Spirit" (ψεύσασθαι τὸ πνεῦμα τὸ ἅγιον, 5:3)[1] and "test" or "tempt" the Spirit of the Lord (5:9), and Peter insists that they have lied not to men but to God (5:4). When Peter is opposed by the Council, he tells them that by preaching about Jesus the Apostles are fulfilling the demand: πειθαρχεῖν δεῖ θεῷ μᾶλλον

---

[1]For a discussion of this interpretation, cf. below, pp. 206-207.

ἢ ἀνθρώποις (5:29). Their mission, in a word, comes from God
and their preaching is an act of obedience to God. As we have
seen above, Peter then joins the witness of the Holy Spirit to
that of the Apostles, the Spirit which is given to those who
obey God (5:32). Immediately upon hearing this, the leaders
wish to kill the Apostles (5:33). What Luke implies by this
sequence is of course not only that the Apostles are obedient
to God and have received his Spirit, but that the leaders are
not obedient to God, since they not only do not have the Spirit
given to those who obey, but are <u>actively opposing</u> the witness
borne by the Spirit Himself. They have therefore put themselves, as Gamaliel will point out in 5:39, in the position of
being θεομάχοι.

    2. <u>Stephen</u>: The relation of Stephen and the Seven
to the Apostles will be discussed later in this study.[1] At the
moment, we are simply interested in the literary descriptions
of Stephen and Philip, the only two of the Seven who emerge
with any individuality, and both of whom fundamentally advance
the plot of the story. Both Stephen and Philip are chosen for
their position because they are certified as being πλήρεις
πνεύματος καὶ σοφίας (6:3). The Seven supposedly were
appointed to handle the distribution of goods, but we hear
nothing more of that. Stephen is described again in 6:5 as
ἄνδρα πλήρης πίστεως καὶ πνεύματος ἁγίου, and instead of waiting on tables, Στέφανος δὲ πλήρης χάριτος καὶ δυνάμεως ἐποίει
τέρατα καὶ σημεῖα μεγάλα ἐν τῷ λαῷ (6:8). Stephen, in a word,
is said to do precisely what the Apostles did in 2:43; 4:16,
22, 30; 5:12. Also like the Apostles, Stephen speaks the Word
with authority. Paul later gives him the title of μάρτυς
(22:20), which again links him to the peculiar function of the
Apostles.

    Stephen's word too arouses opposition (not from local
Jerusalemites), but his opponents οὐκ ἴσχυον ἀντιστῆναι τῇ
σοφίᾳ καὶ τῷ πνεύματι ᾧ ἐλάλει (6:10).[2] Unable to vanquish

---

    [1]Cf. below, pp. 211ff.

    [2]Epp, 117, notes that D's addition of τῷ ἁγίῳ here is con-
sistent with that manuscript's tendency to sharpen the conflict
between the Apostles and leaders of the Jews, and accentuate
the role of the Holy Spirit. If the D reading were correct and

him in argument, his foes move to dispose of him. They bring
forth witnesses to accuse Stephen of blasphemy against Moses
and God (6:11), stir up the populace and leaders, and bring
Stephen before the Sanhedrin (6:12).[1] Commentators have asked
whether the ensuing scene is a trial or a mob action that ends
in Stephen's death.[2] Luke appears to include elements of both.
But what is most significant is that although (as in the trial
of Jesus) the λαός is peripherally involved, the whole focus of
the account is on the formal rejection of Stephen by the
Sanhedrin, the leaders of the people.[3]

The whole scene can only be grasped dramatically by
including an interpretation of Stephen's speech, but that must
for the moment wait. We can note, however, that Stephen

---

not tendentious, we would have in this passage the same dramatic pattern as that found in 5:32f.

[1]It has frequently been noted that Luke places against
Stephen the charges found in the Synoptic (Mk 14:58, Matt
26:61) trial of Jesus. For the teaching against the Law and
the Temple, see the arrest of Paul (21:28). Cf. Haenchen, 273-
274, and M. Simon, St. Stephen and the Hellenists in the
Primitive Church (London: Longmans, Green and Co., 1958) 20ff.

[2]For a discussion of particulars, cf. Haenchen, 273-274,
and B. W. Bacon, "Stephen's Speech: Its Argument and Doctrinal
Relationship," Biblical and Semitic Studies (Yale Bicentennial
Publications; New York: Charles Scribner's Sons, 1901) 214ff.

[3]Because of the conclusions we will later draw about the
response of the leaders and the people in Jerusalem, we must be
very clear about the role of the people in the Stephen account.
Whatever the emphasis of Luke's sources (if any), the way Luke
has shaped the story reveals the following clear progression:
a) the antagonism to Stephen does not arise spontaneously from
the populace of Jerusalem but from Jews of the Diaspora. This
is emphasized by the lengthy description of their origin in
6:9. b) They are responsible for every action until Stephen
appears before the Council. Notice that all the verbs have
them as their subject: ὑπέβαλον (6:11), συνεκίνησαν, συνήρπασαν,
ἤγαγον (6:12). c) The role of the λαός is passive; they do not
rise up in anger, but are stirred up. d) From v. 13, Luke
deliberately places Stephen before the Council, the official
leaders of the people. This is stated in solemn fashion in
6:15. It must above all be noted that Luke has arranged it so
that Stephen's speech is not addressed to the Jews of Jerusalem
in general, but to the leaders of the people (7:1-53), and it
is they who formally reject him, and (if we are to follow the
logical inference of the verbs) stone him (7:57-58). In view
of this careful composition, it cannot be held that Stephen's
speech is a word of rejection addressed to all the Jews, or all
the Jews of Jerusalem; it is addressed to the leaders alone.

concludes his speech by accusing his listeners (who, by Luke's composition are the leaders of the people) of resisting the Holy Spirit: ὑμεῖς ἀεὶ τῷ πνεύματι τῷ ἁγίῳ ἀντιπίπτετε, ὡς οἱ πατέρες ὑμῶν καὶ ὑμεῖς (7:51). Luke then shows that this is the case by elaborating their response to this accusation: ἀκούοντες δὲ ταῦτα διεπρίοντο (cf. 5:33) ταῖς καρδίαις αὐτῶν καὶ ἔβρυχον τους ὀδόντας ἐπ' αὐτόν (7:54).

But the dramatic contrast is heightened still further. Stephen is once again described as ὑπάρχων δὲ πλήρης πνεύματος ἁγίου (7:55), and sees a vision of the Son of Man (7:56, understood by Luke to be of course Jesus, 7:59). At this, the rejection of the leaders moves to action: They cry out in a loud voice, they stop up their ears, and they physically attack him (ironically, ὁμοθυμαδόν, 7:57).

Stephen is a man of the Spirit, who speaks God's Word. By rejecting his Word, his opponents resist the Spirit of God, and reject God Himself. The consequence for them of this action is evident only from the content of the speech, to which we shall return. More succinctly than in the descriptions of the Apostles, then, but perhaps even more impressively, the dramatic description of Stephen portrays him as a Man of the Spirit who performs signs and wonders, speaks God's Word, and stimulates a response of acceptance or rejection.

3. Philip: The description of Philip is even briefer than that of Stephen, but because of its brevity the inclusion of much of the stereotyped pattern is the more striking. Philip, like Stephen, was chosen because he was πλήρης πνεύματος καὶ σοφίας (6:3). We understand that he was among those scattered by the persecution which followed the death of Stephen (8:1) and which apparently did not affect the Apostles. Philip advances the plot of Acts significantly by carrying the Gospel to Samaria. Philip is not called a witness but he is one who "evangelized the Word" (8:4, 35, 40) and in 21:8 is called εὐαγγελιστής. Like the Apostles, he preached τὸν λόγον τοῦ θεοῦ (8:14).

If Stephen stimulated primarily a negative response, Philip's mission in Samaria was enormously successful, not only because the Samaritans were impressed by what they heard, but also because of the σημεῖα ἃ ἐποίει (8:6). Indeed, it was

Philip's powerful deeds which aroused the admiration of Simon
Magus: θεωρῶν τε σημεῖα καὶ δυνάμεις μεγάλας γινομένας
ἐξίστατο (8:13).[1] That Philip was a Man of the Spirit is
shown also by the fact that the Spirit speaks to him directly
(8:29), moves him from place to place physically (8:39), and
perhaps indirectly by the fact that he had four prophetess
daughters (21:9).

Though Philip's mission is presented essentially in positive terms, his very success stimulated the incident of Simon
Magus (8:18ff), which describes the rejection of one, who if
not resisting the Spirit of God, at least badly misunderstood
the δωρεὰν τοῦ θεοῦ (8:20). This passage will be examined much
more closely later in the study, because of the function of
possessions within it.

4. Barnabas and Paul: To a considerable extent, the
descriptions of Barnabas and Paul overlap, since Luke frequently speaks of them together. Yet in the story of Acts,
Barnabas plays what must be considered an absolutely key role,
as the hinge between the Twelve and Paul. We shall have
occasion to examine this at greater length later. In one of
the few passages devoted to Barnabas alone (apart from his gift
of possessions in 4:37), we learn that he was sent by the
Jerusalem Church to look into the new developments at Antioch.
At this point he is described as ἀνὴρ ἀγαθὸς καὶ πλήρης
πνεύματος ἁγίου καὶ πίστεως (11:24). The mission of evangeli-
zation which he and Paul undertake is impelled by the Spirit:
αὐτοὶ μὲν οὖν ἐκπεμφθέντες ὑπὸ τοῦ ἁγίου πνεύματος (13:4).

Luke describes Barnabas and Paul at Iconium in this way:
διέτριψαν παρρησιαζόμενοι ἐπὶ τῷ κυρίῳ τῷ μαρτυροῦντι τῷ λόγῳ
τῆς χάριτος αὐτοῦ διδόντι σημεῖα καὶ τέρατα γίνεσθαι διὰ τῶν
χειρῶν αὐτῶν (14:3). This description contains essentially the
pattern of the Men of the Spirit. Barnabas and Paul proclaim
with boldness (παρρησία) the Lord. He Himself bears witness to
their preaching, by the signs and wonders He works through
their hands. Once more, we see that the function of signs and
wonders is confirming the power of the word and the authority

---

[1]In Luke's writing, δυνάμεις (cf. Acts 2:22; 19:11) has
the same connotation as τέρατα καὶ σημεῖα. Cf. W. Grundmann,
"δύναμις," TDNT 2 (1964) 299-302.

54

of its proclaimers. It is important to note as well that the
continuation of this same passage completes the pattern:
ἐσχίσθη δὲ τὸ πλῆθος τῆς πόλεως καὶ οἱ μὲν ἦσαν σὺν τοῖς
'Ιουδαίοις οἱ δὲ σὺν τοῖς ἀποστόλοις (14:4) Their word causes
a split response of acceptance and rejection among their
listeners.

When it came time for Barnabas and Paul to defend their
mission among the Gentiles before the elders in Jerusalem,
signs and wonders are again mentioned as the certification of
their preaching: ἐσίγησαν δὲ πᾶν τὸ πλῆθος καὶ ἤκουον Βαρναβᾶ
καὶ Παύλου ἐξηγουμένων ὅσα ἐποίησεν ὁ θεὸς σημεῖα καὶ τέρατα ἐν
τοῖς ἔθνεσιν δι' αὐτῶν (15:12). Together with Paul, Barnabas
is said to evangelize (13:32; 14:7; 14:15, 21; 15:35; 16:10),
teach (11:26; 15:35) and "speak the Word" (13:5, 7, 15, 26, 46,
48; 14:3, 25; 15:35; 16:6, 32).

In addition to the characterization of Paul in passages
shared with Barnabas, we can note the following said of him
alone. In 19:11 we find: δυνάμεις τε οὐ τὰς τυχούσας ὁ θεὸς
ἐποίει διὰ τῶν χειρῶν Παύλου. Paul is a Man of the Spirit, and
like the Apostles his every move is governed by the Spirit. He
receives it first at the hands of Ananias in Damascus, and is
sent on his mission with Barnabas by the Spirit (13:4). When
Paul confronts the magician Elymas he is, as Peter was before
the Council, πλησθεὶς πνεύματος ἁγίου (13:9). He is prevented
from speaking the Word in Asia by the Holy Spirit (16:6, 7).
It is the Holy Spirit which impels him toward Jerusalem (20:22)
and testifies to the afflictions which await him there (20:23).

Paul is proclaimed a μάρτυς by the risen Lord Himself in a
vision (22:15; 26:16).[1] Paul evangelizes (cf. the passages
above with Barnabas, and 17:18), teaches (passages above and
18:11; 20:20; 21:21, 28; 28:31), preaches (9:20; 19:13; 20:25;
28:31) and "speaks the Word" (17:11, 13; 18:11; 19:10; 20:32)
with boldness, μετὰ πάσης παρρησίας ἀκωλύτως (28:31).

Even more dramatically than the Apostles in Jerusalem,
Paul causes a division among his hearers wherever he preaches.
The pattern is set already in Paul's "inaugural" sermon at
Antioch in Pisidia (13:16ff). Paul's sermon closes on an

---

[1]Cf. n. 3, pp. 46-47 above, and Trocmé, 66.

initial note of warning (13:40). There is at first a positive
response to the sermon among the Jews and God-fearers (13:42),
but when Paul's preaching attracts "nearly the whole city" to
the synagogue, ἰδόντες δὲ οἱ Ἰουδαῖοι τοὺς ὄχλους ἐπλήσθησαν
ζήλου καὶ ἀντέλεγον τοῖς ὑπὸ Παύλου λαλουμένοις βλασφημοῦντες
(13:45).[1] We notice first that "jealousy" causes their rejection of Paul, just as it had for the leaders in Jerusalem
(5:17), and that they "blaspheme." This can of course simply
mean "to revile," but in the light of Luke's overall portrayal
of the Men of the Spirit, it probably is intended to mean
blasphemy against God.[2]

Paul now responds to their rejection by threatening them
with their own rejection from the Gospel: ὑμῖν ἦν ἀναγκαῖον
πρῶτον λαληθῆναι τὸν λόγον τοῦ θεοῦ.[3] ἐπειδὴ ἀπωθεῖσθε αὐτὸν
καὶ οὐκ ἀξίους κρίνετε ἑαυτοὺς τῆς αἰωνίου ζωῆς ἰδοὺ στρεφόμεθα
εἰς τὰ ἔθνη (13:46). We shall note the same combination of
expressions again when we look at Stephen's Speech (7:39).

The rejection of Paul's words, we see, is the rejection of
God's Word, and they who reject God's Word spoken by His witness are themselves rejected. This threat addressed to the
Jews along with the promise to turn to the Gentiles is greeted
with joy by the Gentiles (13:48), but arouses the Jews to an
active, physical rejection of Paul (cf. the same dramatic
progression in the Stephen episode, and the Nazareth pericope).

---

[1]Apart from some instances where the term lacks any
pejorative force and simply refers to place of origin (2:5, 10,
14; 10:22, 38, 39; 11:19), Ἰουδαῖος appears in Acts as a
designation for those among the historic Israel who are
opponents of the Gospel. It occurs twice in the account of
Herod's persecution (12:3, 11), but appears primarily (and from
the very beginning) in Paul's career (e.g., 9:22, 23; 13:6, 45,
50, etc.). Cf. Conzelmann, The Theology of St. Luke, 145.

[2]The textual variants do not substantially affect the
meaning. We should note that the "blaspheming" is directed
against τοῖς λαλουμένοις ὑπὸ Παύλου, that is, the content of
Paul's preaching (cf. also 18:6; 26:11). As in the case of
Peter and Stephen, the rejection of God's witness is the same
as the rejection of God. Cf. Haenchen, 414; Lake-Cadbury, 159.

[3]Paul here states as a principle what Peter in 3:26
expressed as fact: the priority both chronologically and by
necessity (ἀναγκαῖον) of the preaching to Israel.

This in turn causes Paul and Barnabas to shake the dust off
their feet unto them (13:51), a ritual act of rejection, the
formula for which has already been provided, as we have seen,
by Luke 9:5; 10:11.

We have already mentioned the split in the city of Iconium
over the preaching of Paul and Barnabas (14:4). Jews from
Antioch and Iconium follow Paul to Lystra and stone him (14:19).
In Thessalonica, Paul again meets with considerable success
(17:4) which causes the Jews to be jealous (17:5) and create a
major disturbance (17:5-9). The Beroean Jews receive the
message of Paul gladly (17:11-12), but the Thessalonian Jews
follow Paul there, create a disturbance (17:13), forcing Paul
to move on.

Paul's preaching in Corinth convinces both Jews and Greeks
(18:4), but when "the Jews" resist and blaspheme his words
about Jesus being the Christ (18:6),[1] Paul again formulates a
ritual rejection and declares his intention of going to the
Gentiles (18:6). Again in Ephesus Paul begins his preaching
in the Synagogue and remains there for three months, which
indicates some sort of acceptance. But when the members of
the Synagogue harden their hearts and do not believe, Paul
separates himself and his disciples from the synagogue (19:8-9).
Nevertheless, Luke notes that everyone in Asia heard the Word,
both Jews and Greeks (19:10).

In the final scene of Acts, Paul is again trying to per-
suade the Jews, this time the leaders of the Roman Jews. Some
of them are persuaded, others are not (28:24). In spite of
this mixed response, Paul applies to them the Isaiah blindness
text (Is 6:9-10) and declares for the third and final time in
the most formal fashion that τοῖς ἔθνεσιν ἀπεστάλη τοῦτο τὸ
σωτήριον τοῦ θεοῦ. αὐτοὶ καὶ ἀκούσανται (28:28).

The three ritual "turnings to the Gentiles" of Paul and
Luke's manner of portraying Paul's Jewish opponents hounding
him from city to city, finally and climactically causing his
arrest in Jerusalem (21:17) both tend to give a rather simple
impression of the acceptance/rejection pattern in regard to
Paul: the Jews of the diaspora refused to accept Paul's word

---

[1]Cf. n. 2, p. 55, above.

(the Word of God) and are thereby rejected; the Gentiles
receive the Word with gladness and thereby become a "People
for His Name from among the Nations" (15:14).

Yet in reality Luke's picture of the relations between
Paul and the Jews is more complex. First we note that Luke is
insistent upon the fact that there were many conversions among
the Jews, even in the diaspora (cf. 13:43; 14:1; 17:1, 4, 10,
12; 18:4; 19:10). In fact, Paul was not rejected by the Jews
in every place he spoke; many of the disturbances which force
him to move on are caused by that segment of "unbelieving Jews"
(cf. 14:2, 19) who followed him. Even in the final scene, as
we have noted, the Jewish leaders of Rome do not totally reject
Paul's words: καὶ οἱ μὲν ἐπείθοντο τοῖς λεγομένοις οἱ δὲ
ἠπίστουν (28:24). On the other hand, Luke does not give a
uniformly positive picture of the Gentile response either. The
Gentile magistrates whom Paul encounters may be models of judi-
cial attentiveness and may be charmed by his words, but they
are not converted. We note too that not only Jews but also
Gentiles instigated the riot at Iconium (14:5), that the owners
of the slave-girl in Philippi cause Paul's imprisonment (16:
19ff), that the silversmiths of Ephesus organize against Paul's
preaching (16:23ff), and that the Greeks of Athens greet his
words about the resurrection with mockery (17:32).

This complexity forces us to look at the matter more
closely. If Luke wanted to say simply that because the Jews
as a whole rejected the Gospel the Gentiles received it, why
is his picture so complex? Why does he recount the conversions
among the diaspora Jews at all? Why does he have Paul keep
going back to the synagogue to preach? Why does he have three
separate rejection sayings? Why does he insist on specifying
the origin by place of those who followed Paul around and
caused him such trouble? It seems that to represent fairly
Luke's thought, we must take two factors with seriousness:
the first is that he did have Paul recite the rejection sayings,
and did conclude the work with a saying which obviously functions as a prophetic entry to the Church of the Gentiles, a
legitimation for the Gentile Church. By means of these sayings,
Luke has given a certain formal pattern to the career of Paul.
Secondly, however, we must take seriously the careful shading

of his narrative, and two other statements by Paul: that it was <u>necessary</u> to preach the Gospel to the Jews first of all (13:46), and that the salvation of God "had been sent (ἀπεστάλη)" to the Gentiles (28:28). From the first saying, we gather that for Paul, as for the Apostles in Jerusalem, there was a need for the promises of God to be offered to and fulfilled among the Jews first of all; in his narrative recounting the conversions among the Jews in the diaspora, Luke has shown that this was at least partially realized in the diaspora as it was more fully in Jerusalem. From the second saying, we see that it is not the rejection of the Jews as such which motivates the Gentile mission; the salvation had been sent to them before the rejections of the Jews. The salvation of the Gentiles was always part of God's plan.

What is of immediate significance for this study, however, is that Luke consistently employs the pattern of acceptance and rejection for Paul as he did for the Apostles in Jerusalem, and that for him as for them, the rejection of the words of the Man of the Spirit is in effect the rejection of God's Word. When the Jews of the diaspora reject the preaching of Paul, in other words, Luke identifies this simply as a rejection of the Gospel itself.

We have seen by this literary analysis that Luke has employed a certain stereotyped pattern of description for the Apostles, Stephen, Philip, Barnabas and Paul. They are all Men of the Spirit who, whatever the differences of office or teaching, speak the Word of God with boldness and power, certify that preaching by the performance of signs and wonders, and stimulate among their hearers a response of acceptance and rejection. This literary characterization is the more striking in that it applies to all the major characters of Acts, all those who advance the narrative in a significant way, and (with the partial exception of Apollos, 18:24ff) only to them.[1]

---

[1]The short account about Apollos is interesting for several reasons. The fact that he is not one of Luke's heroes, that is, one who advances the narrative in a fundamental way, speaks well for the historicity of his description, as does the association with the Corinthian Church, which is of course supported by I Cor. The description of Apollos is not as stereotyped as the main characters. He is ἀνὴρ λόγιος, δυνατὸς

Throughout the analysis to this point we have been using
the expression "Men of the Spirit," in an attempt to use as
neutral an expression as possible and avoid precipitous conclusions not based on the text. But it is clear by now that
every part of the stereotyped description impels us to the
conclusion that Luke is presenting his central characters in
the drama of Acts as prophetic figures, indeed as Prophets.
This conclusion is based on the following three major points:
a) the programmatic prophecy of Joel already united (by means
of Luke's adaptations) the gift of the Spirit as the Spirit of
Prophecy with the manifestation of signs and wonders; b) in the
narrative Luke has brought together in the closest fashion the
elements of speaking God's Word with boldness, and the working
of signs and wonders in certification of that preaching; c)
consistent with this, Luke has portrayed the response to these
characters as an acceptance or rejection of God's Spirit and
Word. We are justified in concluding in a preliminary fashion
therefore that the major characters of Acts are portrayed
deliberately as Prophets[1] and that this dramatic description
is applied consistently whether it refers to the Twelve, the
Seven, or the great missionaries to the Gentiles, Barnabas and
Paul.

___

ἐν ταῖς γραφαῖς and ζεῶν τῷ πνεύματι, but he is not "filled
with the Holy Spirit," does not work "signs and wonders," and
is not a witness. The character of this description throws
into sharper relief that of the Men of the Spirit.

[1]Cf. Cerfaux, Recueil 2, 164; Jervell, 93. It might be
objected that Luke does not give these figures the title of
prophets, while he does give it to others in Acts (11:27; 13:1;
15:32; 21:9, 10). Cf. E. Ellis, "The Role of the Christian
Prophet in Acts," Apostolic History and the Gospel ed. by W.
Gasque and R. Martin (Exeter: Paternoster Press, 1970) 55-67.
But it is most important not to confuse the use of titles with
modes of literary presentation. If, for example, we accept
Χριστός as the most important title for Jesus, we should still
have to ask about the literary shape of his presentation:
what sort of Χριστός? The references to prophets in Acts are,
with the exception of Agabus, made in passing and none of the
figures so identified significantly advances the story. Even
Agabus appears as a prophet like Nathan, making his prophecy
and withdrawing. The case with the characters we have been
discussing is quite different. Though we must pursue the question, what sort of prophetic image is here being employed, the
prophetic character of their presentation is not in doubt.

It is now possible to ask whether we have gone as far as
we can with this analysis. Can we determine whether Luke has
portrayed his characters in this fashion arbitrarily, or is
there some further, more fundamental model upon which they are
based?

D. Jesus as the Model for the Apostles in Acts

The author of Acts answers in the most meticulous fashion
our question about the Spirit-filled men; their power comes not
from themselves but from the Spirit of God, which is the Spirit
which Jesus Himself received from the Father and poured out on
them (2:33).[1] The power at work in them is therefore the power
at work in Jesus. We can indicate this briefly by a short
series of passages in chs. 3-4.

When Peter sees the crowds thronging to him after the
healing of the lame man, he tells them that the act of healing
was accomplished not by their ἰδίᾳ δυνάμει ἢ εὐσεβείᾳ, but that
the healing was an act of the God of their fathers who
ἐδόξασεν τον παῖδα αὐτοῦ ᾿Ιησοῦν (3:12-13). After the speech,
Peter and John are brought before the Council and asked
explicitly, ἐν ποίᾳ δυνάμει ἢ ἐν ποίῳ ὀνόματι ἐποιήσατε τοῦτο
ὑμεῖς; (4:7), and Peter's response is straightforward: γνωστὸν
ἔστω πᾶσιν ὑμῖν καὶ παντὶ τῷ λαῷ ᾿Ισραὴλ ὅτι ἐν τῷ ὀνόματι
᾿Ιησοῦ Χριστοῦ τοῦ Ναζωραίου . . . . οὗτος παρέστηκεν ἐνώπιον
ὑμῶν ὑγιής (4:10).

When the Apostles return to pray for the bestowal of the
Spirit that they might preach the Word boldly, it is to be
accomplished ἐν τῷ τὴν χεῖρά σου ἐκτείνειν σε εἰς ἴασιν καὶ
σημεῖα καὶ τέρατα γίνεσθαι διὰ τοῦ ὀνόματος τοῦ ἁγίου παιδός
σου ᾿Ιησοῦ (4:29).

We should not be surprised then, if the description of the
Men of the Spirit should find its basis in the description of
Jesus, and this is what we discover. The information about
Jesus in Acts is of course derived from the discourses. We
shall look here at the discourses in the first part of Acts,
where the delineation of the Apostles is to be found. Let us
recall again what was said in the introduction to this study

---

[1]Lampe, "Holy Spirit," 193; von Baer, 19.

about the way in which Luke unites discourses to narratives.
As we shall see, what is said about Jesus in the discourses of
Acts finds its fulfillment in the narrative about the Apostles.

In his Pentecost sermon, Peter describes Jesus in this
way: ἄνδρα ἀποδεδειγμένον ἀπὸ τοῦ θεοῦ εἰς ὑμᾶς δυνάμεσι καὶ
τέρασι καὶ σημείοις οἷς ἐποίησεν δι᾽ αὐτοῦ ὁ θεὸς ἐν μέσῳ ὑμῶν
καθὼς αὐτοὶ οἴδατε (2:22). The following points should be
noted concerning this description. a) Coming as it does
immediately after the Joel citation with its Lukan alterations,
the description of Jesus carries unmistakeable allusions to the
association of signs and wonders with Moses.[1] b) Jesus has
been attested to, shown forth or certified (ἀποδεδειγμένον) by
God by his signs, mighty works, and wonders; these authenticate
his mission.[2] c) The signs and wonders are actually worked by
God through Jesus. (Cf. also 10:36.) Like the Apostles in
Acts, then, Jesus in his earthly ministry is the agent of God's
activity. d) This authentication of Jesus has been established
for the people (εἰς ὑμᾶς) and the wonders have been performed
among the people (ἐν μέσῳ ὑμῶν),[3] just as the signs and wonders
of the Men of the Spirit in Acts are worked ἐν τῷ λαῷ, and
those of Moses (Deut 34:12) were worked ἔναντι παντὸς ᾽Ισραήλ.
This authentication is well-known to them (καθὼς αὐτοὶ
οἴδατε).[4] Particularly if we are to regard the discourse of
ch. 2 as a "keynote address"[5] functioning as programmatic for
the rest of Acts, it is significant that Jesus is here described in terms so similar to those used by Luke for the Men of
the Spirit who are the witnesses to Jesus.

In Peter's speech to the household of Cornelius, we find

[1]Wilckens, 32, 123; Zehnle, 34; Dupont, Beatitudes II,
135, n. 2; Cerfaux, Recueil 2, 98; Rese, 49; Lake-Cadbury, 23.

[2]The reading ἀποδεδειγμένον is to be preferred to D's
δεδοκιμασμένον, though Lake-Cadbury, 22-23, prefers the latter.

[3]The reading of D* ἡμᾶς must be a correction. Cf.
Haenchen, 180; Lake-Cadbury, 23.

[4]Jervell, 97, correctly notes that it is characteristic of
Luke to have the whole ministry of Jesus exposed to all the
people and not just the Apostles.

[5]Zehnle, 95.

the following description of Jesus' earthly ministry:[1] 'Ιησοῦν
τὸν ἀπὸ Ναζαρὲθ ὡς ἔχρισεν αὐτὸν ὁ θεὸς πνεύματι ἁγίω καὶ
δυνάμει ὃς διῆλθεν εὐεργετῶν καὶ ἰώμενος πάντας τοὺς
καταδυναστευομένους ὑπὸ τοῦ διαβόλου ὅτι ὁ θεὸς ἦν μετ' αὐτοῦ
(10:38). As the Apostles received the Spirit to work signs and
healings in the Name of Jesus (4:29), Jesus Himself was
anointed with the Holy Spirit to work signs and healings. As
the preaching of the Apostles has been called an "evangelizing,"
so is the Word spoken to Israel by Jesus: τὸν λόγον ὃν
ἀπέστειλεν τοῖς υἱοῖς 'Ισραὴλ εὐαγγελιζόμενος εἰρήνην διὰ
'Ιησοῦ Χριστοῦ (10:36).[2]

An essential element in the description of the Men of the
Spirit was the divided response of acceptance and rejection
their word stimulated. This same pattern forms the very core,
the essential element of the discourses about Jesus. In the
case of Jesus, this pattern goes: He who was rejected by the
people has been accepted by God (that is, raised by God from
the dead). The formulation is very consistent. Thus in 2:23:

> τοῦτον τῇ ὡρισμένῃ βουλῇ καὶ προγνώσει τοῦ θεοῦ ἔκδοτον
> διὰ χειρὸς ἀνόμων προσπήξαντες
> ἀνείλατε
> ὃν ὁ θεὸς ἀνέστησεν.

In 2:36, we find the reverse order:

> κύριον αὐτὸν καὶ χριστὸν
> ἐποίησεν ὁ θεός
> τοῦτον τὸν 'Ιησοῦν
> ὃν ὑμεῖς ἐσταυρώσατε.

---

[1]Wilckens, 105-107, has shown the strong Lukan character
of this description. It should especially be noted how the
description echoes the Is 61 citation of Luke 4:18 (the
anointing by the Spirit, the preaching of peace); cf. Dupont,
Beatitudes II, 132ff.

[2]Cf. the fine article by J. Comblin, "La Paix dans la
Théologie de Saint Luc," ETL 32 (1956) 439-460, which, coming
from a different direction, touches on many of the points made
in this part of our study. We should note too in this description the way in which Luke has Peter speak of God working
through Jesus. It was διὰ 'Ιησοῦ Χριστοῦ that God proclaimed
peace to the people. And, ὁ θεὸς ἦν μετ' αὐτοῦ, a frequent
expression in the LXX for the agents of God (cf. e.g., Gen
39:2 [Joseph, also in Acts 7:9!], Exodus 8:12 [Moses], Jer 1:8,
19; 15:20; 20:11 [Jeremiah]). It is less accurate to call this
"die lukanische Subordinationschristologie," (Wilckens, 108;
Conzelmann, Apg 73) than to see it positively as part of Luke's
coloration of the picture of Jesus.

In 10:39:

> ὃν καὶ ἀνεῖλαν κρεμάσαντες ἐπὶ ξύλου
> τοῦτον ὁ θεὸς ἤγειρεν τῇ τρίτῃ ἡμέρᾳ . . .

Peter's discourse in 3:12ff deserves closer analysis as a whole.[1] We have seen already that the occasion for the speech is the healing of the lame man, which Peter explains is an act not of their own power but of God glorifying Jesus. Peter then moves directly into the pattern of the rejection of Jesus, which is expressed with particular fullness.

> ὃν ὑμεῖς μὲν παρεδώκατε καὶ ἠρνήσασθε
>   κατὰ πρόσωπον Πιλάτου
>   κρίνοντος ἐκείνου ἀπολύειν
>   ὑμεῖς δὲ τὸν ἅγιον καὶ δίκαιον ἠρνήσασθε
>   καὶ ᾐτήσασθε ἄνδρα φονέα χαρισθῆναι ὑμῖν
> τὸν δὲ ἀρχηγὸν τῆς ζωῆς ἀπεκτείνατε (3:13-15a)

The acceptance by God is expressed succinctly:

> ὃν ὁ θεὸς ἤγειρεν ἐκ νεκρῶν (3:15b).

The first part of the speech concludes by Peter's returning to the first point: it is by faith in the Name of Jesus that the man has been made healthy.[2] We shall want to recall

---

[1]Zehnle, 41, finds the discourse of ch. 3 "a decidedly inferior piece of literary composition," and argues (71ff) that Luke has, with only partial success, reworked materials from an earlier source into an example of early preaching to the Jews (131f). Without trying to answer all his arguments, the following should be noted: a) Zehnle objects (42f) to the order of the Jesus-kerygma in 3:13-15 because it does not follow the "classic" structure of 2:23-24; yet 2:36 has the same reversed order. b) He sees no connection between the speech and its context; yet the connection with the healing is obvious in the saying on the raising up of the Prophet, (the allusion to the resurrection here cannot be dismissed simply on the word of Haenchen), and the rejection of the leaders in 4:1 clearly follows upon 3:22. c) His attempt to link all the uses of "God of our fathers" in Acts to the hypothetical source is strained. A more reasonable hypothesis is that the phrase was one Luke liked. d) Zehnle rightly stresses the Moses typology present in both chs. 3 and 7, but is wrong in concluding (78), "The extended Moses-Jesus parallel woven so essentially into the fabric of Acts 3 and 7, yet totally absent from the rest of Acts, is probably to be credited to source material of a primitive nature." This is an unfortunate example of the sort of conclusions reached when only titles are accepted as significant identifying agents.

[2]The Greek of v. 16 is notoriously difficult, and provided Torrey, Composition and Date of Acts, 14-16, one of his more cogent "mistranslations." For other possibilities, cf. Lake-Cadbury, 36-37, and Haenchen, 207. The thought is clear enough, and the inclusio formed by vv. 13 and 16 establish a dramatic

64

the wording of the acceptance/rejection pattern when we look at
the speech of ch. 7. We should note here, however, that the
framing of the acceptance/rejection pattern by the two statements about the present power of Jesus to effect healing (life)
lends it a particular force.

Peter's next words are instructive for revealing Luke's
understanding of how the rejection of Jesus fitted into God's
plan. We saw already in 2:23 that the rejection was pre-
ordained by God, that is in some sense necessary. Now in 3:17-
18, we find that the culpability of people and leaders alike is
lessened for two reasons: first, because they acted out of
ignorance (οἶδα ὅτι κατὰ ἄγνοιαν ἐπράξατε ὥσπερ καὶ οἱ ἄρχοντες
ὑμῶν) 3:17;[1] second, because their rejection of Jesus had in
some sense brought to fulfillment God's plan for the Christ
revealed by the prophets. We cannot go here into a discussion
of the Lukan formulations similar to this, that the Christ had
to suffer (cf. e.g., Lk 24:44, Acts 17:3), but it is clear that
the rejection of the Christ by the people formed an essential
element in Luke's understanding of God's plan.[2]

The remainder of the speech presents the plea for repentance, which is again presented with considerable fullness. We
should note carefully that in fact, this is the last full-
fledged offer of repentance to the Jews, which contains a
positive element. Paul's conclusion at Antioch in Pisidia is
much more of a warning than a plea. The motivation for repentance here is twofold, positive and negative. Positively,
repentance will lead to the days of refreshment which will

framework around the statement of rejection-acceptance: the
"leader of life" who was killed, now brings healing through the
power of His name.

[1]This ignorance motif (found also at Luke 23:34 if we
accept the more likely reading) is appropriate precisely and
only here in the narrative, even when applied to the leaders.
But while ignorance is an excuse in the time of the first
rejection it has (as we shall see in ch. 7) no place in the
second and final offer of repentance.

[2]The form of argumentation used by Luke in these formulations is the subject of a study now being carried out by my
colleague, William Kurz, S.J.

culminate in the restoration of all things.[1] But those who do
not repent will be cut off from God's people. It is the
second of these motivations which is of special interest to
us here.

Luke has brought together two disparate OT texts to make
one statement.[2] The first, from Deut 18:15-19, concerns the
"Prophet like Moses," a text closely related to Deut 34:10-11,
which we have seen adumbrated in the Pentecost speech. Luke
has condensed the text of Deut to read: προφήτην ὑμῖν
ἀναστήσει κύριος ὁ θεὸς ὑμῶν ἐκ τῶν ἀδελφῶν ὑμῶν ὡς ἐμέ.
αὐτοῦ ἀκούσεσθε κατὰ πάντα ὅσα ἂν λαλήσῃ πρὸς ὑμᾶς (3:22).
As the passage stands in Deut, it already has attached to it
a threat: ὃς ἐὰν μὴ ἀκούσῃ ὅσα ἐὰν λαλήσῃ ὁ προφήτης ἐπὶ τῷ
ὀνόματί μου ἐγὼ ἐκδικήσω ἐξ αὐτοῦ (Deut 18:19). Instead of
including this threat, Luke uses a text from Lev 23:29, which
in its original context applied not to the hearing of a prophet
but to the keeping of the Law, but which contained the severest
possible penalty for non-observance. As Luke renders it:
ἔσται δὲ πᾶσα ψυχὴ ἥτις ἐὰν μὴ ἀκούσῃ τοῦ προφήτου ἐκείνου
ἐξολεθρευθήσεται ἐκ τοῦ λαοῦ (3:23).[3]

---

[1]The promise of the times of refreshment is linked to the
citation from Gen in v. 25, and together with 3:23 forms a
double-edged prophecy of promise and threat. Cf. Lindars, 208.

[2]It can be argued that Luke was using the citation as
found in a previous source, such as a book of "testimonies."
Cf. Wilcox, 46; Lake-Cadbury, 22; Holtz, 74; J. Fitzmyer, "4Q
Testimonia and the New Testament," TS 18 (1957) 537; J. de
Waard, A Comparative Study of the Old Testament Text in the
Dead Sea Scrolls and in the New Testament (Studies in the texts
of the desert of Judah 4; Leiden: E. J. Brill, 1966) 24, 79.
On the other hand, since we do not have an ending of the cita-
tion like this one extant, the alteration may also have been
carried out by Luke on the basis of the LXX.

[3]Lake-Cadbury, 38. De Waard's suggestion (23-24) that
from a Vorlage like 4QTest with a scriptio plena a scribe could
have derived εξολεθρευθήσεται = 'wryš from 'dryš, and ἐκ τοῦ
λαοῦ from m'mw is appealing, but of course remains as hypothetical as the view that Luke himself combined verses from Deut
and Lev. Lindars, who calls the mixed citation a "pesher
adaptation in a Septuagint milieu," (207), points out that the
Lev 23 verse "concentrates attention on one point, the solemn-
ity of the threat," (208). Cf. also J. Dupont, "Les Discours
de Pierre dans les Actes et le chapitre XXIV de l'évangile de
Luc," L'Evangile de Luc, 352, n. 67.

66

The "Prophet like Moses" can here only refer to Jesus.[1]
Yet, according to Luke, Jesus has already been rejected by the
people in the past, and they have not been cut off; they are
even now being offered the chance of repentance. We notice
further that all the prophets spoke of "these days" (τὰς ἡμέρας
ταύτας 3:24), that is, the time of the listeners, the time when
the speech is made.[2]

What Luke appears to be saying, then, is that the "Prophet
like Moses" whom God has raised up is presented to the people
again for the possibility of acceptance or rejection,[3] and that
at stake for them is inclusion among the messianic people
(sharing in the times of refreshment), or definitive exclusion
from the people. But how is the Prophet like Moses present in
this way? In the power of the Spirit at work through His witnesses, the Apostles, in their signs and wonders, in their Word
about Jesus! Thus we see the significance of this speech with
its peculiar christology following upon the healing narrative
of ch. 3. The possibility of acceptance and rejection is still
alive for the people, because Jesus is alive, and at work
through the deeds of his witnesses. That this is in fact
Luke's understanding is not based just on this text, but from
the whole analysis of the Men of the Spirit we have done.

This text makes explicit the final part of the pattern of
acceptance/rejection; those who reject the prophetic word are
themselves cut off from the people, are themselves rejected.

---

[1] For a discussion on the relationship of the Deut text to
the expectation of an eschatological prophet, cf. H. Teeple,
The Mosaic Eschatological Prophet (SBLMS 10; Philadelphia:
Society of Biblical Literature, 1957) 84ff; R. Schnackenburg,
"Die Erwartung des 'Propheten' nach dem Neuen Testament und den
Qumran-Texten," Studia Evangelica I, ed. by K. Aland, F. Cross,
et al. (TU 73; Berlin: Akademie-Verlag, 1959) 622-639; and the
material on the Moses traditions in W. Meeks, The Prophet King
(NovTSup 14; Leiden: E. J. Brill, 1967).

[2] Cf. H. Flender, St. Luke, Theologian of Redemptive
History trans. by R. and I. Fuller (London: S.P.C.K., 1967) 97;
Rese, 69; Conzelmann, Apg., 41; L. Gaston, No Stone on Another
(NovTSup 23; Leiden: E. J. Brill, 1970) 280.

[3] Zehnle's view (93) that the earthly mission of Jesus and
His coming at the end-time correspond to the two sendings of
Moses is incorrect. It is the resurrection of Jesus, His
establishment in power, which corresponds to the second sending
of Moses.

The raising up of the prophet thus contains a deliberate ambiguity, or double reference.[1] God "raised up" Jesus as a prophet in his earthly ministry, to work signs and wonders among the people as Moses did, and to be rejected a first time by the people he had come to save, a rejection, however, which was not definitive because of the ignorance of the people and the role they had to play in fulfilling God's plan. Having been rejected and put to death, Jesus is "raised up" by God as Prophet in a definitive and eschatological way. He is now present among the people in the powerful signs and wonders worked by his witnesses and in the Word about Him spoken by them. Those who reject the Prophet now (that is, those who reject the prophets who are his witnesses) reject him definitively, and are as radically rejected themselves.

Luke's use of the "Prophet like Moses" text together with the threat from Leviticus is of great importance for this study. Not only does it establish the pattern of acceptance/rejection thematically, so that we are able to read the subsequent narrative in the light of this pattern, it also, and more importantly, defines the role of Jesus and of his Apostles within the people. "Prophet" is perhaps not the most important of the Lukan christological titles,[2] but as we have seen here and shall see again in ch. 7, it is a title which significantly defines the work of Jesus. More significantly, the model of understanding toward which the title itself points clearly expresses an essential element of Luke's thinking about Jesus.[3]

---

[1] Dupont, Etudes, 149; F. Gils, Jésus Prophète d'après les Evangiles Synoptiques (Orientalia et Biblica Lovaniensia II; Louvain: Publications Universitaires, 1957) 33-34. Contra: Zehnle, 93; Rese, 70, n. 19; Haenchen, 209.

[2] Cf. Rese, 121-133; C. F. D. Moule, "The Christology of Acts," SLA 159-185; Wilckens, 155-178; F. Hahn, Christologische Hoheitstitel (FRLANT 83; Göttingen: Vandenhoeck & Ruprecht, 1963) 380-404.

[3] It lies outside our purpose to discuss whether the Christology of ch. 3 is "primitive" or "archaizing." Among the many studies dealing with this, cf. A. Wilder, "Variant Traditions of the Resurrection in Acts," JBL 62 (1943) 308-318; J. A. T. Robinson, "The Most Primitive Christology of all?" JTS n.s. 7 (1956) 177-189; Bauernfeind, Die Apostelgeschichte, 65-68, and "Tradition und Komposition in dem Apokatastasis-spruch Apostelgeschichte 3, 20f," Abraham Unser Vater ed. by

The pattern of acceptance/rejection is found twice more
applied to Jesus in the first part of Acts, not in formal discourses, but in responses of Peter to the Council. We have
already seen how Luke stresses the division in the people
following Peter's speech in ch. 3: Many of the people accept
the word and believe; the leaders however are moved to anger at
Peter's words and bring him before the Council. After Peter
responds to their question about what power and name effected
the healing of the lame man, he continues: ὃν ὑμεῖς
ἐσταυρώσατε ὃν ὁ θεὸς ἤγειρεν ἐκ νεκρῶν (4:10), and then
identifies Jesus as ὁ λίθος ὁ ἐξουθενηθεὶς ὑφ' ὑμῶν τῶν
οἰκοδόμων ὁ γενόμενος εἰς κεφαλὴν γωνίας (4:11).[1] The following points should be noted: a) Peter is addressing the leaders
of the people directly. He says, "you crucified Him." b) Luke
uses the Ps 118:22 text as a Scriptural foundation for the
pattern of acceptance/rejection. c) But he has made a very
small addition to the text of the psalm. He adds ὑμῶν.[2] These
leaders whom Peter addresses are themselves the builders who
have rejected Jesus. d) In addressing the leaders, Peter
neither downplays their guilt by the plea of ignorance,[3] nor

---

O. Betz (Arbeiten zur Geschichte des Spätjudentums und
Urchristentums V; Leiden: E. J. Brill, 1963) 13-23; Moule,
167f; Zehnle, 89-94; Wilckens, 152-155. It can however be
noted that these discussions do not take enough into account
that a literary motive may shape the christological statements
of a particular passage. In ch. 3, the placement of the
speech at a point in the story where conflict and rejection
intensify, may substantially contribute to the sort of christological emphasis Luke wished to make.

[1]The use of ἐξουθενηθεὶς here may have been influenced by
Is 53:3. Cf. Lindars, 170; Dupont, Etudes, 261, 301; Rese,
113-114; Cerfaux, Recueil 2, 140-141.

[2]The word is obviously not in the LXX, and is not omitted
by any NT ms of note. It is strange that this alteration has
not received more attention, for it indicates Luke's willingness to emend a text according to context, and sharpens considerably the motif of the rejection of the leaders. Epp, 71,
lists 4:11 as one of the ἡμεῖς/ὑμεῖς variations of D which
represent "a case of patent absurdity as far as the sense
goes." Either his reference to 4:11 is a misprint, or he is
mistaken, for the D reading here is not distinctive.

[3]Cf. Dupont, "Les Discours," 338.

holds out to them the chance of repentance.[1] Why? Because in
4:1, they have already rejected the word spoken by Peter. We
are to understand therefore that by rejecting the word of the
Prophet, they are in the position of being rejected themselves.

The confrontation scene of ch. 5 follows the summary
statement of 5:12-16 which shows the steadily increasing power
of the Apostles among the people. The leaders are filled with
jealousy at this (5:17) and again drag the Apostles before the
Council. Now, however, they themselves make explicit what was
implied in Peter's last words to them. They accuse the
Apostles not only of continuing to teach in Jesus' name, but
of ἐπαγαγεῖν ἐφ' ἡμᾶς (that is, the leaders) τὸ αἷμα τοῦ
ἀνθρώπου τούτου (5:28). Peter, we notice, does not deny this
accusation. After stating that they must obey God rather than
men (the significance of which we have already mentioned), he
adds: ὁ θεὸς τῶν πατέρων ἡμῶν ἤγειρεν Ἰησοῦν ὃν ὑμεῖς
διεχειρίσασθε κρεμάσαντες ἐπὶ ξύλου. τοῦτον ὁ θεὸς ἀρχηγὸν
καὶ σωτῆρα ὕψωσεν τῇ δεξιᾷ αὐτοῦ δοῦναι μετάνοιαν τῷ Ἰσραὴλ
καὶ ἄφεσιν ἁμαρτιῶν (5:30-31). In this context, Peter's use
of the acceptance/rejection pattern in regard to Jesus has the
effect of affirming precisely what they feared. He brings on
their heads the blood of this man. Jesus has been raised up,
we see, to offer repentance and remission of sins to Israel.
But Peter does not extend this offer to the leaders. In our
previous analysis, we saw the significance of Peter's allying
the testimony of the Spirit to that of the Apostles in this
place, and the murderous rage of the Council as affirming their
rejection of the Spirit.

The major points made about Jesus in the discourses are
clear enough. He is the Prophet like Moses who worked signs
and wonders among the people; He was rejected by the people,
but raised up by God; He is the source of the Spirit working
through the Apostles; He is present in their work and words as
the "raised Prophet," the second rejection of whom leads to a
final cutting off from the people.

---

[1]Reading ἡμᾶς in v. 12 with the majority of witnesses,
against the ὑμᾶς of B.

E. Moses as the Model of the Prophet

To complete this first stage of our literary investigation we must now consider another major discourse in the first part of Acts, the Speech of Stephen (7:2-53), a speech which is not about Jesus, but which sheds a great deal of light on the structure of Luke's understanding of Jesus. Our interest here is again focussed on a particular literary description and dynamic. Therefore, at the risk of neglecting other important aspects of the speech,[1] we will concentrate on the description of Moses, 7:17-44. We have already been invited by Luke in 3:22-23 to see Jesus as the Prophet like Moses. In Stephen's speech Moses is given considerable attention, and we are therefore able to see the way in which we are to understand Moses as the type of Jesus.[2]

Consistent with our approach to the text as a whole, we begin with the presupposition that the Stephen speech substantially represents the language[3] and

---

[1]Against the view that the largest portion of the Stephen Speech is irrelevant, alien, or both (cf. e.g., Dibelius, 167; Ehrhardt, "Construction and Purpose," 67; Holtz, 85-86; A. Klijn, "Stephen's Speech--Acts VII 2-53," NTS 4 [1957-8] 26-27), Dahl, "The Story of Abraham," 139ff, shows that throughout the speech the typical Lukan pattern of prophecy-fulfillment dominates the retelling of the biblical narrative.

[2]Wilson, The Gentiles and the Gentile Mission, 134, says that typological interpretation of the speech "is as unconvincing as it is ingenious. The only reference to Christ apart from 7:52 is 7:37; other than this, typology is present only in the sense that the treatment of Jesus was typical of the way Israel had always treated its leaders and prophets." This opinion is as unconvincing as it is cavalier. Among the many who recognize some elements of typology in the speech (though differing widely concerning its significance), cf. Dahl, "The Story of Abraham," 144; Conzelmann, Theology, 166, n. 2; Dupont, Etudes, 149, 251; Easton, The Purpose of Acts, 48; Zehnle, 89; Rese, 80; Gils, 33ff; Gaston, 280-281; G. W. H. Lampe, "The Lucan Portrait of Christ," NTS 2 (1955-6) 166-168.

[3]Cf. W. Mundle, "Die Stephanusrede Apg.7: Eine Martyrerapologie," ZNW 20 (1921) 133ff; J. Bihler, Die Stephanusgeschichte (Münchener Theologische Studien I, Historische Abteilung 30; München: Max Hueber, 1963) 86 and 249; cf. also the conclusion of Bacon ("Stephen's Speech," 236), "The Speech of Stephen is linguistically of a piece with the first and last chapters of Luke and various other passages peculiar to Luke and Acts. It is the type of Hellenistic Greek framed on the model of the LXX."

thought[1] of Luke. The analysis of this speech is of particular
importance for this study because it leads us close to what
might be called the structure of Luke's thinking about Jesus
and his place in God's plan. We have seen time and again how
Luke has emphasized that Jesus is to be understood on the basis
of the Scriptures. The speech of Stephen shows us how Luke
read the Scripture, and how the understanding of Jesus might be
derived from that reading. Much of the story of Moses in this
speech is, after all, simply a recountal of the story in Exodus.
But Luke's distinctive understanding of that story is revealed
in the elements he selects for recountal, how he structures
these elements dramatically, and how he comments on them, that
is, interprets their significance.[2] It is in these factors
that we find revealed his understanding that "Moses and all the
Prophets" foretold that the Christ might be rejected.

Luke has structured the story of Moses in this speech so
that it takes place in two stages, represented by an initial
rejection of Moses (7:17-29) and a second rejection (7:30-43).

----

[1]The positions in regard to the sources behind Luke's
composition here are, with sharper focus, typical for the arguments concerning the whole of Acts. Thus it can be argued that
the semitisms of the speech and the peculiar form of citations
makes it likely that Luke was using a written source whose
citations differed from the LXX (Wilcox, 162 and 181-182; Holtz,
172). On the other hand, these features can be accounted for
by Luke's "septuagintalizing" style (Bihler, 81-86). Cf.
Dupont, "Les Discours," 356, nn. 77-78. The speech has been
said to show unmistakable resemblances to hellenistic Jewish
materials (Bacon, 237ff; O'Neill, Theology, 77ff; Cadbury, The
Book of Acts in History, 102-104), to the distinctive outlook
of the Qumran sectarians (Klijn, 28-31; O. Cullmann, "The
Significance of the Qumran Texts for Research into the Beginnings of Christianity," JBL 74 [1955] 213-226), and to the
Samaritan writings (M. Scharlemann, Stephen: A Singular Saint
[Analecta Biblica 34; Rome: Pontifical Biblical Institute,
1968]; Simon, St. Stephen and the Hellenists, 78-97). Whatever
the arguments for the influence of one tradition or another,
two things are certain: a) the structure of the speech, and in
particular of the biblical narration, is completely consistent
with the Lukan outlook; b) there are too many and too intricate
literary relations between the speech and the whole of Luke-
Acts for Luke's contribution to have been only a light reworking of a source.

[2]Cf. B. S. Childs, Exodus (The Old Testament Library;
Philadelphia: Westminster, 1974) 33-35, and Biblical Theology
in Crisis (Philadelphia: Westminster, 1970) 164-171, for perceptive comments on the handling of the Moses account in Exodus
and Acts 7.

This structuring is itself the single most revealing aspect of
Luke's understanding.[1] The two stages are linked by the key
verse 35. Rather than attempt here a full exegesis of each
verse, we will make a series of comments, the pertinence of
which should be evident, and note certain relations to the text
of Luke-Acts elsewhere.[2]

Stage One (7:17-29):

1. Moses was born at that time (ἐν ᾧ καιρῷ,
7:20), when the promise given to Abraham was approaching fulfillment (7:17).[3] This is Luke's interpretation.[4] He follows
Exodus in describing it as a time of oppression for the people
(7:19).

2. Moses is described as ἀστεῖος τῷ θεῷ (7:20),
and instructed in all the σοφία Αἰγυπτίων (7:22). Cf. Lk
2:41-52.

3. As he approached maturity (cf. 22a), Moses
was δυνατος ἐν λόγοις καὶ ἔργοις αὐτοῦ (7:22). Cf. Lk 24:19.

4. Moses' first approach to his people is
called a "visitation": ἀνέβη ἐπὶ τὴν καρδίαν αὐτοῦ
ἐπισκέψασθαι τοὺς ἀδελφοὺς αὐτοῦ τοὺς υἱοὺς Ἰσραήλ (7:23).[5]

---

[1]The pattern is partially found in the story of Joseph.
In v. 9, the first rejection (for "jealousy" as a motif in
Luke, cf. Acts 5:17; 13:45), followed by the rise to power of
Joseph, and his saving of his father and brothers, v. 13.

[2]Some of the literary relations mentioned below have been
pointed out by Bacon, 239ff; Gils, 33ff; Zehnle, 76-78;
Comblin, "La Paix," 447ff; Lampe, "Lucan Portrait," passim.

[3]Dahl, "The Story of Abraham," 143-144, has demonstrated
that the promise to Abraham (7:6-7) functions thematically
throughout the speech, so that the successive stages in Israel's
history are seen in relation to the fulfillment of that promise.

[4]Similarly, the Canticle of Zachary speaks of the salvation of the people as the result of God's remembering his promise made to "Abraham our father" (Lk 1:72-73), and in Acts
3:25 Peter tells his listeners that they are the sons of the
prophets as heirs of the covenant God made with the fathers in
swearing an oath to Abraham.

[5]God's coming to save His people is frequently spoken of
in the OT as a "visitation" (e.g., Gen 21:1; 50:24-25; Ex 3:16;
4:31; 13:19; 32:34, etc.). This same expression is used at
three critical places in Luke's Gospel (1:68; 7:16; 19:44). We
notice as well that the language of "visitation" is applied to

5. Moses' killing of the Egyptian is understood
by him to be an act of salvation for his brothers,[1] but they do
not understand: ἐνόμιζεν δὲ συνιέναι τοὺς ἀδελφοὺς αὐτοῦ ὅτι ὁ
θεὸς διὰ χειρὸς αὐτοῦ δίδωσιν σωτηρίαν αὐτοῖς, οἱ δὲ οὐ συνῆκαν
(7:25).[2]

6. Moses seeks to make peace between quarelling
brothers[3] but is rejected: ὁ δὲ ἀδικῶν τὸν πλησίον ἀπώσατο
αὐτόν (7:27). The words of this rejection come from the LXX of
Ex 2:14: τίς σε κατέστησεν ἄρχοντα καὶ δικαστὴν ἐφ' ἡμῶν. It
interesting, of course, that these words find an echo in Lk
12:10, but what is of significance for the understanding of the
Moses story is that these are the words reprised in 7:35.

7. This initial rejection results in Moses'
departing from the people for a time, becoming an alien (7:29).

The first stage of the Moses story, therefore, hinges on
a) Moses' power and mission and b) the rejection of him by his
people.

Stage Two (7:30-43):

1. Vv. 30-34 are taken largely from the text of
Exodus. Moses encounters the "God of your fathers, the God of
Abraham, Isaac and Jacob" (cf. Acts 3:13) who sends Moses to be
his agent of redemption (ἀποστελῶ σε εἰς 'Αἴγυπτον) (7:34).

2. Although vv. 35-39 form a rhetorical unit,[4]
v. 35 undoubtedly provides the key to Luke's understanding of
Moses' significance:

τοῦτον τὸν Μωϋσῆν ὃν ἠρνήσαντο
εἰπόντες
τίς σε κατέστησεν ἄρχοντα καὶ δικαστήν

---

the time of the first rejection, the time of Jesus' earthly
ministry.

[1]For "salvation" as thematic in Luke (Lk 1:47, 69, 71, 77;
2:11, 30; 3:6; 19:19; Acts 5:31), cf. Bacon, 233-235 and
especially Marshall, Luke 94ff.

[2]This is an obvious use of the ignorance motif found in
Acts 3:17. As in that place, ignorance is seen as appropriate
to the first rejection but not the second.

[3]The classic expression of Jesus' ministry as a preaching
of peace is of course Acts 10:38 (together with Lk 4:18f). For
the connection of "visitation" and "peace," cf. Lk 19:41-44.

[4]Cf. Haenchen, 282.

τοῦτον ὁ θεός
ἄρχοντα καὶ λυτρωτὴν[1] ἀπέσταλκεν
σὺν χειρὶ ἀγγέλου.

It should be immediately clear that this verse not only recalls
the acceptance/rejection passages such as 3:13-15 in language
and form, but also in precise meaning: He whom man rejected,
God has established. The initial rejection of Moses by his
brothers is not definitive; he is sent to them again by God,
this time with power (σὺν χειρὶ ἀγγέλου). This corresponds
exactly to the pattern we have seen used of Jesus in the discourses.[2] The second sending of Moses, then, is structurally
the same as the resurrection of Jesus; it is an establishment
in power, and a second chance for the people to accept him as
the agent of God's salvation.

 3. V. 36 is of course based on the Exodus
account and the Deuteronomic traditions about Moses, but here
it is used thematically, as it is when used of the Men of the
Spirit in Acts: οὗτος ἐξήγαγεν αὐτοὺς ποιήσας τέρατα καὶ
σημεῖα ἐν γῇ Αἰγύπτῳ ktl.

 4. V. 37 so interrupts the smooth recital of
Moses' power and deeds which runs from vv. 36-38 that it stands
out with special emphasis. Coming immediately after the
acceptance/rejection (kerygmatic) formula, and the mention of
the signs and wonders performed by Moses, it points us inexorably to the figure of Jesus of whom Moses is the type: οὗτός
ἐστιν ὁ Μωϋσῆς ὁ εἴπας τοῖς υἱοῖς 'Ισραήλ προφήτην ὑμῖν
ἀναστήσει ὁ θεὸς ἐκ τῶν ἀδελφῶν ὑμῶν ὡς ἐμέ. In 3:22, Luke
had already identified Jesus as the Prophet like Moses. Here
we come to understand the precise point of that typology: as
Moses after being rejected by his brothers was established by
God in power as their leader, so was Jesus.

 5. V. 38 completes the portrait of Moses. He
is the one ὃς ἐδέξατο λογία ζῶντα δοῦναι ὑμῖν. Once more, as

---

[1]λυτρώτης only here in the NT. But cf. Lk 24:21,
λυτροῦσθαι, and 1:68; 2:38: λύτρωσις. Bacon, 233, suggests
that the application of this title to Moses "is plainly intended to make him appear more plainly as the type of Christ."

[2]Contra Zehnle, 77, the most striking parallel between ch.
7 and the picture of Jesus is not found in 7:22, but in the
structure of this "kerygmatic" statement in 7:35, which
corresponds exactly to that used of Jesus.

with Jesus and the Men of the Spirit, we find two aspects of
Moses' ministry emphasized: the working of wonders and the
speaking of the Word.[1]

      6. V. 39 spells out in the story of Moses the
second aspect of the theme of acceptance/rejection which we
found in 3:23. Moses spoke to the people living words, but
their reaction? ᾧ οὐκ ἠθέλησαν ὑπήκοοι γενέσθαι οἱ πατέρες
ἡμῶν ἀλλὰ ἀπώσαντο[2] καὶ ἐστράφησαν ἐν ταῖς καρδίαις αὐτῶν εἰς
'Αἴγυπτον! Moses is rejected a second time, and this is the
definitive rejection, for it takes place after he has been
established by God. Vv. 40-41 amplify this rejection, in terms
of the people's idolatry. Instead of obeying the one through
whom God worked signs and wonders, they worshipped the works of
their own hands.

      7. The pattern of 3:23 is brought to conclusion
in vv. 42-43. Those who rejected the Prophet Moses and the
words he spoke are themselves rejected by God: ἔστρεψεν δὲ ὁ
θεὸς καὶ παρέδωκεν αὐτοὺς λατρεύειν κτλ, with the result, as
the prophecy from Amos 5:25-27 indicates, that they are removed
from the land in exile.[3]

We have not attempted in this analysis to deal with important questions about the speech, for example, how it might
answer the charges brought against Stephen. But the literary
analysis of the figure of Moses shows clearly that whoever
wrote this part of the speech wrote also the parts of Acts we
have so far studied. More importantly, the analysis has
revealed Luke's fundamental conception of the prophetic model.
Whether his description of Moses is derived from his

---

[1]V. 38 refers back to the end of v. 35 (Bihler, 56).
Another similarity to Jesus: Moses receives the living words
to give them; Jesus in 2:33 receives the Holy Spirit to pour it
out.

[2]ἀπώσαντο here corresponds exactly to ἀπώσατο in 7:27, the
first rejection.

[3]God's "turning away" (ἔστρεψεν) in 7:42 corresponds to
the peoples' "turning away" (ἐστράφησαν) in 7:39. As they have
rejected, so are they rejected. (We note the same pattern in
Paul's statement in 13:46: ἀπωθεῖσθε . . . . στρεφόμεθα). The
conclusion of the first section was Moses' exile; the conclusion of the second, the peoples' exile.

understanding of Jesus,[1] or whether Moses as Luke appreciates
him from his reading of the Scriptures has provided the
literary model for Jesus Himself, it is clear at least that
Luke has so described each that they must be seen together.

Now when we recall that this story about Moses is being
told by one who himself πλήρης χάριτος καὶ δυνάμεως ἐποίει
τέρατα καὶ σημεῖα ἐν τῷ λαῷ, and who spoke τῇ σοφίᾳ καὶ τῷ
πνεύματι, and is addressed to the men who have brought him to
trial, the complex and intertwining levels of meaning to be
found in Stephen's final accusation in the speech emerge:
those to whom he is speaking are stiffnecked and uncircumcised
in heart and ear. Just as their fathers, they always resist
the Spirit of God. The fathers killed the prophets, and they
have murdered the Just One, Jesus (7:51-52).

And when we see that this accusation is immediately
followed by the leaders' fury and grinding of teeth over
Stephen's words, we recognize how artfully Luke has meshed
these levels: a) Moses is the type of the prophet. He was
rejected by the fathers, and thus they were rejected by God;
b) Jesus is the Prophet like Moses. The present generation
has rejected Him a first time by killing Him; c) now Stephen
the Man of the Spirit (Prophet) speaks the Word, and is being
rejected by those who hear him. This is their second rejection, and the final one. By seeking to kill this man who
speaks in the Spirit, and even as they boil in fury at his
words is filled with the Spirit (7:55), they fulfill the words
of his final accusation, that they always resist the Spirit of
God. That they are thereby rejected from God's people is left
unexpressed, but how can the point be missed?

Finally fitting together the narrative about Stephen and
his speech has also served to unite the literary themes we have
been analyzing separately. We have seen first in the clearest
fashion how the speech functions as a prophecy for the narrative. Secondly, we have found expressed a lineage of spiritual
authority and a lineage of rejection. Moses, Jesus, Stephen:
each a speaker of God's Word and a worker of wonders, each in
his time rejected by the people.

---

[1]Gils, 35, considers that the titles were applied to Moses
because of Luke's understanding of Jesus.

F. Conclusions to Chapter One

Our initial examination of Acts 4:32ff in relation to the
other passages concerning possessions in the first chapters in
Acts revealed certain patterns of association which connected
the Apostles, the use of possessions, the Jerusalem community,
and a dynamic of inclusion/exclusion.

Beginning the process of placing these passages within an
appropriate literary context, that is the story of Luke-Acts,
we undertook an analysis of the Apostles in literary or dramatic terms. We found that the Apostles at this level of
literary description were examples of a larger category,
which we tentatively termed "Men of the Spirit," and that all
the figures in this category shared a certain stereotyped description, which included being filled with the Holy Spirit,
speaking God's Word, performing signs and wonders, and stimulating a response of acceptance/rejection. They were, we
concluded, described as Prophets.

Seeking a possible model for this description, we
discovered that in the discourses of Acts, Jesus is described
in terms identical to those used of the Men of the Spirit. We
also found that Moses is portrayed as a type of Jesus, who
thereby can be designated a Prophet like Moses.

In these descriptions, we suggest, there is nothing
accidental, but rather there is revealed a literary method or
pattern. By means of this pattern, the author has established
both a typology and succession of authority. Moses is the type
of Jesus, Jesus is the fulfillment of that type. Jesus is in
turn the type of the Apostles. But He is more. He is also the
direct source of their authority, both through his direct
appointment and through bestowing on them the Spirit He
received from the Father. But what of the other Men of the
Spirit? That they share in the Spirit of Jesus is clear. But
He did not appoint them as He did the Apostles. How can the
transfer of authority to them be expressed? This problem, and
the way in which Luke has expressed this transfer of authority,
will be an important consideration as this study progresses.

This rather lengthy analysis has been only the first step
toward placing 4:32ff and the other passages dealing with
possessions within the story of Luke-Acts. But by concentrating

on the main characters, we have found a way of grasping that
story in its essential dynamism. We have found that the story
progresses by means of the dynamic of acceptance and rejection
by the people of the Men of the Spirit who proclaim the Word
about Jesus. But what about the Gospel? We cannot lop off the
whole first part of the story and focus simply upon Acts. We
have already found, indeed, that in the discourses about Jesus,
this same pattern of acceptance/rejection forms the nucleus of
Luke's understanding of Jesus' mission. We have legitimate
hope, then, of finding in the story about Jesus in the Gospel
that which is contained in nuce in the discourses.[1] We are
further impelled to analyze the Gospel under the perspective
of the dynamic of acceptance/rejection because of the fact that
Luke has clearly structured the acceptance/rejection of Jesus
as taking place in two stages (like that of Moses); the first
during his earthly ministry, the second through his witnesses.
We will try to discover to what extent this same literary
pattern of acceptance and rejection has shaped the narrative
of Luke's Gospel, to what extent the earthly ministry (the time
of the first rejection) foreshadows and anticipates the time of
the second rejection. We turn then to the Gospel, reading it
insofar as we can, as the story of "the Prophet and the People."

---

[1]The attempt to use the Acts discourses as a framework for
examining Luke's Gospel has been undertaken in a broad fashion
by Lampe, "The Lucan Portrait," 160-175.

CHAPTER TWO

If Acts refers back consistently to the story told by the
Gospel when it presents the story of the second rejection of
the Prophet like Moses, it is not surprising that the Gospel
story should anticipate to some degree the pattern established
in Acts, by presenting Jesus' earthly ministry as the Visitation by God of His People in the person of the Prophet and the
rejection of that visitation by the People. What may be
surprising, however, is the extent to which the literary
pattern of the Prophet and the People has shaped the Gospel
narrative.

Why surprising? Because in the telling of the story of
Jesus, Luke enjoyed not nearly the literary freedom he could
exercise in Acts. He had before him not only a great body of
material already shaped by oral or written transmission, but
also the Gospel of Mark which provided a kerygmatic if not
biographical framework for the story of Jesus.[1] Luke enriched
his narrative with a substantial amount of new material, but it
is clear that he was indebted to his sources for much of his
story,[2] and to a considerable extent to the framework provided

_____

[1]The two-source hypothesis has come under continuing and
recently vigorous challenge. Cf. e.g., B. C. Butler, The
Originality of St. Matthew (Cambridge: University Press, 1951);
A. Farrer, "On Dispensing with Q," Studies in the Gospels, 55-
88; N. Turner, "The Minor Verbal Agreements of Mt. and Lk.
against Mk.," Studia Evangelica I, 223-234; and W. Farmer, The
Synoptic Problem (New York: The Macmillan Co., 1964). It
remains an elegant hypothesis, and one which is less cumbersome
for handling the data. In this study, however, "Q" will simply
mean material common to Matthew and Luke, with no implied
judgment on the order, origin or even existence of this hypothetical document.

[2]Cf. the listing of passages and discussions in J. M.
Creed, The Gospel according to St. Luke (London: Macmillan and
Co., 1930) lvi-lxx; E. Ellis, The Gospel of Luke (The Century
Bible; London: Nelson, 1966) 25-30; B. S. Easton, The Gospel
according to St. Luke (New York: Charles Scribner's Sons, 1926)
xiii-xxx; W. Grundmann, Das Evangelium nach Lukas
(Theologischer Handkommentar zum Neuen Testament III; Berlin:
Evangelische Verlaganstalt, 1963) 7-17. For those passages

him by Mark as well.[1]

A literary analysis of the Gospel, then, must be in effect a redactional study, one which at the same time avoids the easy temptation of literary fancifulness and attends to the often minute deviations from the parallels which betray the author's hand and intention.[2] The nature of a writing must to a great extent determine our procedure for interpretation. In Acts, it was possible to proceed on the assumption that the narrative was shaped totally by Luke, and we found through our analysis which began with the smallest details and led to the largest patterns, that this presumption had been sound. The same presumption cannot be made for the Gospel. The interpreter must therefore take into account the frequently difficult questions relating to the sources of Luke and his use of them.

We have an advantage in interpreting Luke, however, which is not granted us by Matt or Mk. We cannot neglect the important, indeed overriding, fact that the author has himself already interpreted the Gospel in the book of Acts. In Acts, Luke has already provided a perspective which must be taken

which have no parallel either in the other synoptics, John, or as is frequently the case with Luke, The Gospel of Thomas, we are in a situation similar to Acts; we may suspect a written source, but are quite unable to determine with finality what may have been totally composed by him and what may only have been reworked.

[1]This position presents fewer problems than the so-called Proto-Luke theory of, e.g., B. H. Streeter, The Four Gospels (New York: The Macmillan Co., 1925) 199ff, and V. Taylor, Behind the Third Gospel (Oxford: Clarendon Press, 1926). Even though he recognized the difficulties of this theory, L. Gaston, No Stone on Another, 244-256, proceeded to analyze an enormous amount of materials in Luke through this perspective, thereby vitiating the effect of many fine individual insights. It must be said, however, that Luke by no means follows the Markan framework slavishly. Cf. Ellis, Luke, 27.

[2]Caution must be expressed concerning two unspoken presuppositions which color many studies called redactional. First, the tendency to equate the unique with the essential; in fact an author's thought is as much represented by material taken over unchanged (or minimally changed) from the tradition, as it is by his changes. Second, the tendency to restrict the interest of the redactor to the polemic or paraenetic; other factors may also be at work, notably the aesthetic. A life-situation of crisis that is being addressed by the evangelist cannot be presumed, but must be shown.

seriously as the most reliable hermeneutic key to the meaning
of the Gospel as the author himself understood it. The present
study is an attempt to read the Gospel through the perspective
established by the discourses and narrative of the first part
of Acts.

Two examples can be cited to illustrate how significant
the perspective of Acts can be. It has been pointed out by
commentators that the concluding words from the cloud in the
transfiguration account of all three synoptics (Lk 9:35, Matt
17:5, Mk 9:7), αὐτοῦ ἀκούετε, could be a reminiscence of the
Deut 18:5-9 passage speaking of the Prophet like Moses.[1] From
an internal analysis of the passage, and from a comparison with
the parallels, this suggestion can stand only as a possibility,
however plausible. But when the passage is read in the light
of Acts 3 and 7, and the picture of Jesus as the Prophet like
Moses in Acts, the reference to Deut 18 in the Lukan version
seems certain.[2] On the other hand, the perspective of Acts
can provide a certain negative check on interpretations of
passages in the Gospel. For example, the view that in 10:1ff
Luke intended to portray the ideal attitudes toward possessions
for the missionaries of his own day[3] must not only deal with
the obvious problem that Lk 22:35 explicitly revokes these
norms, but that the descriptions of missionaries in Acts
(especially Paul) present quite another picture of the
missionaries' use of possessions.

---

[1]Cf. e.g., V. Taylor, The Gospel according to St. Mark
2nd ed. (London: Macmillan, 1966) 392; X. Leon-Dufour, Études
d'Evangiles (Paris: Editions du Seuil, 1965) 93; H. Teeple,
The Mosaic Eschatological Prophet, 84.

[2]The discussion of the ἔξοδος which Jesus would fulfill
strengthens the allusion in Luke. Cf. J. Mánek, "The New
Exodus in the Books of Luke," NovT 2 (1958) 8-23; E. Lohse,
"Lukas als Theologe der Heilsgeschichte," 263; Lindars, New
Testament Apologetic, 204; Gils, Jésus Prophète, 36; Schubert,
"Structure and Significance of Luke 24," 181-182.

[3]Cf. H.-J. Degenhardt, Lukas Evangelist der Armen, 60-66,
who sees Lk 10:1ff as a description based on and directed to
missionaries of Luke's time. He handles the revocation of
22:35 by distinguishing the ideal for missionaries in peace
(10:1ff) and persecution (22:35), but does not deal with the
problem that neither picture corresponds to any description of
missionaries in Acts.

Since our purpose here is not an exhaustive analysis of
every aspect of the Gospel which anticipates the pattern of
Acts, but rather the discernment of an intelligible literary
pattern within which the materials on possessions can be seen
in their literary function, our treatment of the Gospel
materials will be selective. We shall consider several sec-
tions of the Gospel in which the hand of the author appears to
be especially evident, and try to determine to what extent
these passages reflect and express the pattern of the Prophet
and the People (the acceptance and rejection of the Prophet by
the people) found to be so dominant in Acts. We shall focus
not simply on explicit statements which contain the title
Prophet, but on the thematic significance of these and other
statements in relation to the narrative as a whole.

A. Luke 24:19ff.

A unique feature of the resurrection narratives in Luke
is the way in which they have a double function within the
Gospel. As in the other Synoptics and John, the appearances
of the Risen Lord serve to establish the reality of the
resurrection and prophesy the future ministry of the disciples.[1]
But in Luke the resurrection narratives also serve to interpret the significance of the earthly ministry and the suffering
of Jesus.[2] The Emmaus story (24:13-35) is of particular
interest in this respect. The story is clearly a Lukan composition.[3] Within a narrative which contains elements of a

---

[1]Matt 28:9-10; 16-20; Mk 16:15-18 (?); Jn 20:17; 19-21;
21:15ff. Cf. C. H. Dodd, "The Appearance of the Risen Christ:
An Essay in Form-Criticism of the Gospels," Studies in the
Gospels, 9-35; R. H. Lightfoot, Locality and Doctrine in the
Gospels (New York: Harper and Brothers, 1937), 1-105.

[2]Schubert, "Structure and Significance," has convincingly
demonstrated that the Lukan resurrection appearances reach
their climax in the teaching of the risen Christ concerning the
fulfillment of the Scriptures by His suffering, and notes (185)
that the "forward and backward look are important aspects both
of Luke's literary method and of his Theology of History." Cf.
also Ellis, Luke, 265; and Lightfoot, Locality and Doctrine,
who points out that the Lukan alteration of the angel's message
at the tomb (Lk 24:6-7) functions as an explicit fulfillment of
Jesus' own prophecy.

[3]In agreement with Schubert, "Structure and Significance,"

pilgrimage tale, a recognition story and a cultic etiology,[1] the dialogue between Jesus and the two disciples is the central focus of the pericope.

In v. 19, the disciples[2] recount to their mysterious companion their expectations regarding Jesus and the shattering reversal of those expectations, a reversal only slightly quali- fied by the strange events they had heard of occurring at the tomb (vv. 22-24). Jesus' response to them serves both to clarify their expectations and interpret the true significance of the reversal (vv. 24-26).

Their description of Jesus in vv. 19-20 is very close to those used of Jesus and Moses in Acts. As in the Acts dis- courses, the place of Jesus' origin is appended to his name as a kind of title.[3] He had shown himself to be[4] ἀνὴρ προφήτης δυνατὸς ἐν ἔργῳ καὶ λόγῳ, a phrasing almost identical to Acts

---

172-174; Dodd, "Appearance," 13; A. Ehrhardt, "The Disciples of Emmaus," NTS 10 (1963) 184ff; R. Leaney, "The Resurrection Narratives in Luke (xxiv 12-53)," NTS 2 (1955-6) 110-111. Contra, P. Winter, "The Treatment of his Sources by the Third Evangelist," ST 8 (1955) 168. The recent study by J. Wanke, Die Emmauserzählung (Erfurter Theologische Studien 31; Leipzig: St. Benno-Verlag, 1973) provides an exhaustive analysis of the vocabulary and style of the passage, and concludes that the passage is Lukan.

[1]For a survey of opinions concerning the literary form of the passage, cf. Wanke, 1-32. Interesting remarks are also offered by Dodd, 14; Ehrhardt, 184; Schubert, 172; E. Kloster- mann, Das Lukasevangelium (HNT II, 1; Tübingen: J. C. B. Mohr [Paul Siebeck], 1919) 601-602; W. Grundmann, Lukas, 442-443, and "Fragen der Komposition des lukanischen 'Reiseberichte,'" ZNW 50 (1959) 253.

[2]The δύο ἐξ αὐτῶν of v. 13 refers to τοῖς λοιποῖς in v. 9. Considering the emphasis in Acts upon the Apostles as witnesses, it is interesting that in the Gospel there is only one appear- ance to the Apostles alone, and that is mentioned in passing (24:34). The Emmaus disciples would have to be included among those who "ate and drank with Him after He rose from the dead," (Acts 10:41).

[3]Acts 2:22; 3:6; 4:10; 6:14; 22:8; 26:9. Cf. Wilckens, Die Missionsreden, 122-123.

[4]The ὃς ἐγένετο here is not simply copulative, but has the strength of "manifested" or "proved," as in Lk 10:36. Cf. Klostermann, 605; Easton, 360; Creed, 296; A. Plummer, A Critical and Exegetical Commentary on the Gospel according to St. Luke 9th ed. (ICC; New York: Charles Scribner's Sons, 1910) 553.

7:22, and close in significance to 2:22, as the following words
indicate. The phrase ἐναντίον τοῦ θεοῦ καὶ παντὸς τοῦ λαοῦ
corresponds to the ἀποδεδειγμένον ἀπὸ τοῦ θεοῦ . . . ἐν μέσῳ
ὑμῶν of Acts 2:22, and this combination, as we have seen in ch.
1, also recalls that of Deut 34:10-12 in regard to Moses. The
disciples had hoped that this prophet would be ὁ μέλλων
λυτροῦσθαι τὸν Ἰσραήλ (v. 21). The use of the verb λυτρόομαι
here recalls Lk 1:68 and 2:38, and as we have seen, reflects
the description of Moses in Acts 7:35 as ἄρχοντα καὶ λυτρωτήν.

Now it must be kept in mind that this description of Jesus
would still be fresh in the minds of Luke's readers when they
heard the words of Acts 3:22-23 and 7:22. By means of this
description, Luke has invited his readers to view the earthly
ministry of Jesus as that of a Prophet, and has prepared them
to understand the preaching of the raised Jesus as the Prophet
whom God has raised up as the continuation of this same
ministry, but now in power, carried on by His witnesses.

V. 21 recounts the setback to the disciples' expectations
caused by the death of the Prophet. We should note that the
rejection of Jesus is here attributed solely to the leaders of
the people (οἱ ἀρχιερεῖς καὶ οἱ ἄρχοντες ἡμῶν),[1] a distinction
made more dramatic by being placed in immediate contrast to the
expectation of Jesus' disciples (ἡμεῖς δὲ ἠλπίζομεν). We have
seen already how in the first part of Acts Luke progressively
shifts the blame for the rejection of Jesus from the people as
a whole to their leaders.

Jesus' response to the disciples is not a repudiation of
the terms of their expectation,[2] but a rebuke (ὦ ἀνόηται κτλ,

---

[1]Cf. Dupont, "Les Discours de Pierre dans les Actes et le
chapitre XXIV de l'évangile de Luc," 339; G. Rau, "Das Volk in
der lukanischen Passionsgeschichte: Eine Konjecture zu Lk.
23:13," ZNW 56 (1965) 46; A. Loisy, L'Evangile selon Luc
(Paris, 1924) 576.

[2]It is necessary to emphasize this point. Luke is not
replacing the unworthy title "Prophet," associated with
nationalistic hopes, with the more proper title of "Christ,"
(so Wanke, 61, 64), for in his thought both titles are appropriate designations for Jesus. Nor should we conclude that the
expectation of the "release of Israel" expresses a nationalistic hope (Grundmann, 446), for in Lk 1:74 it is clear that the
redemption of the people means for Luke freedom to worship and
not a national liberation. The assumption that the evangelists

v. 25) for their failure to grasp[1] the full implications of the
mission of the Prophet, that in fact rejection was an essential
part of His mission, and that through suffering the Messiah
would enter into Glory. When Jesus interprets the Scripture in
such fashion as to show "from Moses and all the prophets" how
the Scriptures spoke τὰ περὶ ἑαυτοῦ, it appears very likely
that in Luke's own understanding this interpretation would be
along the lines of the interpretation he himself would soon
make of the figure of Moses as the type of the Prophet rejected
by men but accepted by God.

The resurrection sayings of Jesus in Lk 24:44ff complement
the sayings found in the Emmaus story, for after again revealing to the disciples the meaning of the Scriptures in regard to
Himself, Jesus prophesies the mission to be carried out by His
witnesses (v. 49), after their being clothed with power from on
High (v. 49), a prophecy which in effect provides the program
for Acts, and anticipates the course of its narrative from
Jerusalem to Rome (v. 47).

Luke's resurrection accounts therefore play an important
transitional role in the work Luke-Acts as a whole. They

---

sought to correct christologies by their critical use of titles
requires careful examination. To take only this instance: How
do we know that "the Prophet" was for the NT writers necessarily a title of less profundity or dignity than "the Christ?"
If Luke did not like the title "Prophet," why didn't he just
eliminate it? Respect for his sources cannot be the reason,
for Luke is not hesitant about dropping other things. But in
fact, the emphasis on Jesus as prophet is nowhere as heavy as
in those passages unique to Luke! It is also doubtful that the
readers of the Gospel were quite so sensitive to the nuances of
meaning found in a particular title, as the modern exegete. It
would take an attentive listener indeed to discern, for example,
that in 7:13 of the Gospel Luke corrected the use of Prophet in
7:16 by calling Jesus Lord. Yet this has been seriously
suggested. If Luke wanted to correct the use of the title of
Prophet, he botched the job badly by using the title in such
climactic places in the Gospel and Acts. Finally, we must
again assert that a lopsided emphasis on titles as the main
vehicle of christological expression has led to the neglect of
the obvious consideration that Luke has consistently and
dramatically presented Jesus as a prophet. If Jesus is for
Luke the Χριστός, He is a prophetic Χριστός, and if He is
κύριος then He is such as the risen Prophet.

[1]Dupont, "Les Discours," 339, sees here the same ignorance
motif as in the speeches of Acts.

interpret the first volume and anticipate the second. In the interpretation of the story of Jesus, we have found the same picture as in the discourses of Acts: Jesus is the Prophet sent by God to redeem the People, certified by God through the working of powerful deeds and the speaking of powerful words, and rejected by that part of the people represented by the leaders, only to be raised up by God to be preached by His witnesses to the ends of the earth.

B. Luke 2:25-35:

This study cannot provide a complete analysis of the literary role of the infancy narratives within Luke-Acts, nor even a justification for considering them an integral part of the work.[1] It is certainly as justifiable to proceed on the assumption that they are Lukan in composition and play a significant and coherent role in the work, as to dismiss them out of hand and interpret Luke-Acts as though they did not exist.[2]

---

[1]For representative positions regarding the original language of Luke 1-2, cf. on the one hand the many essays of P. Winter, including "Some Observations on the Language in the Birth and Infancy Narratives of the Third Gospel," NTS 1 (1954-5) 111-121; "The Proto-Source of Luke I," NovT 1 (1956) 184-199; "On Luke and Lukan Sources," ZNW 47 (1956) 217-242; and on the other, H. J. Cadbury, "Luke--Translator or Author?," American Journal of Theology 24 (1920) 436-455; N. Turner, "The Relation of Luke I and II to Hebraic Sources and to the Rest of Luke-Acts," NTS 2 (1955-6) 100-109; H. Sparks, "The Semitisms of St. Luke's Gospel," JTS 43 (1942) 129-138; P. Benoit, "L'Enfance de Jean-Baptiste selon Luc I," NTS 3 (1956-7) 169-194. Useful reviews of work done on these chapters can be found in R. Mc. Wilson, "Some Recent Studies in the Lucan Infancy Narratives," Studia Evangelica I, 235-253, and in the major study of R. Laurentin, Structure et Théologie de Luc I-II (EBib; Paris: J. Gabalda, 1957).

[2]The consistent exclusion of the infancy narratives from consideration is one of the recognized failings of Conzelmann's Theology of St. Luke. When the evidence of those chapters threatens the schema he has developed from the rest of the Gospel, he invokes the source problem (cf. 24, 48-49, 75, n. 4, 118, 172) which is scarcely satisfactory. Attempts made to rehabilitate the infancy accounts in line with the Conzelmann perspective have not been very successful; cf. H. Oliver, "The Lukan Birth Stories and the Purpose of Luke-Acts," NTS 10 (1963) 202-226 and W. B. Tatum, "The Epoch of Israel: Luke I-II and the Theological Plan of Luke-Acts," NTS 13 (1966-7) 184-195. The independent essay of P. Minear, "Luke's Use of the Birth Stories," SLA, 111-130, is far more helpful.

In fact, however, when we do proceed on the assumption that the
infancy narratives are Lukan, we discover many literary relationships with the rest of the Gospel and Acts which in the
final analysis receive proper explanation only by the hypothesis of a common author.[1]

The canticles and prophecies of the infancy narratives are
of particular importance. Like the resurrection narratives in
Luke, they provide a double function of interpretation. In the
first place, they connect the story about Jesus to the story of
the People Israel in the Scriptures, so that from the very
beginning, the reader understands "the events brought to fulfillment among us" (1:1)[2] as a continuation of the story of God
and His People in the Old Testament.[3] More pertinent to the
present study, the canticles of the infancy narratives serve
as prophecies which interpret beforehand the events occurring
in the subsequent narrative.[4] They provide a clear example of
Luke's use of literary prophecy discussed in the introduction
to this study. By means of these prophecies, Luke provides his
readers with an interpretation of the events still to come.

Both because of their placement at the climax of the
infancy account (separated from the ministry only by 2:4-52)
and content, the canticle and prophecy of Simeon in 2:25-35
invite particular attention. The passage as a whole bears

---

[1] Cf. especially the common preoccupations and themes
listed by Laurentin, 101-103; Benoit, 188-189; Minear, 112-118,
and J. Comblin, "La Paix dans la Théologie de Saint Luc,"
439ff.

[2] On πεπληροφορημένων (1:1), H. J. Cadbury, "Commentary
on the Preface of Luke," Beginnings II, 496, says that "The
suggestion that the fulfillment of the Scripture is what Luke
means need hardly be taken seriously, though of course πληρόω
is so used." For Luke's use of πληρόω, cf. 4:21 and 24:44
(both thematically important); Acts 1:16; 3:18; and 13:27, all
with explicit reference to the Scripture. Although other N.T.
uses of πληροφορέω in the passive have the sense of "assurance"
or "conviction" (cf. Rom 4:21; 14:5; Gal 4:12; II Tim 4:5), it
can also mean "fulfillment" (cf. II Tim 4:17). Cf. also Scott
Liddell, s.v., and E. Trocmé, 46-47.

[3] Cf. again the remark of Dahl, "The Story of Abraham,"
152-153, that Luke really intended to write "the continuation
of the biblical history."

[4] Minear, 116.

clear marks of Lukan composition.[1] In a fashion structurally
similar to the discourses of Acts, the canticle first presents
the positive significance of Jesus, and the prophecy made to
Jesus' parents establishes the pattern of acceptance and
rejection.

The following points about the canticle can be quickly
noted: a) The fulfillment of God's promise to Simeon brings
peace, just as the coming of the Messiah to Israel in fulfillment of the promises to Abraham is for the proclamation of the
Good News of peace.[2] b) Simeon stands as a witness and a
proclaimer of this fulfillment. c) The "comfort of Israel"
is defined as the salvation that comes from God, a salvation
which He Himself has prepared. d) The place where this salvation is achieved is first of all Israel itself; the salvation
coming from God in the person of Jesus is the Glory of Israel
(God's People). e) The gentiles are first of all witnesses of
this blessing which has been brought to Israel (v. 31),[3] and

---

[1]Not only does the passage contain a high proportion of
"Lukan" vocabulary (e.g., προσδέχομαι, εὐλαβής, παράκλησις,
εἰσάγω, γονεῖς, εὐλογέω, δεσπότης, εἰρήνη, σωτήριον), but more
significantly, the structure of the passage contains the
"prophecy-fulfillment" pattern in miniature: Simeon awaits
the comfort of Israel (2:25); it is revealed to him that he
will see the Christ of the Lord (2:26); Simeon receives the
child (2:28); He gives thanks to God for fulfilling His word
of promise to him (2:29).

[2]Cf. our remarks on Acts 10:36 and 7:20, 26, above, pp.
62 and 72.

[3]κατὰ πρόσωπον πάντων τῶν λαῶν is very difficult. It
recalls passages like Is 40:5 and 52:10, but why has Luke used
λαῶν instead of ἐθνῶν? H. Schürmann, Das Lukasevangelium
(HTKNT III, Erster Teil; Freiburg: Herder, 1969) 125, suggests
that the replacement of the Isaian ἐθνῶν by λαῶν indicates the
creation of a "new people" among the Gentiles. Similarly,
Plummer, Luke, 69, and Creed, Luke, 41. G. Kilpatrick, "λαοί
at Lk. 2:31 and Acts 4:25, 27," JTS 16 (1965) 127, thinks that
on analogy with 4:27, where λαοί seems to signify the peoples
of Israel, the term here might mean something like "all the
tribes of Israel." Still, it may be wondered whether Luke was
making so conscious an adaptation. The weight of the Isaian
passages themselves would favor seeing the Gentiles as the
referent here. Perhaps the following points can be held with
some assurance: a) Whatever the referent of πάντων τῶν λαῶν,
the salvation spoken of is not extended to them in this verse;
they are seen as witnesses of the salvation. b) The next verse
emphasizes the realization of that salvation within Israel.

then share in it.[1]

The canticle has described the positive significance of
the Savior. But it is the explicit prophecy made to Mary in
v. 34 which plays a particularly significant role in illuminating the way in which the subsequent telling of the story will
be structured dramatically. If we exclude the awkward clause
addressed to Mary,[2] the text reads: ἰδοὺ οὗτος κεῖται εἰς
πτῶσιν καὶ ἀνάστασιν πολλῶν ἐν τῷ Ἰσραὴλ καὶ εἰς σημεῖον
ἀντιλεγόμενον . . . ὅπως ἂν ἀποκαλυφθῶσιν ἐκ πολλῶν καρδιῶν
διαλογισμοί.

1. Although Simeon has expected the παράκλησιν τοῦ
Ἰσραὴλ (2:25) and states that his eyes have seen the salvation
which will be the δόξαν λαοῦ σοῦ Ἰσραὴλ (2:32), the prophecy

Cf. M.-J. Lagrange, Evangile selon Saint Luc (EBib; Paris: J.
Gabalda, 1948) 86. c) It is from Israel that the light of
salvation will reach the Gentiles.

[1]It is difficult to say whether φῶς and δόξαν are to be
seen as in apposition to σωτήριον (Grundmann, Lukas, 91), or
whether in parallelism they form a breakdown of the aspects of
that salvation (Loisy, Luc, 122). In either case, the focus is
on Israel (Lagrange, Luc, 87). The φῶς εἰς ἀποκάλυψιν ἐθνῶν,
from Is 49:6 is difficult to translate precisely (Plummer,
Luke, 69), but the meaning is clear enough. The Gentiles'
participation in salvation is mediated by Israel; it does not
come to them directly. "Nur durch Vermittlung Israels gibt es
also Heil für die Heiden," (Schürmann, Lukas, 126). This
should be noted in view of our later development. There is
consistency to Luke's presentation. There must be a salvation
realized within Israel, a "Glory of Israel," for there to be a
light of revelation to the Gentiles. Neither should it go
unnoticed that Is 49:6 reappears at the beginning of Paul's
ministry (Acts 13:47). For Luke, Paul is the instrument
through whom the light of salvation comes to the Gentiles.

[2]Awkward, that is, grammatically, not theologically. We
should expect ὅπως to follow directly upon ἀντιλεγόμενον. If
we are to interpret the text as it stands, we should consider
that in the infancy accounts Luke describes Mary in terms which
would lead an attentive reader to see her as a type of Israel.
This is especially clear in the annunciation account (1:28)
with its striking verbal allusions to Zeph 3:14 and Zech 2:14
(cf. Laurentin, Théologie, 64ff), and in the Magnificat where
the visitation of God to Mary (1:48) parallels or exemplifies
His raising up the poor and putting down the mighty within
Israel (1:51ff). Here, the piercing or splitting of Mary's
heart by the sword mirrors the division in the people occasion-
ed by the Prophet Jesus. Cf. also L. Gaston, No Stone on
Another, 274.

90

of v. 34 qualifies this in a significant fashion: not all of
Israel will accept this salvation. There is to be a division
within the people.[1] We shall see as the study progresses how
appropriate the images of "rising" and "falling" are to the
respective fates of the Apostles and leaders of the people
"within Israel."

2. Jesus is destined (κεῖται)[2] to cause this division among the people; it is not accidental or fortuitous, but
a part of God's plan. We have already seen how in Acts and Lk
24 the idea of the divine necessity has been attached by Luke
to the pattern of rejection. "This one" (οὗτος) is the focus
of the split within the people Israel. It is in response to
Him that the unbelieving part of the historic Israel will fall
away, be rejected from the people, and the believing people of
God will emerge from that same historic Israel.

3. It is as a σημεῖον ἀντιλεγόμενον that Jesus will
cause this division. The use of σημεῖον here is less related
to the "signs and wonders" of Acts (a phrase that does not
occur in the Gospel), than to Luke's use of σημεῖον in 11:29ff.
From the Lukan redaction of that passage it is clear that the
"sign of Jonah"--which in Matt is made to refer to the
resurrection--is understood as the prophetic mission itself
or the prophetic word.[3] The "contradicted sign" of 2:34, then,
approaches once more the imagery of the prophet.

4. In their response to the Prophet, the διαλογισμοί

---

[1]We follow the terminology of J. Jervell, Luke and the
People of God.

[2]Many commentators (Creed, 42; Plummer, 70; Schürmann,
127; Grundmann, 91; Klostermann, 405; Loisy, 123; Laurentin,
89) see here an allusion to the "stone of stumbling" of Is 8:14.
In spite of Luke's use of Is 8:14 in the parable of the vineyard (20:18), there is no real evidence for such an allusion
here. As Lagrange, 88, notes, the image of the stone may be
appropriate to falling, but not to rising. Laurentin, 90, concludes that the passage remains "à certains égards, un passage
mysterieux." Seeing it as programmatic for the rest of the
Gospel, however, reduces the element of mystery a little.

[3]Contra J. Jeremias, The Parables of Jesus 6th ed. trans.
by S. Hooke (New York: Charles Scribner's Sons, 1963) 108, who
sees the sign of Jonah "as God's legitimation of His messenger
through his deliverance from death." But there does not appear
to be that implication in the Lukan version.

of men's hearts will be laid bare. Luke's use of διαλογίζομαι
is largely negative, in contexts referring to the opponents of
Jesus (5:21, 22; 6:8) and to the disciples when in need of
rebuking (9:46, 47; 24:38).[1] What is significant here is that
the inner condition of men before God is made manifest in their
response to the Prophet.[2] By accepting Him, they show themselves just before God (cf. 7:29-30), but by rejecting him, no
matter how they justify themselves (Lk 16:15, 18:9, etc.), they
are revealed as rejecting God who sent Him (7:29-30, 10:16).

The canticle and prophecy of Simeon therefore stand at the
end of the infancy narrative as a programmatic prophecy for the
rest of the Gospel (and Acts as well). The imagery of the
passage is somewhat different from that we have seen in Acts
and Lk 24; the prophetic imagery in particular is largely
implicit. But the pattern of acceptance and rejection is laid
out explicitly and focussed directly on the person of Jesus.
What makes the prophecy of Simeon so important as a key to the
following narrative is that it directs us to see in the story
of Jesus a story as well of a people divided over the prophet,
a division in which some are to rise and others are to fall.

We have seen from Lk 24:19ff and 2:25ff how Luke has
framed the Gospel narrative within sayings which interpret the
story as that of the Prophet and the People. We turn now to
some significant passages within that story where Luke has
shaped the narrative in accord with that interpretation.

C. Luke 4:16ff:

It is not necessary to emphasize the programmatic nature
of this passage within Luke's Gospel, for it is universally
recognized.[3] Nor is there any doubt that the passage

---

[1]Cf. G. Schrenk, "διαλέγομαι," TDNT 2 (1964) 97-98.

[2]That a prophet should know the thoughts of a man's heart
is axiomatic for Simon the Pharisee in Lk 7:39, and Jesus shows
Himself to be such a prophet by "answering" Simon's unspoken
criticism, 7:40. Cf. also Lk 5:22; 22:21; Acts 5:3.

[3]Cf. H. von Baer, Der Heilige Geist in den Lukasschriften,
63; Conzelmann, Theology, 34; Easton, Luke, 50; Creed, Luke,
65; Grundmann, Lukas, 119; Dupont, Etudes, 406; R. H. Lightfoot,
History and Interpretation in the Gospels (London: Hodder and

92

represents a thoroughgoing redaction of his sources by the
author.[1] A comparison with the parallels shows that Luke has
elevated a controversy story to the level of a fundamental
reflection upon the nature of Jesus' mission and a literary
foreshadowing of the rest of the Gospel and Acts.[2] The passage
is extraordinarily rich, and only the following points immediately pertinent to the present study can be made here:

    1. 4:16-21. Although we speak of Jesus' inaugural
speech, there is no real discourse by Jesus,[3] but simply a
reading from Isaiah 61:1-2,[4] followed by Jesus' announcement
that the Scripture had found fulfillment that day in the hearing of those in the synagogue (v. 21). We shall have occasion
to talk about the Isaiah citation in regard to possessions in
the next chapter[5] but for now the following points can be made:

Stoughton, 1935) 199. A useful review of work done on the
passage can be found in H. Anderson, "The Rejection of Nazareth
Pericope of Luke 4:16-30 in Light of Recent Critical Trends,"
Int 18 (1964) 259-275.

[1]On the question whether Luke used only Mk and expanded
that account (Conzelmann, Theology, 33), or used another source
on the visit (Creed, 64; Plummer, 118), or combined accounts of
two visits (Lagrange, 147), cf. the lengthy discussion of
Schürmann, Lukas, 241-244. The pericope appears to have seams:
a) the disproportion between the words of the congregation and
Jesus' response (vv. 22-23); b) the apparent chronological (or
geographical) anomaly in v. 23; c) the connection between the
proverb of v. 24 and the examples cited by Jesus, vv. 25-27.
These difficulties may be accounted for to some degree by a
reworking of Mk, but J. Bajard, "La Structure de la Péricope de
Nazareth en Lc. iv 16-30," ETL 45 (1969) 165-171, argues that
if the pericope be read apart from the parallels, the Lukan
composition is coherent on its own terms. Cf. also H. J.
Cadbury, The Making of Luke-Acts, 189.

[2]Schürmann, Lukas, 225, calls the pericope "ein Evangelium
im Evangelium," and points out that it is a fulfillment of
Simeon's prophecy about Jesus being a sign of contradiction.
Cf. also Gaston, 313.

[3]Cf. Dupont, "Les Discours," 349.

[4]For the variations from the LXX in this citation, cf. T.
Holtz, Untersuchungen über die Alttestamentlichen Zitate bei
Lukas, 39-41; Plummer, 120. The best mss. eliminate ἰασασθαι
τοὺς συντετριμμένους τῇ καρδίᾳ. Dupont, Beatitudes II, 132, n.
1, discusses the reasons why Luke may have eliminated one of
his favorite motifs from the citation.

[5]Cf. above all the rich presentation of Dupont, Beatitudes
II, 123-142.

a) The Messiahship of Jesus is seen as a literal anointing by
the Holy Spirit (4:18) [cf. Acts 4:27, 10:38]. This statement,
following the repeated emphasis upon Jesus' possession of the
Spirit following His baptism (3:22, 4:1, 4:14), functions as
the Acts 2 speech does in its citation from Joel, as a fundamental premise for the rest of the Gospel. Luke does not again
speak of Jesus being filled with the Holy Spirit after this
passage. He does not have to. This passage notifies the
reader that everything said and done by Jesus throughout the
Gospel is said and done by the Spirit-anointed Messiah.[1]
b) The mission of the Messiah is expressed succinctly as the
preaching of Good News (εὐαγγελίσασθαι) and proclaiming
(κηρῦξαι); the similarity to the mission of the Men of the
Spirit in Acts is clear.[2] c) What the Messiah proclaims
(κηρῦξαι) is a "year acceptable to the Lord."[3] δεκτός is in
the LXX citation; we note it here because of its probable
influence on v. 24.

    2. V. 22 is puzzling because the reaction of the
hearers seems very positive,[4] and we are at a loss to understand how the seemingly innocuous "Isn't this Joseph's son?"
could arouse the strong response of Jesus in v. 23. A comparison with the parallels indicates that Luke may have reduced the
objections of the townspeople to this one line, thereby causing
our confusion.[5] The real problem however is determining the

---

[1] Cf. von Baer, Heilige Geist, 71-72.

[2] Cf. Schürmann, Lukas, 230; Dupont, Beatitudes II, 132.

[3] On this, cf. Schürmann, 230; Lagrange, 139; Grundmann,121.

[4] Bajard, "La Structure," 166, notes that μαρτυρεῖν and
θαυμάζειν have in Luke a positive connotation.

[5] Cf. Mk 6:2-3; Matt 13:54-57. In trying to show that
there is no rupture with the townspeople till v. 28, Bajard
does not give enough weight to this possibility. Gils, Jésus
Prophète, 12ff, suggests the phrase "words of grace" should be
seen as a formula used of persons speaking under the influence
of the Holy Spirit, thus "inspiré et prophetique." H. Flender,
St. Luke Theologian of Redemptive History, 153f, says that the
expression in Luke has the technical meaning of "message of
grace," and that its use here possesses a deliberate ambiguity.
The townspeople focus on the "winsomeness" of Jesus' words, but
fail to accept the challenge put them by those words to recognize Jesus as a prophet.

94

relationship of Jesus' response to the rest of the pericope.
If we read Jesus' response in the light of the controversy
presented by Mk and Matt, it appears that Jesus is rebuking
the nonacceptance of Him as prophet by his townspeople who,
knowing his antecedents, could not accept his role as prophet.[1]
In v. 24, Luke has made an interesting alteration. Matt 13:57
and Mk 6:4 read οὐκ ἔστιν προφήτης ἄτιμος εἰ μὴ ἐν τῇ πατρίδι
[αὐτοῦ]. Luke replaces ἄτιμος with δεκτός, probably influenced
by the Isaiah citation.[2] V. 24 then presents a strong contrast: the Prophet proclaims a year acceptable to the Lord,
but he himself is not acceptable to his people.[3]

3. Luke proceeds to illustrate the prophetic proverb
by means of examples from the Scripture (I Kings 17:1ff, II
Kings 5:1ff). But the connection between the proverb and the
examples is not immediately clear. We would expect the examples to show that prophets who had not been accepted in Israel
were accepted elsewhere. But this is not the case. Elijah and
Elisha are said to help those outside Israel, but this was not
caused by any rejection they experienced within Israel.

We must take careful note of the fact that it is after
these examples are spoken by Jesus, upon hearing these words,
that the people are filled with anger and try physically to
reject Jesus (v. 28). The structural resemblance to Acts
5:29ff, 7:51ff, and 13:41ff is unmistakeable. By means of the
prophetic word, Luke has Jesus reveal the latent hostility of

[1]Conzelmann's suggestion (Theology, 34-35), that the
deliberate use of the future ἐρεῖτε in v. 23 looks forward to
the scene in 8:19-21 is much too subtle, particularly since
there is no reason for suspecting that the latter passage means
that the relatives of Jesus "want to take Him to Nazareth in
order that he may work miracles in what they consider the
proper place." On this, cf. Anderson, "The Rejection," 273.
It is better to see the future tense as related to Jesus' use
of the prophet proverb in v. 24. That is, a prophet will not
be accepted in his own land no matter what works he performs
(you will say to me = you will demand proof). The very asking
for such signs (seeking such authentication) indicates their
rejection of Him as prophet.

[2]Dupont, Beatitudes II, 295, n. 2; Gils, Jésus Prophète,
10; Bajard, "La Structure," 168-169.

[3]As Schürmann, Lukas, 237, points out, the use of πατρίς
in the proverb, followed by the examples of vv. 25-27, raises
the issue of rejection from that involving Jesus' "Vaterstadt"

the people and incite it to full and physical rejection. It is
the prophetic word itself which causes rejection. This is the
significance of the examples.

But what is the relation of the content of the examples to
this rejection? Immediately, the examples rebuke the narrow
jealousy of the townspeople toward Capernaum by showing how
God's will to save through the prophets is wider than the
bounds of the prophet's homeland. But there is more to it than
that. What Luke seems to be doing is using the people of
Nazareth as the type of those who reject the prophet within
Israel. But seeing the townspeople as a type of those who
reject the prophet should not lead immediately to the presumption that because of the rejection by the Jews, the Gentiles
will receive the Good News of salvation.[1] This would accord
neither with the content of the examples, nor Luke's insistence
elsewhere that the Jews as a whole did not reject the Good News.
What the examples appear to indicate is that it is God's will
from the beginning to show mercy to the Gentiles, and it is
this prophetic word which stimulates the jealousy and rejection
of that part of the people represented by Jesus' townspeople.

4. Once more, then, at the very beginning of Jesus'
public ministry, Luke delineates the pattern of the Prophet and
the People. The prophetic nature of Jesus is strongly portrayed. Luke expanded the prophet proverb shared with the
tradition into a full exposition.[2] Jesus is anointed as a
prophetic Messiah,[3] and his mission can be understood in the
light of the prophets of old. Luke's use of the Elijah and
Elisha examples is particularly interesting. We have seen that
the figure of the "Prophet like Moses" has provided Luke with
the basic framework for his understanding of Jesus. But Luke
does not use this figure in a strictly typological fashion.

---

to that involving his "Vaterland."

[1]Here contra Dupont, Etudes, 406-407; Wilson, The Gentiles
and the Gentile Mission, 40-41.

[2]Cf. J. Goudoever, "The Place of Israel in Luke's Gospel,"
Placita Pleiadia (Leiden: E. J. Brill, 1966) 113.

[3]This is the obvious import of the Isaiah citation. Cf.
Dupont, Beatitudes II, 123-142.

For Luke, the Prophet Jesus is not to be seen as any one prophet redivivus, but as the realization of God's Prophet, the
great Prophet. He is therefore free to employ all the prophets
of the Scriptures as partial types of Jesus. If Moses is most
significant for his working of signs and wonders, and for
providing the pattern of acceptance and rejection, it is
Elijah and Elisha who provide Luke with the most images to
flesh out his characterization of Jesus as the Prophet.[1] In
fact, we shall see next how the Elijah-Elisha cycle has affected Luke's structuring of ch. 7. As important as the prophetic
language used of Jesus in this passage, however, is the second
part of the Lukan pattern, that the prophet in the time of his
first visitation is rejected by His people. He is the Prophet
who proclaims a year acceptable to the Lord, but who is Himself
rejected by His People.

D. Luke 7:1-8:3:

Although chapter seven contains a considerable amount of
material in common with Matthew,[2] it is clear that the materials have been very carefully shaped by Luke into a unity.[3] It
is particularly interesting that chapter seven is thematically
so closely related to the Nazareth pericope.[4]

---

[1]For the traditions concerning Elijah as the eschatological prophet, cf. H. Teeple, The Mosaic Eschatological Prophet,
2-9. Elements of Elijah typology in Luke's Gospel have been
discussed by Lampe, "The Holy Spirit in the Writings of St.
Luke," 166, 176; I. de la Potterie, "L'Onction du Christ," NRT
80 (1958) 225-252; L. Gaston, No Stone on Another, 285ff; P.
Dabeck, "Siehe es erschienen Moses und Elias," Bib 23 (1942)
175-189; J.-D. Dubois, "La Figure d'Elie dans la Perspective
Lucanienne," RHPR 53 (1973) 155-176.

[2]Lk 7:1-10 = Matt 8:5-13; Lk 7:18-35 = Matt 11:2-9.
There are some similarities between Lk 7:36-50 and the anointing story of Matt 26:6-13, Mk 14:3-9 and Jn 12:1-8, but the
story has quite a distinct focus in Luke.

[3]The placement of the two uniquely Lukan segments (7:11-17
and 36-50) puts a distinct stamp on the Baptist sayings. This
has been noticed by Gaston, No Stone on Another, 287, but
without elaboration.

[4]Schubert, "Structure and Significance," 180, has stated
that ch. 7 is an important stage in the development of Luke's
"proof-from-prophecy" theology, following on the Nazareth
pericope. Our conclusions in this regard were reached

1. The two miracles: The healing of the Centurion's slave is paralleled by Matt 8:5-13 (and Jn 4:43-54). Two aspects of the Lukan version are striking: the role of the Jewish elders in interceding for the Gentile petitioner (7:3-5)[1] and the fact that all communication between Jesus and the Centurion takes place through intermediaries (7:6, 10).[2] As in Matt, the saying which concludes the story contrasts the faith of the Centurion to that found in Israel.[3] These notes in themselves are not particularly striking until we see how Luke has combined this story with the raising of the widow's son (7:11-16). For the second story, unique to Luke, is clearly reminiscent of the miracle of Elijah in raising to life the son of the widow of Sarepta in I Kings 17.[4]

If we read the two stories together, we see that they form

---

independently of Schubert, and go somewhat further. A. Ehrhardt, "The Disciples of Emmaus," 187, n. 2, refers to Schubert's article, and dismisses it by saying that Luke has here done little more than rearrange Q material, which may already have contained a "proof-from-prophecy" theology. Luke has certainly done more than rearrange Q material here.

[1]In the passion narrative and Acts, the Elders are among the Jewish hierarchy hostile to Jesus and the Apostles (Lk 20:1; 22:52; Acts 4:5, 8, 23).

[2]Cf. Schürmann, Lukas, 391. As Lagrange, Luc, 207, points out, the words of the Centurion are so personal that they would seem to indicate a face to face encounter. The insertion of intermediaries would appear to be a Lukan touch (Creed, 100). Easton, Luke, 96, asks, "Would the Gentile Luke, who was writing for Gentiles, go out of his way to insert with considerable emphasis that Christ could only be approached through the mediation of Jewish elders?" In fact, the idea of Jewish mediation of salvation to the Gentiles is not at all foreign to Luke. Gaston, 314, suggests that the story points forward to the conversion of Cornelius, and that within the structure of "proto-Luke," has the function not of foreshadowing the calling of the Gentiles, but of shaming Israel.

[3]Lagrange, Luc, 208, sees in v. 9 a nuance more favorable to the Jews than Matt 8:10. Certainly Luke lacks here the "rejection" motif of Matt's next verses, 11-12.

[4]καὶ αὐτὴ ἦν χήρα (I Kings 17:10); καὶ ἔδωκεν αὐτὸν τῇ μητρὶ αὐτοῦ (I Kings 17:23). Among those finding a direct literary allusion here, cf. Gils, Jésus Prophète, 26; Schürmann, Lukas, 402; Grundmann, Lukas, 159; Creed, Luke, 104; Gaston, No Stone on Another, 286. Lagrange, Luc, 211, denies any dependence on the Kings story, but probably in reaction to Loisy.

a rough correspondence to the examples of Elijah and Elisha
cited in the Nazareth pericope, 4:25-27. As Elisha worked a
wonder for the Gentile commander Naaman (II Kings 5:1-15)
through the intercession of the Jewish maiden and instructed
Naaman through delegates, so Jesus cures the slave of the
Gentile Centurion through the intercession of Jews and communi-
cates with the Centurion through legates. As Elijah raised the
widow's son to life, so does Jesus raise the widow's son to
life. A rough equivalence, indeed. Especially in the first
story, the details do not match up at all. Yet we must
remember that the story of the Centurion was one Luke had from
the tradition, and that his redaction does move it closer to a
correspondence with the Elisha story. The second story is his
own, and there the literary relationship is obvious. Therefore
while the possibility that Luke was intentionally mirroring ch.
4 with both these stories should not be pushed too far, it
remains an intriguing one, and not too hastily to be dismissed,
especially in the light of the obvious connection drawn to ch.
4 by 7:22.

     2. Jesus the Prophet: The response of the people to
Jesus' raising the boy to life is a praise of God in two statements which express a single idea: ὅτι προφήτης μέγας ἠγέρθη[1]
ἐν ἡμῖν καὶ ὅτι ἐπεσκέψατο ὁ θεὸς τὸν λαὸν αὐτοῦ.[2] The people
recognize the prophetic implications of Jesus' act, and there
is no indication in the text that Luke regarded such an identification of Jesus as inaccurate or in need of correction.[3]
Whether or not 7:1-10 is meant to mirror 4:27, there can be no
doubt that by 7:16 Luke has consciously pointed the reader back
to 4:25-26, and in 7:11-15 portrayed Jesus in accordance with

---

    [1]The passive indicates divine action. The "raising up"
here follows the LXX expression found especially in Judges
(e.g., 2:16, 18; 3:9, 15) of leaders of Israel. Cf. also
Deut 34:10-12.

    [2]For God's "visiting" his people through the Prophet, cf.
Lk 1:68; 19:44; Acts 7:23. This verse is clearly related
thematically to Lk 24:19.

    [3]Contra Schürmann, Lukas, 403, the use of κύριος in v. 13
can hardly be taken as a correction of the title προφήτης.
Cf. our remarks in n. 2, pp. 84-85, above.

the example there.[1]

      3. Acceptance and rejection of God's Prophets:
Jesus has been hailed in 7:16 as the great Prophet. This proclamation not only concludes 7:1-15, it colors the narrative
which follows. The sending of messengers from John to Jesus
with the question whether Jesus was the "coming one" is
paralleled by Matt 11:2-6, but Luke has greatly highlighted
the incident: a) The question is asked twice (7:19, 20);
b) Luke specifies that ἐν ἐκείνη τῇ ὥρᾳ Jesus was working the
deeds to which 7:22 refers, and of course Luke has just
recounted two of them. c) In Luke, 7:22 clearly functions as
a reminder of the programmatic prophecy of 4:18ff. The deeds
which were to signify the mission of the Messiah, the anointed
prophet in Israel, are now in fact being fulfilled by Jesus.[2]
Together with 7:16, the thematic summary of 7:22 gives a
prophetic coloration to Jesus' ministry which is unmistakable.
Furthermore, as we shall see, Jesus is again spoken of in
7:36-50 as a prophet.

      This context is important for the series of sayings about
John the Baptist (7:24-35). The sayings themselves are largely
paralleled by Matt 11:2-19, but the Lukan placement of the
material is quite different from Matthew's.[3] By placing the
sayings on the Baptist in the context of prophetic language
used of Jesus, Luke is able to affirm that John is himself a
Prophet (7:25-26), indeed the forerunner of the Messiah (7:27),
with a very special place in the βουλὴ τοῦ θεοῦ (7:30), while
at the same time relativizing John's significance. John is a

_____

[1]Ben Sira 48:1-16 presents a "re-reading" of the Elijah-
Elisha cycle remarkably close to Luke's own. We see Elijah
"raised up" as a Prophet (48:1). He "raises from the dead,"
(48:5), ascends in a fiery chariot (ἀναλημφθείς 48:9; cf. Lk
9:51), and restores the tribe of Jacob (48:10). His successor
Elisha is filled with the spirit (ἐνεπλήσθη πνεύματος αὐτοῦ,
48:12). Most interesting is the way in which the preaching of
Elijah and Elisha causes rejection: οὐ μετενόησεν ὁ λαός
(48:15), but a rejection which is not total: τινὲς μὲν αὐτῶν
ἐποίησεν τὸ ἀρεστόν τινὲς δὲ ἐπλήθυναν ἁμαρτίας (48:16).

[2]Cf. Schubert, "Structure and Significance," 180.

[3]Matt 11:2-9 is framed by the saying on receiving a
prophet (10:40) and the woes to the unrepentant cities (11:20-
24) but does not present Jesus as a Prophet as in Luke.

Prophet, and more than a Prophet. But he is not the "great Prophet" whose presence among the people effects God's "Visitation."[1] The Lukan construction of the two miracle stories, the proclamation of 7:16, the thematic statement of 7:22, and the story of 7:36ff all throw attention on the figure of Jesus as Prophet over against John. Yet, Luke sees John as standing in that same tradition of prophets whose mission has caused a division in the people. In this respect, vv. 29-30 deserve closer attention.

Though these verses clearly are Lukan in composition[2] and represent Luke's judgment on the situation,[3] if we read them in context they appear as the words of Jesus and as representing his judgment on the situation of John and the people.[4] a) The λαός and τελῶναι are distinguished from the Pharisees and Lawyers in their response to John. This division corresponds to the narrative up to this point both about John (cf. 3:7-14) and Jesus (5:21, 33; 6:2, 7). Until the Jerusalem narrative, the Pharisees and Lawyers appear as the prime opponents of

---

[1] A full discussion of the place of John in Luke's writing lies outside the scope of this study. It should be noted, however, that it is only by excluding the infancy narratives and a dubious interpretation of 16:16, that Conzelmann can state that Luke excludes John from the time of salvation. Luke does avoid identifying John explicitly with Elijah; yet he sees John as acting in the Spirit of Elijah (1:17, 76). The same distinction is found in his presentation of Jesus. Luke uses the prophetic imagery of Moses and Elijah in his presentation of Jesus, but does not regard Him as any of these prophets redivivus. Again, the distinction between identification and literary presentation is important. In view of Luke's use of the prophetic model for all his major characters, it would be strange if he did not present John as a prophet as well, particularly since he was so strongly viewed as such by the tradition. But he must also show that John was not the prophet by whom God's visitation was effected. For a balanced presentation on the role of John in Luke's writing, cf. Marshall, Luke, 145-147.

[2] Cf. Dupont, Beatitudes III, 216. Vv. 29-30 thematize elements of the narrative found only in Luke (cf. 3:12; 3:21). Matt 21:32 has a similar saying, but with a different perspective than Luke's.

[3] We cannot agree with Flender, Luke, 48, who considers that Luke, in contrast to Mark, passes lightly over the issue of the people's response to John.

[4] Grundmann, Lukas, 166; Schürmann, Lukas, 421.

Jesus. The division in the People is a division between the
leaders and the people.[1] b) In being baptized by John, the
people and taxcollectors ἐδικαίωσαν τὸν θεόν, an expression
important in the light of v. 35 below.[2] c) The Pharisees and
Lawyers, on the other hand, τὴν βουλὴν τοῦ θεοῦ ἠθέτησαν εἰς
ἑαυτούς[3] by not being baptized. Here we find the typical
Lukan pattern. In rejecting God's emissary, they have rejected
God's plan for them. The εἰς ἑαυτούς is significant; in Luke's
understanding, God's plan was for them to be part of His
People.[4] By rejecting the Prophet, they have effected their
own rejection from the People.

Because of this thematic interpolation by Luke, vv. 31-35
(again from Q) now become in his version an elaboration of vv.
29-30, and in the light of those verses, the charge against
"this generation" applies to the leaders of the people rather
than to the people as a whole, for the leaders are those who
have rejected both John and Jesus, for however different
reasons.[5] The careful fashion in which Luke has brought these
materials together is again illustrated by v. 34. The description of Jesus as ἄνθρωπος φάγος καὶ οἰνοπότης[6] φίλος τελωνῶν
καὶ ἁμαρτωλῶν is paralleled in Matt 11:19, but in Luke it is

_____

[1]Schürmann, Lukas, 420, correctly sees this passage as
part of the unfolding fulfillment of Simeon's prophecy.

[2]Cf. Descamps, Les Justes et la Justice dans les évangiles
et le christianisme primitif, 96.

[3]For Luke's use of βουλὴ τοῦ θεοῦ, cf. Acts 2:23; 13:36;
20:27. ἀθετέω here is not simply "frustrate" (so Lagrange,
Luc, 222), but "reject," as in Lk 10:16.

[4]John's mission was to ἑτοιμάσαι κυρίῳ λαὸν
κατεσκευασμένον (Lk 1:17).

[5]For a discussion of the parable, cf. Lagrange, Luc, 223-
225, and Jeremias, Parables, 160-162. However difficult the
precise meaning of the parable, it is clear from the Lukan
redaction that it is the leaders who reject the style both of
John and Jesus, and who are, as Jeremias nicely puts it,
"spoilsports."

[6]The strength of this accusation is stressed by Jeremias,
Parables, 160: "The designation of Jesus as ἄνθρωπος φάγος καὶ
οἰνοπότης is derived from Deut 21:20 and stigmatizes Him on the
strength of this connection as a 'refractory and rebellious
son,' who deserved to be stoned."

102

immediately picked up and dramatized by the narrative of
7:36ff. V. 35 contains another small but significant alteration. It is not, as in Matt 11:19, ἀπὸ τῶν ἔργων αὐτῆς that
σοφία is justified, but in Luke ἀπὸ πάντων τῶν τέκνων αὐτῆς.
The connection with v. 29 is clear,[1] whether we read σοφία as
meaning God, or the βουλὴ τοῦ θεοῦ (cf. Lk 11:49). Luke is
here making a statement about who are to be counted among God's
children, that is, His People. His People are those who accept
the prophets John and Jesus.[2]

The acceptance and rejection of the Prophet Jesus is now
expressed dramatically by the story of the sinful woman (7:36-
50), again unique to Luke.[3] The following points should be
noted: a) The woman is identified as γυνὴ ἁμαρτωλός which
establishes a literary connection with 7:34. b) Simon is
identified as a Pharisee (7:36) which connects him to the
thematic statement of 7:30. c) Simon doubts if Jesus is really
a prophet, since he does not seem to be aware of the character
of the woman (7:39). d) Jesus immediately shows that He is a
prophet who can reveal men's thoughts by answering Simon's
unspoken criticism (cf. again the prophecy of Simeon, 2:35).
e) Simon's refusal of the signs of hospitality is contrasted
to the honor shown Jesus by the woman. f) The woman is saved
because of her faith (i.e., acceptance of Jesus) (7:50).
g) Simon's fate is not expressed, but in the light of 7:29-35,
the reader is left in no doubt that this particular Pharisee
is among those who have rejected God's plan for them by not
recognizing the Prophet, and who is therefore himself being
rejected from the People.

We notice too that in the immediately following passage
(8:1-3), again unique to Luke, we find Jesus accompanied by
women who by any standard would have to be included among the
ἁμαρτωλοί, and who express their acceptance of Jesus by supporting Him from their possessions. We shall say more about this
passage in the next chapter.

_____

[1]Descamps, Les Justes, 96; Schürmann, Lukas, 428.

[2]Lagrange, Luc, 226.

[3]Cf. n. 2, p. 96, above.

7:1-8:3 is remarkable for the way in which Luke has
carefully combined traditional materials and his own sources
(compositions?) into a tightly organized unity expressing a
coherent point of view. Nor does this section stand isolated.
We have seen how the themes of this chapter pick up especially
the programmatic statements of 2:34 and 4:18ff, and serve to
interpret the course of the narrative from chs. 5-7. Especially characteristic of the Lukan method is to have speech
fulfilled in action. Here we have found the programmatic
statements of 4:18ff fulfilled in 7:1-16, and explicitly shown
to be such by 7:22. Then the sayings of Jesus in 7:29-35 are
fulfilled again by 7:36-8:3. There is no need to belabor the
clear literary kinship this section demonstrates to the other
passages we have considered till now. Here, once more, Jesus
is presented as a Prophet identified by mighty works and words,
who experiences rejection. The important clarification of the
pattern offered by this chapter is that the rejection of the
Prophet is not seen as total, and that the division in the
people spoken of by Simeon is now expressed thematically as a
split between the leaders (the Pharisees and Lawyers) and the
People (and Tax-collectors).

E. Luke 9-19:

The central section of Luke's Gospel presents many problems for interpretation. On the one hand, it is clear that a
great amount of materials in these chapters comes from Luke
himself or his unique sources, and that the arrangement of
these materials is due to him. On the other hand, it has
proven very difficult to determine what if any literary or
formal shape has been given to the materials by Luke. He is
in these chapters no longer following the outline of Mk. But
is there another framework of his own to be found, or are the
materials of these chapters to be regarded as a rather clumsy
collection of passages over which Luke had no control?

A simple quantitative analysis shows the extent to which
these chapters are specifically Lukan. There are in this
section fifteen passages that are paralleled neither by Matt or

104

Mk.[1] A comparison of the ordering of the material which Luke shares with either Mk or Matt indicates that if there was a common source, Luke was using it in a very free fashion.[2] It is manifestly impossible to consider at length this great body of material. Since there is so much talk about possessions in these chapters, however, we will be doing considerably more content analysis in the next chapter. For the present, we must ask as so many others have done[3] whether there is

[1]Lk 9:51-56; 10:1-12, 17-20, 25-42; 11:27-28; 12:13-21, 35-40; 13:1-7; 14:1-14; 15:8-32; 16:1-8, 19-31; 17:11-19; 18:1-14; 19:1-10.

[2]There are in Lk 9:51-19:10 only some 57 verses found in Mk, and these in a different order, with the exception of Lk 18:15-35 = Mk 10:13-52, where Lk again picks up Mk's ordering. Considerable material in these chapters is found in Matt (or Q) but a listing of the parallels shows that the ordering is drastically different from Matt. Even where a substantial amount of Q material is grouped together, the precise order is different in Lk than Matt. For example: a) the continuation of Matt 11:20-27 is broken in Lk 10:13-24 by the return of the Seventy(-Two); b) the large body of material shared by Lk 11:14-32 = Matt 12:22-30; 43-45; 38-42 is found in different sequence and interrupted by the unique Lukan saying on true blessedness, 11:27-28; c) the material on care and anxiety (Lk 12:22-34 = Matt 6:25-34; 19-21) is in different order; etc.

[3]Cf. e.g., W. Gasse, "Zum Reisebericht des Lukas," ZNW 34 (1935) 293-299; H. Conzelmann, "Zur Lukasanalyze," ZTK 49 (1952) 16-33, and Theology of St. Luke, 60ff; J. Schneider, "Zur Analyze des lukanischen Reiseberichtes," Synoptische Studien ed. by J. Schmid and A. Vögtle (München: Karl Zink Verlag, 1953) 207-229; J. Blinzler, "Die literarische Eigenart des sogennanten Reiseberichts im Lukasevangelium," Synoptische Studien, 20-52; C. F. Evans, "The Central Section of St. Luke's Gospel," Studies in the Gospels, 37-53; E. Lohse, "Mission-arisches Handeln Jesu nach dem Evangelium des Lukas," TZ 10 (1954) 1-13; B. Reicke, "Instruction and Discussion in the Travel Narrative," Studia Evangelica I, 206-216; W. Grundmann, "Fragen der Komposition des lukanischen 'Reiseberichte'," ZNW 50 (1959) 252-271; W. Robinson, "The Theological Context for Interpreting Luke's Travel Narrative (9:51ff)," JBL 79 (1960) 20-31; M. D. Goulder, "The Chiastic Structure of the Lucan Journey," Studia Evangelica II (TU 87, Part I; Berlin: Akademie Verlag, 1964) 195-202; J. Davies, "The Purpose of the Central Section of St. Luke's Gospel," Studia Evangelica II, 164-169; D. Gill, "Observations on the Lukan Travel Narrative and some related Passages," HTR 63 (1970) 199-221; G. Ogg, "The Central Section of the Gospel according to St. Luke," NTS 18 (1971-2) 39-53; G. Trompf, "La Section Médiane de l'Evangile de Luc: l'Organisation des Documents," RHPR 53 (1973) 141-154; M. Miyoshi, Der Anfang des Reiseberichts (AnBib 60; Rome: Biblical Institute Press, 1974).

discernible in this section an intelligible and plausible
literary structure.

    1. The Journey Motif: The first and most obvious
structure Luke has used in this section is that of a continuing
journey from Galilee to Jerusalem. In typical Lukan fashion
the solemn proclamation of 9:51 acts as programmatic for what
follows; even if there were no more mention of a journey, we
would understand that Jesus was on his way to Jerusalem. But
Luke repeatedly draws the reader's attention to this fact
(9:51, 53, 56, 57; 10:1, 38; 13:22, 31, 33; 14:25; 17:11;
18:31, 35, 36; 19:1, 11, 28) building inexorably to the entry
into Jerusalem. The Journey motif is not so much geographical
in character as it is dramatic.[1] The high point of Luke's
narrative takes place in Jerusalem, and by means of the pro-
longed journey motif he is able to build dramatically to that
climax. In addition, the placement of material such as the
call to the would-be disciples (9:57-62) within the journey
lends it an urgency and dramatic force lacking in the Matthean
parallel (Matt 8:19-22).

    The Journey motif itself is not unrelated to the theme of
the Prophet and the People.[2] The solemn opening of the journey

---

[1]Two remarks may be made concerning the many studies that
have focussed on this aspect of the section. a) It is not
necessary to show that Luke's grasp of geographical data is
confused or wrong (cf. esp. Gasse, "Reisebericht," 299;
Conzelmann, Theology, 68-69; Trocmé, Le "Livre des Actes," 83)
in order to conclude that the journey motif serves another
purpose than the historical (cf. Marshall, Luke, 70-72, against
Conzelmann). b) It should not immediately be concluded that
the alternative to the historical is the polemic or paraenetic;
the journey motif may make good sense simply at the level of
the story.

[2]The call of the disciple in 9:62 echoes the call of
Elisha by Elijah in I Kings 19:19-21; cf. Miyoshi, Anfang,
55-58. Similarly, the disciples wanting to rain down fire on
the Samaritan village, II Kings 1:10ff. Cf. Gaston, No Stone
on Another, 289. A. Denaux, "L'hypocrisie des Pharisiens et le
dessein de Dieu; Analyse de Lc., XIII, 31-33," L'Evangile de
Luc, 245-285, has shown how the warning of the Pharisees in
13:31 and Jesus' response that a prophet cannot be killed outside Jerusalem (13:33) should be seen within the context of the
journey narrative, reaching the sound conclusions that a) the
Pharisees' action here is hostile, not friendly, b) because
they wish to reverse his progress toward Jerusalem, c) not
recognizing that He is a prophet fulfilling God's plan for Him,

in 9:51, ἐγένετο δὲ ἐν τῷ συμπληροῦσθαι τὰς ἡμέρας τῆς
ἀναλήμψεως αὐτοῦ καὶ αὐτὸς τὸ πρόσωπον ἐστήρισεν τοῦ πορεύεσθαι
εἰς 'Ιερουσαλήμ, has frequently been analyzed in terms of its
resemblance to prophetic language: the use of στηρίζω so frequent in Ezechiel and the possible relationship of the
ἀνάλημψις to either Moses or Elijah.[1] But there is one text
of Ezechiel which does not seem to have attracted much attention, and which bears a strong resemblance to what Luke sees
as happening in this section: διὰ τοῦτο προφήτευσον υἱὲ
ἀνθρώπου καὶ στήρισον τὸ πρόσωπον σοῦ ἐπὶ 'Ιερουσαλήμ καὶ
ἐπίβλεψον ἐπὶ τὰ ἅγια αὐτῶν καὶ προφητεύσεις ἐπὶ τὴν γῆν τοῦ
'Ισραήλ. καὶ ἐρεῖς πρὸς τὴν γῆν τοῦ 'Ισραήλ ἰδοὺ ἐγὼ πρὸς σὲ
καὶ ἐκσπάσω τὸ ἐγχειρίδιόν μου ἐκ τοῦ κολεοῦ αὐτοῦ καὶ
ἐξολεθρεύσω[2] ἐκ σοῦ ἄδικον καὶ ἄνομον (Ez 21:7ff). We are not
of course suggesting an "Ezechiel Typology" here, but the combination of ideas in the passage does accord well with the
picture Luke presents of Jesus moving on to Jerusalem. He is
prophesying to Israel, and there is a judgment taking place;
at the end, those who do not heed Him will in fact be "rooted
out" of the people.

The Journey motif is a discernible and important structural element in this section. But although a considerable
amount of material can be interpreted in light of that motif,[3]
there remains a large amount of material only loosely related
to the journey, if at all--a mass of material which retains the
impression of being static, of being arranged more formally[4]
than dramatically. This is especially so for the sayings

_____

d) and by so doing they reject both the prophet and the fulfillment of God's plan.

[1]Cf. Dabeck, "Siehe es erschienen," 182; Evans, "Central
Section," 39; Davies, "Purpose," 165ff; Miyoshi, Anfang, 9.

[2]Cf. Acts 3:23.

[3]Cf. Robinson, "Theological Context," 22ff; and especially,
Gill, "Observations," 199ff.

[4]Goulder, "Chiastic Structure," 195ff, has shown that
10:23-18:30 contains a chiasm. But what the significance of
that structure might be, and how it relates to the obvious
structure of the journey, and how it might illuminate the
meaning of the passages within the chiasm, he does not say.

material which for the most part can be related only tenuously
to the Journey motif.

2. The Division in the People: There is a second
structure discernible in this section of the Gospel, one which
begins not at 9:51, but with the sending of the Twelve in 9:1.
From this point till the entry into Jerusalem, Luke arranges
his materials in an intriguing fashion. There are four
elements to consider:[1] a) Jesus is almost always speaking; a
great portion of the materials in these chapters are sayings.[2]
b) Jesus is not alone. Journeying with Him are the disciples,
who become more highly visible from this point.[3] c) There is
constantly around Jesus an indeterminate group of people called
"the crowd."[4] d) Jesus has repeated confrontations with the
Pharisees and Lawyers.[5]

Luke arranges these four elements in a pattern of contrasts, which possesses its own dramatic force. He is throughout this section, with only few exceptions, very careful to
note precisely who is involved in a particular scene, and
above all, what is said to whom. If we pay close attention to
these editorial indications,[6] we find that Luke has arranged

---

[1]Cf. Reicke, "Instruction," 215.

[2]The didactic nature of this section has been frequently
noted, but usually with a concentration upon the instructions
to the disciples and not on the sayings as a whole. Cf. Lampe,
"The Holy Spirit in the Writings of St. Luke," 190; Grundmann,
"Fragen," 259; Schneider, "Analyze," 219; Reicke, "Instruction,"
209; Gill, "Observations," 200; Trompf, "La Section Médiane,"
141ff.

[3]μαθητής referring to Jesus' disciples occurs 21 times in
these chapters, only 12 times elsewhere in the Gospel; more
significantly, only in these chapters (8 times) the expression
"Jesus said to His disciples," followed by a body of teaching,
is used. Cf. also Flender, Luke, 73.

[4]In this section, the expression ὄχλος for those around
Jesus is used 18 times; λαός only three times (9:13; 11:53;
18:43).

[5]These four elements have been isolated by Reicke,
"Instruction," 210ff, but he does not attempt to place them in
a formal pattern as we do. He also concentrates on the relevance of the sayings in this section for Luke's contemporary
situation rather than their possible significance for the telling of the story.

[6]A. Mosely, "Jesus' Audiences in the Gospels of St. Mark

Jesus' sayings and deeds in an alternating, contrasting
pattern, which might be described broadly as an alternation
between the inside and the outside. Jesus addresses the crowd,
for example, then turns from the crowd to address his disciples,
then turns from them to attack the Pharisees, etc. At times
this pattern is more sharply indicated than at others, but as
a formal pattern, it is present throughout these chapters.[1]

If we step inside the formal pattern, we discover that to
a considerable degree (an impressive degree when the traditional nature of much of the material is recognized), the
content of the sayings addressed to each group is appropriate
to the nature and stance of the group. To the disciples, Jesus
speaks what is essentially a positive catechesis concerning
his identity, their mission, the nature of service and authority within the community, confessing Christ in persecution, the
nature of the end-time, etc.[2] To the crowds, Jesus speaks
words of warning, threat, and calls to repentance.[3] Against

---

and St. Luke," NTS 10 (1963) 139-149, has shown how careful
Luke is in this respect. Jeremias, Parables, 33ff, discusses
the tendency of the evangelists to alter the setting or audience for parables according to their purpose, and Dupont,
Beatitudes I, 74, shows how Luke differs from Matt in this
respect.

[1]As with most formal patterns applied to the Gospels, the
breakdown is not absolute, nor are the classifications inargu-
able. The following listing of passages together with a rough
designation of audience or participants at least shows that
there is a definite alternation, frequently enough a sharp one,
between the insiders and outsiders around Jesus. The list
follows the indications of Luke, rather than editorial divi-
sions: 9:1-6 (disciples); 9:7-9 (Herod); 9:10-22 (disciples);
9:23-27 (crowd); 9:28-36 (disciples); 9:37-42 (disciples,
crowd); 9:43-56 (disciples); 9:57-62 (would-be-disciples =
crowd); 10:1-12 (disciples); 10:13-15 (unbelieving cities =
opponents); 10:16-23 (disciples); 10:25-37 (Lawyer = opponent);
10:38-11:13 (disciples); 11:14-36 (crowd); 11:37-53 (Pharisees,
Lawyers); 12:1-12 (disciples); 12:13-21 (crowd); 12:22-53
(disciples); 12:54-13:30 (crowd); 13:31-14:24 (Pharisees);
14:25-35 (crowd); 15:1-32 (Pharisees); 16:1-13 (disciples);
16:14-31 (Pharisees); 17:1-10 (disciples); 17:11-19 (Samaritans); 17:20-21 (Pharisees); 17:22-18:8 (disciples); 18:9-14
(Pharisees). Luke picks up the order of Mk again in 18:15.

[2]Cf. 9:1-6, 18-21, 28-26, 43-55; 10:1-12, 17-23; 10:38-
11:13; 12:1-12, 22-53; 16:1-13; 17:1-10; 17:22-18:8.

[3]Cf. 9:23-27, 57-62; 10:13-15; 11:14-36; 12:13-21; 12:54-
13:30; 14:25-35.

the Pharisees and Lawyers, Jesus uses the language of attack
and condemnation, tells parables in which the element of
rejection is dominant and parables in defense of His mission
against their attacks.[1]

It may be helpful to look briefly at two series of passages which demonstrate the force of Luke's literary technique.

a. Luke 15:1-16:31. Luke notes in 15:1 that
ἐγγίζοντες πάντες οἱ τελῶναι καὶ οἱ ἁμαρτωλοὶ ἀκούειν αὐτοῦ.
The author of 7:29 is clearly speaking here.[2] These "outcasts"
are the ones who justify God by heeding the voice of the
Prophet. And again as in 7:30ff it is the Pharisees (now
grouped with the Scribes) who grumble at this easy access of
the outcasts to Jesus (15:2). In response to their complaint,
Jesus speaks three parables of "the lost" in defense of his
mission to the outcasts, the last two stories peculiar to Luke,
and both involving possessions. These parables simply end in
15:32, with no indication given of the Pharisees' reaction.[3]

Luke then has Jesus turn to the disciples. ἔλεγεν δὲ καὶ
πρὸς τοὺς μαθητάς the story of the dishonest steward (16:1-13),
which again involves possessions and to which we will return in
the next chapter. For now we can note that Jesus contrasts the
attitudes of the "sons of Light" to that of the "sons of this
age," that is, between insiders and outsiders; this is an
'insider' story. A series of morals concludes the parable, the
last and strongest of which states the impossibility of serving
both God and Mammon (16:13).

Immediately following this (!), in 16:14, Luke notes:
ἤκουον δὲ ταῦτα πάντα οἱ φαρισαῖοι φιλάργυροι ὑπάρχοντες καὶ
ἐξεμυκτήριζον αὐτόν. This verse brings together the formal
pattern and content, and shows in the clearest fashion Luke's
method. The Pharisees are those who reject the word of the

---

[1]Cf. 10:25-37; 11:37-53; 13:31-14:24; 15:1-32; 16:14-31;
17:20-21; 18:9-14.

[2]Cf. the discussion in Dupont, Beatitudes II, 234, n. 2.

[3]In view of the setting Luke has established for the
parable of the Lost Son, it is difficult to avoid the impression that the plaint of the elder son, οὐδέποτε ἐντολήν σου
παρῆλθον, deliberately reflects the attitude of the Pharisees
to whom the story is told. Cf. Jeremias, Parables, 131.

Prophet (7:30). In this case, the Prophet was speaking of the
service of God and possessions. The Pharisees mock this
teaching, indeed mock Jesus. They are therefore characterized
as φιλάργυροι. Their avidity prevents them from being able to
accept what even the tax-collectors (!) could accept. That
this rejection of Him and his word leads to their own rejection
by God is explicitly stated by Jesus in 16:15. The phrase οἱ
δικαιοῦντες ἑαυτούς used by Luke to characterize the Pharisees
here provides us with a literary clue for recognizing them when
they are not mentioned by name. More importantly, it again
contrasts the Pharisees who justify themselves but who do not
accept the prophet with those "sons of wisdom" (7:35) who hear
the prophet and thereby justify God (7:29). Luke then follows
with a story told to the Pharisees (which we will discuss in
the next chapter), which not only contains the theme of rejection, but clearly is applied to their rejection of the prophet
Jesus: Εἰ Μωϋσέως καὶ τῶν προφητῶν οὐκ ἀκούουσιν οὐδ' ἐάν τις
ἐκ νεκρῶν ἀναστῇ πεισθήσονται (16:31), a grim foreshadowing of
the time of the second rejection in Acts.

           b. Luke 17:20-18:4. This sequence begins with
a question by the Pharisees concerning the coming of the Kingdom (17:20). Jesus answers οὐκ ἔρχεται ἡ βασιλεία τοῦ θεοῦ
μετὰ παρατηρήσεως. There is already in this answer to be found
a subtle rebuke. For παρατήρησις in Luke's Gospel characterizes the Pharisees' and other leaders' attitude towards Jesus
(cf. 6:7; 14:1; 20:20). Jesus' answer then can mean in effect,
"You won't find the Kingdom the way you are looking for it"
(that is, by hostile questioning). He continues that it won't
be found "here" or "there" but ἰδοὺ γὰρ ἡ βασιλεία τοῦ θεοῦ
ἐντὸς ὑμῶν ἐστιν (17:21). Without trying to resolve all the
problems concerning this text,[1] it would seem possible to
suggest that given the whole course of the narrative in the
Gospel, we might understand the ἐντὸς ὑμῶν as "among you," in
the sense of "all around you." That is, while the Pharisees
are probing and testing and rejecting the Prophet, there are

------

[1]For a review of interpretations of this famous crux, cf.
B. Noack, Das Gottesreich bei Lukas (SBU 10; Uppsala: C. W. K.
Gleerup, 1948), and C. Roberts, "The Kingdom of Heaven (Lk
XVII,21)," HTR 41 (1948) 1-8.

those, the "outcasts," who are heeding him, and the Kingdom is
in the process of being formed.

Having rejected the approach of the Pharisees and intimated their rejection from the Kingdom, Jesus εἶπεν δὲ πρὸς τοὺς
μαθητὰς (7:22) an extended and positive catechesis concerning
the end-time. We will discuss in the next chapter the significance of the possessions material in this passage. The positive teaching of the disciples continues till 18:8. Then comes
another uniquely Lukan parable, that of the Pharisee and tax-
collector. We know from the introduction πρὸς τινας τοὺς
πεποιθότας ἐφ᾽ ἑαυτοῖς ὅτι δίκαιοι εἰσὶν καὶ ἐξουθενοῦντας
τοὺς λοιποὺς (18:9) that this story is addressed directly to
the Pharisees. Once more, like the story of Lazarus and the
Rich Man, it is a story of acceptance and rejection. Those who
justify themselves instead of God will be rejected. In the
light of what we have seen in 7:29-35 and 15:1-16:31, it should
be clear that the contrast between the Pharisee and tax-
collector in the parable emerges not simply as an isolated and
tidy moral lesson on humility, but as a powerful indictment of
the entire stance of the Pharisees and a forceful statement
concerning the division in the People.[1]

3. In chapters 9-19, therefore, the Journey motif
and the placement of materials in a pattern of contrast work
together to establish a highly dramatic structure to the
narrative. The characterization of Jesus in these chapters is
highly prophetic.[2] But although the narrative does focus
strongly on the person of Jesus and His goal (Suffering-Glory)[3]
Luke's arrangement of materials has also highlighted the story
of the division in the people caused by the Prophet. As Jesus

---

[1]Cf. Descamps, La Justice, 96-98.

[2]Apart from the brief remarks made at the start of this
chapter, we have not considered the significance of the transfiguration account for the theme of the Prophet and the People.
Schubert, "Structure and Significance," 181-182, has done this
already, and we have chosen to focus more explicitly on passages he has not. Cf. also our remarks above on 9:51ff, and
13:31ff. Grundmann, "Fragen," 259, speaks of Luke's presentation of Jesus in these chapters as one of a "prophetischer
Lehrer."

[3]Conzelmann, Theology, 65; Grundmann, "Fragen," 255-256;
Robinson, "Theological Context," 23ff.

112

moves on Jerusalem to fulfill his destiny, he is at once
a) calling to the crowds for conversion and warning them of
being lost if they do not convert; calling to individuals from
among the crowd to become his disciples; b) experiencing
rejection at the hands of the Pharisees/Lawyers and in turn
threatening them with rejection;[1] c) instructing his disciples.
In a word, the core of the faithful people is being prepared on
the road to Jerusalem. Those who are going to reject are
rejecting, those who are going to convert are being called;
those who are following are being instructed. To grasp this
we must see how effectively Luke has managed to convey the process of growth. Luke has Jesus begin in Galilee with the
Twelve and a handful of sinful women following him (8:1-3).
But as he enters Jerusalem, ἅπαν τὸ πλῆθος τῶν μαθητῶν accom-
panies Him in triumph, rejoicing and glorifying God for the
wonders they had seen (19:37); the band of disciples has become
a "multitude."

But as 19:37 describes the fullness of the positive
response to Jesus, 19:39ff completes the pattern of acceptance/
rejection. As the crowd cheers, it is τινες τῶν φαρισαίων who
speak the words of rejection: "Teacher, rebuke your disciples."
The Pharisees, the leaders of the people, stand aloof and
reject the proclamation of the Prophet Jesus as King.

Jesus responds to this rejection with words which must be
considered as climaxing the previous stage of the ministry and
prophesying what is to follow (19:41ff). The Prophet has
finally arrived in Jerusalem to proclaim to her peace (19:42),
to effect for her God's saving "Visitation" (19:44), but He
will be rejected by her, with the result that she too will
suffer rejection (19:43-44).

4. The New Leadership in Israel: The shape of
Luke's narrative in chs. 9-19 continues the fulfillment of
Simeon's prophecy that many would rise and fall in Israel.
Up to the Jerusalem ministry we have seen that those who are
falling, those who are being rejected from the people, are the
leaders of the people, in particular the Pharisees and Lawyers.
But who are those who are "rising" in Israel? In this section,

---

[1]Cf. A. George, "Israël dans l'Oeuvre de Luc," RB 75
(1968) 495-498.

Luke begins to anticipate, prepare for, the role of the Twelve
and the other Men of the Spirit in Acts. They are to be the
new authority over Israel. This anticipation is seen most
clearly of course in the statements of the Last Supper and in
the programmatic statements of ch. 24, but already in this
section, the emergence of a new leadership within Israel is
being adumbrated.

This can be seen first in the sending of the Twelve
(9:1-6). We read: ἔδωκεν αὐτοῖς δύναμιν καὶ ἐξουσίαν ἐπὶ
πάντα τὰ δαιμόνια καὶ νόσους θεραπεύειν. καὶ ἀπέστειλεν αὐτοὺς
κηρύσσειν τὴν βασιλείαν τοῦ θεοῦ καὶ ἰᾶσθαι. The clear intent
of this is that the Twelve are to exercise the same powers and
possess the same authority that Jesus did (cf. 4:33, 36; 5:17;
6:18-19; 7:21; 8:2, 29; 9:42), by preaching and healing the
sick. Nor is it accidental that these are the "signs and
wonders" performed by the Apostles and Men of the Spirit in
Acts. The close connection between the authority of Jesus and
that of the Twelve is underscored by the sequence of verses in
9:6, 10 and 11. The Twelve are said to go out εὐαγγελιζόμενοι
καὶ θεραπεύοντες πανταχοῦ (9:6). When they return, they
report to Jesus all that they had done (9:10), and immediately,
Luke says of Jesus ἐλάλει αὐτοῖς (the crowds) περὶ τῆς
βασιλείας τοῦ θεοῦ καὶ τοὺς χρείαν ἔχοντας θεραπείας ἰᾶτο
(9:11). It is striking and scarcely accidental that Luke here
portrays Jesus and the Apostles as carrying out the same
ministry.

Further, we notice that as the Twelve preach and heal with
the authority of Jesus, so they will, like Him, stimulate both
acceptance and rejection among the people (9:4-5), and those
who reject them will be themselves rejected, as signified by
the ritual acts of separation (9:5).

We have already seen how Luke connects the mission of the
Twelve to the incident of the feeding of the Five Thousand
(9:11ff), a connection which he alone makes so closely.[1] In

---

[1]In Matt 14:13ff the feeding of the five thousand follows
the rejection of Jesus at Nazareth (13:53-58) and the death of
John the Baptist (14:1-12); the feeding of the four thousand
(15:32-38) follows the story of the Canaanite woman (15:12-28)
and a summary account of healings (15:29-31). In Mk 6:30-44
the feeding of the five thousand does follow the sending of

this feeding the Twelve (or the disciples--Luke does not have
perfect clarity of terms here)[1] are placed in the role of distributing food to the people, a role particularly interesting
in the light of Acts 4:32ff, and to which we shall return in
the next chapter.

The account of the sending of the Seventy (-Two)[2] in
10:1-12 is given an explicit function by Luke within the story.
These men were sent out to prepare the way for Jesus' coming (10:
2); they do this by proclaiming the coming of the Kingdom and
by healing (10:9). Why does Luke include this second sending?
Many think that it functions as a foreshadowing of the mission
to the Gentiles carried out by the hellenistic missionaries.[3]
This may be possible, though it is not clear how Luke would
have us understand the sending in that fashion.[4] These points
however are certain: a) Although they are not said to receive
"power" from Jesus as did the Twelve,[5] they perform essentially
the same functions--preaching and healing. b) Luke does not
draw as close a literary connection between them and the
ministry of Jesus as he did for the Twelve. c) On the other
hand, the pattern of acceptance and rejection is drawn even

---

the Twelve (6:6-12), and is loosely connected with it (cf.
6:30), but the connection is loosened by the account of the
death of John (6:14-29). The feeding of the four thousand
(8:1-10) is unconnected to the sending.

[1]V. 10 οἱ ἀπόστολοι; v. 12, οἱ δώδεκα; v. 13 αὐτοὺς =
δώδεκα; v. 14, μαθητάς; v. 16, μαθηταῖς; v. 17, δώδεκα (κόφινοι).
Degenhardt, Lukas Evangelist der Armen, 29 and 38, places too
much weight on the distinction of terms here.

[2]For a discussion of the textual problems, cf. B. Metzger,
"Seventy or Seventy-Two Disciples?" NTS 5 (1958-9) 299-306.

[3]Grundmann, "Fragen," 260; Lohse, "Lukas als Theologe,"
272; Lohse, "Missionarisches Handeln," 12; Zehnle, Peter's
Pentecost Discourse, 107, 130; Grundmann, Lukas, 208; Creed,
Luke, 144. Flender, Luke, 23, moves out of the realm of sober
exegesis when he declares, "The mission of the Seventy becomes
the sign of the consummation in heaven." A listing of other
symbolic suggestions can be found in Metzger, "Seventy," 302-04.

[4]Cf. the remarks by Lagrange, Luc, 291-292, and Metzger,
"Seventy," 304.

[5]The ἀνέδειξεν is of course very official in tone. Cf.
Grundmann, Lukas, 208; H. Schlier, "δείκνυμι," TDNT 2 (1964)
30.

more sharply in regard to the seventy(-two) than in the case of the Twelve (cf. 10:10-12). Indeed, it is after their sending that Luke places the condemnation of the unbelieving cities, concluding with the saying which summarizes perfectly his understanding of the relationship between Jesus and His witnesses: ὁ ἀκούων ὑμῶν ἐμοῦ ἀκούει καὶ ὁ ἀθετῶν ὑμᾶς ἐμὲ ἀθετεῖ. ὁ δὲ ἐμὲ ἀθετῶν ἀθετεῖ τὸν ἀποστείλαντά με (10:16).[1] d) Here as elsewhere in the Gospel and Acts, it would seem to be a mistake to speculate too closely about what contemporary offices or ministries Luke may have had in mind in these descriptions.[2] We shall return in the next chapter to a consideration of possessions in these passages. Leaving aside that element, what we find in these descriptions is the typically Lukan stereotype for spiritual authority: Those who are sent out by Jesus [both the Twelve and the Seventy(-Two)] work wonders, preach the Word, and stimulate both acceptance and rejection; and those who reject them reject Jesus and those who reject Jesus reject God.

Two further passages pertinent to the transfer of authority to the Twelve (12:35-48 and 19:11-27) will be discussed in the next chapter because of their connection with possessions.

F. Luke 19:45-23:49:

In the Jerusalem ministry, the bulk of Lukan materials are paralleled by Matt and Mk. There are however numerous redactional touches continuing the patterns established in the earlier chapters. Rather than interpret successive passages, we will comment on selected features of Luke's presentation in order to bring to a more rapid conclusion this literary analysis of the Gospel.

1. The Division in the People: In agreement with the parallels, Luke emphasizes in the Jerusalem section of his Gospel the positive response of the λαός (this word again in

---

[1] The saying of Matt 10:40 parallels only the first, positive part of the statement. For ἀθετῶν, cf. Lk 7:30.

[2] Cf. e.g., Degenhardt, Lukas, 65. On the other hand, the sending by twos does appear to reflect at least a common practice of early Christian missionaries; cf. J. Jeremias, "Paarweise Sendung im Neuen Testament," New Testament Essays, 136-144.

frequent use), in contrast to the opposition to Jesus by the
leaders of the people.[1] The leaders are constantly trying to
trap Jesus, but are stymied because of His popularity with and
their fear of the people (cf. 19:47-8; 20:6, 19, 26; 22:2, 6).
The only puzzling feature in Luke's presentation, and it is
very puzzling, is that the identity of the opponents changes.
We have seen throughout the Gospel and in particular in chs. 7
and 9-19, that the Pharisees and Lawyers stood against Jesus as
the main, indeed, almost only opponents. But in Jerusalem, the
Pharisees appear as opponents only once, and even there we
would not recognize them were it not for their literary
characterization: παρατηρήσαντες . . . . ἑαυτοὺς δικαίους
εἶναι (20:20).[2] Their place is taken by the High Priests,
Elders, Scribes, and Sadducees, the πρῶτοι τοῦ λαοῦ (19:47)
and ἄρχοντες τοῦ λαοῦ (23:13, 35) [cf. 20:1, 19, 27, 46; 22:2,
66; 23:4]. Is there some literary logic behind this dramatic
shift in characters? Or is Luke adhering in this section to
the cast of characters provided him by the tradition? We do
not know.[3] The presentation here is consistent with the

---

[1]Cf. A. George, "Israël," 199ff; J. Kodell, "Luke's use of
Laos 'People', especially in the Jerusalem Narrative," CBQ 31
(1969) 327-343.

[2]Cf. 14:1; 16:15; 17:20; 18:9. The identification of the
Pharisees is explicit in Matt 22:15-16 and Mk 12:13. George,
"Israël," 502, suggests Luke avoided this identification
because he did not wish to involve the Pharisees in a dispute
which would lead eventually (23:2) to Jesus' condemnation.

[3]It is widely held that Luke was more favorable to the
Pharisees than other groups in Judaism. The statement of
Flender, Luke, 108, is somewhat representative: "The Pharisees
disappear from the passion narrative. They are exonerated from
any guilt over the crucifixion. They represent the group among
the Jewish leaders which is receptive to the Christian message.
Gamaliel is a particular case in point." It is indeed puzzling
that Luke drops his favorite opponents when the Jerusalem
ministry begins. Perhaps the fact that some Pharisees became
believers (Acts 15:5), that Paul was a Pharisee, and that they
believed in the resurrection, all affected this picture. Or
perhaps Luke simply did not wish to counter the weight of the
tradition which placed the blame for Jesus' death on the members of the Council. But it is not the case that Luke portrays
the Pharisees as such with much favor. We have seen already
the thematic statement of 7:29-30, and the incident of 13:31ff.
Luke does have Jesus dine with Pharisees, but every such
occasion is a time of testing and conflict. Gamaliel, as we

continuation of the Jerusalem ministry in Acts, where a
Pharisee only appears once (5:34) and the opponents of the
Apostles are the Priests, Elders and Sadducees. In spite of
the shift of characters, however, there is continuity with the
first part of the Gospel in this respect, that the division in
the people remains a split between the leaders and the people.

    2. The guilt of the people: In the light of the
discourses of Acts, which, as we have seen, attribute the blame
for the death of Jesus to the whole people on two occasions
(2:23, 36 and 3:14) and which cushion the blame in the second
instance by the excuse of ignorance, while at the same time
progressively shift the blame to the leaders of the people
(4:10-11; 5:28-32; 7:51ff), it is important to see how Luke
handles this issue in the actual narrative of the rejection of
Jesus.

    The whole weight of the tradition before Luke, of course,
clearly implicated the people in the death of Jesus, and he
could scarcely avoid that imputation entirely.[1] In Luke, it
is found most clearly in the sentencing of Jesus, where the
Priests, leaders and λαός are said to present (23:13)[2] and
Luke adds that πανπληθεί they cried out repeatedly for Barabbas
to be released in place of Jesus (23:18). On the other hand,

----

shall see in chapter four, is <u>not</u> favorable to the Christian
cause, and his speech is given by Luke a highly ironic twist.
The believing Pharisees of Acts 15:5 are not presented in an
especially good light. The famous ploy of Paul in Acts 23:6
puts the Pharisees in humorous, ironic, but scarcely believing
stance. The case for Luke's favorable treatment of the Pharisees remains to be proven; it definitely should not be assumed.

[1]Conzelmann, _Theology_, 87ff, rightly stresses that Luke
minimizes the guilt of Pilate out of an apologetic motive. So
also G. Kilpatrick, "A Theme of the Lucan Passion Story and
Luke XXIII.47," _JTS_ 43 (1942) 34-36. Conzelmann is less than
accurate, however, when he speaks of a "one-sided emphasis on
the guilt of the Jews," for he does not distinguish sharply
enough between Luke's presentation of the people on the one
hand and the leaders on the other.

[2]The mention of the presence of the people here seems so
out of harmony with Luke's presentation that it has been
suggested, despite the meager mss evidence in support, that an
early copyist's mistake had changed τοῦ λαοῦ to καὶ τὸν λαὸν in
23:13. So George, "Israël," 504; Rau, "Das Volk in der
lukanischen Passionsgeschichte," 50; Dupont, _Beatitudes_ III,
58, n. 4.

Luke avoids the explicit assumption of guilt by the people so
emphatically stated in Matthew's account: καὶ ἀποκριθεὶς πᾶς
ὁ λαὸς εἶπεν τὸ αἷμα αὐτοῦ ἐφ' ἡμᾶς καὶ ἐπὶ τὰ τέκνα ἡμῶν
(Matt 27:25).

In addition, Luke so shades his narrative that the role
of the populace in the series of events leading to the death of
Jesus appears minimal, and the impression left at the end is
that of a people sorrowful at the death of the prophet and
ready for repentance.[1] The following individual points support
this suggestion: a) In the betrayal scene (22:2), Luke has the
leaders fear the people (as in 20:19) and not just a θόρυβος
among the people as in Matt 26:5 and Mk 14:2. In addition,
Luke adds ἄτερ ὄχλου to the plan of the leaders in 22:6. b) In
the Gethsemane scene, Luke identifies the ὄχλος of 22:47 with
the leaders in 22:52, whereas in Matt 26:47 and Mk 14:43 the
mob was sent out by the leaders. c) In the Council of course,
the people played no role, only the leaders (22:54, 66). But
in Luke's version, neither are there false witnesses from among
the people (as there are in Matt 26:59, Mk 14:56).[2] d) In the
first scene before Pilate (23:1-5), the ἄπαν τὸ πλῆθος αὐτῶν
(v. 1) can by context refer only to the members of the Council.
Although the ὄχλος is mentioned in Pilate's response (23:4),
the charge clearly comes from the leaders, for they speak of
"our nation" and "the people" as entities almost separate from
themselves, which of course in Luke's understanding they were.
e) On the way to Calvary, Luke adds this scene not found in the
parallels: ἠκολούθει δὲ αὐτῷ πολὺ πλῆθος τοῦ λαοῦ καὶ γυναικῶν
ἂι ἐκόπτοντο καὶ ἐθρήνουν αὐτόν (23:27). The threatening
response of Jesus (v. 28) does not imply a rejection of those
who wept for him, but a promise of disaster to befall the
nation which rejected him. f) At the crucifixion, Matt 27:39
and Mk 15:29 have οἱ παραπορευόμενοι blaspheming Jesus as well
as the High Priests, Scribes and Elders. Luke, however,
distinguishes the people from its leaders: καὶ εἰστήκει ὁ λαὸς

---

[1] Some of the details noted here have also been mentioned
by Rau, "Das Volk," 41ff.

[2] We have seen already that Luke introduces the false
witnesses into the Stephen story, Acts 6:13.

θεωρῶν. ἐξεμυκτήριζον δὲ καὶ οἱ ἄρχοντες . . . (23:35).
g) Finally, at the death of Jesus, Luke notes that πάντες οἱ
συμπαραγενόμενοι ὄχλοι ἐπὶ τὴν θεωρίαν ταύτην θεωρήσαντες τὰ
γενόμενα τύπτοντες τὰ στήθη ὑπέστρεφον (23:48).

By this last stroke, Luke prepares for the conversions
among the people in Acts. The people already at the crucifixion were struck with sorrow at what had happened, and those who
had come as if to a spectacle returned sadly, beating their
breasts in a gesture of repentance. The same, we notice, is
not said of the leaders. We can state with some confidence
that all these details add up to the minimalization of the
guilt of the people in the death of Jesus. When seen together
with the dominant pattern found throughout the Gospel, wherein
the acceptance by the people of the prophet is contrasted to
the rejection of Him by the leaders, this conclusion appears
even better founded.

3. The New Leadership over Israel: In the central
section of the Gospel we saw how Luke began to anticipate the
change in leadership over the people. There are two passages
in the Jerusalem section of the Gospel which are pertinent to
that motif.

The removal of the old leaders from their authority over
Israel is expressed parabolically by the story of the vineyard
(20:9-19); cf. Matt 21:33-46, Mk 12:1-12). All the versions
agree that the story was aimed at them (Lk 20:19, Mt 21:45,
Mk 12:12).[1] Matt 23:43 elaborates the point of the story as
the explicit stripping of the Kingdom from Israel as a whole
and its bestowal on a worthy nation. Luke does not follow
Matthew in speaking of the rejection of the People as a whole,
but speaks instead of the rejection of the leaders.[2] It is the

---

[1]Luke has the parable addressed πρὸς τὸν λαόν (v. 9), but
by context (20:1) and v. 19, it is clear that the leaders not
only overheard the parable but were its main target. Cf.
Jeremias, Parables, 76.

[2]Contra Plummer, Luke, 458. It is particularly interesting that Luke's citation of Ps 118:22 is picked up in Acts 4:11
and applied there, as we have seen, directly to the leaders.
The use of the mixed citation (Is 8:14; Dan 2:34, 44) here in
20:18 completes the pattern of rejection: those who reject
God's emissaries are themselves rejected.

120

tenders of the vineyard who are destroyed,[1] who lose their
authority; the vineyard endures and is given to others for
tending. The parable is clearly meant to be understood
allegorically. If we so see it, it is clear that in Luke's
understanding Israel itself remains, even though the heir has
been rejected; but the authority over Israel will be changed.

We have already seen in 9:1-6 that the Twelve were
invested with the authority of Jesus to preach and to heal.
At the Last Supper, Jesus explicitly places them in a position
of authority over the twelve tribes of Israel (22:30), an
appointment which is of the greatest importance for understanding the portrayal of the Twelve in the first part of
Acts.[2] We shall return to this passage in the next chapter,
but in the present context, the following should be noted:
a) The saying on the authority of the Twelve is placed in a
context (22-28) in which authority has been defined in terms
of διακονία, an association which will have implications for
Acts. b) Jesus gives now (διατίθεμαι) to them what He received
from the Father. It is a present appointment with future implications. The bestowal is not in the future, but now. c) What
is given the Twelve is the power to rule (anarthous βασιλείαν),
an authority which is specified in terms of judging
(κρίνοντες).[3] d) Contrary to Matt 19:28, Luke does not
specify that this rule will begin when the end-time comes
and when the Son of Man is seated in Glory; the much vaguer
ἐν τῇ βασιλείᾳ μοῦ (if indeed it is not to be taken to refer
only to eating and drinking at the table) leaves open the
question of the time of fulfillment; as we know, it takes
place in Acts. e) The scope of the Twelve's authority is

---

[1]We will have occasion in the next chapter to remark on
the overseeing of property as an image of authority and on the
concomitant loss of self and property.

[2]Cf. Jervell, Luke and the People of God, 94; S. Brown,
Apostasy and Perseverence in the Theology of Luke, 64ff. For
a thorough analysis of the saying, cf. J. Dupont, "Le Logion
des douze Trônes (Mt. 19:28, Lk. 22:28-30)," Bib 45 (1964)
355-392.

[3]After discussing the difficulties of finding the precise
meaning here, Dupont, "douze Trônes," 381, correctly concludes
that in Luke, "Les Apôtres deviendront les chefs des douze
tribus, ils les gouverneront."

Israel. This limitation raises implications for the spread of
the Gospel beyond Israel, as we shall see. f) The following
verses (31-32) single out the role Peter will play in strengthening his brothers, again a clear foreshadowing of the
situation in Acts.

The two passages, then, when taken together, complete the
pattern of falling and rising. The old leaders of the people
have rejected the Prophet, the Son, the Heir; they are to be
removed from their place of authority. But the People Israel
remains. In the place of the old leaders, Jesus appoints the
Twelve to rule over Israel.

G. Conclusions to Chapters One and Two:
     This analysis of Luke-Acts was motivated by the hope of
discovering a literary pattern which would better enable us to
grasp the significance of Luke's language about possessions in
Acts 4:32ff and a series of related passages. Beginning with
certain clues provided by those passages themselves, and moving
through successive stages of analysis, we have slowly and pain-
stakingly delineated such a literary pattern, which we have
called the pattern of the Prophet and the People.

The main elements of that pattern are clear enough by now
to enable us to forego further repetition. But some remarks
should be made about the literary character of the pattern.
This pattern is not one which was imposed from the beginning
on the text by an alien theological, historical or even
literary preconception, but is one which emerged from the text
itself. As such, it has revealed not some mechanical formality,
but what is probably the instinctive style and outlook of the
author. The pattern is flexible and alive. It does not run
counter to, but rather is the very mainspring of the story,
that which gives the story both coherence and color. It is a
pattern which weds both structure and content, and to that
extent offers us some insight into the concerns and intentions
of the author.

From all that we have seen, it is evident that the fate of
Israel was no less a concern for Luke than it was for Paul,
though in a very different way. We have seen how in spite of
the conclusion of Acts, when Paul proclaims that the Word of

Salvation will go to the Gentiles and "they will listen," Luke attempts to show by any number of ways that all of Israel did not reject Jesus or the Word about Him. In his story, Luke does not describe a total or definitive rejection by all the Jews, but a division in the Jewish people. And in every way, he tries to show that the majority of the Jews accepted the Word.

Why was he concerned to show this? We can perhaps find a clue in Luke's insistence that the "things brought to fulfillment among us" were in fact the fulfillment of God's promises made to Abraham in the Old Testament (cf. 1:55, 73; Acts 3:25, 7:2, 16, 17; 13:26). These promises concerned Israel. But for the promises to Abraham to have been fulfilled, for God's promise therefore to have proven true, there must have been an Israel within which those promises were realized in a real way.

This is basically a question of theodicy. If Israel totally rejected God's visitation and was itself totally rejected from salvation, then God Himself was untrue to His Word. But if God was untrue in his promise to Israel, how can the Gentiles have ἀσφάλεια in their own belief?

The Gospel now is among the Gentiles. In all likelihood, Luke wrote from within a church that was almost totally Gentile and wrote for the sake of those Gentiles.[1] But if there is one thing clear about the personality of Luke, it is that he was steeped in the perspective of the Scriptures, and, more, had an outlook that emphasized above all else continuity. His work is a testimony to this outlook which expresses itself in the continuity of the promises and their fulfillment, the continuity of the People of God, the continuity of the Prophetic mission.

---

[1] The independent and valuable insights of Jervell, Luke and the People of God, which have considerably influenced the present study, do not depend for their validity on Jervell's insistence that the Christian milieu in which Luke wrote contained a Jewish element which was if not numerically at least theologically decisive (147), or that Luke's defense of Paul could make sense "only for a milieu of essentially Jewish Christian stamp," (176). Nevertheless, Jervell's stress upon the positive response of Israel within Luke-Acts must be maintained as a needed corrective to the more common view as articulated, e.g., by S. Wilson, The Gentiles and the Gentile Mission, 219ff.

For Luke, the notion of a break, of an hiatus in the working out of God's plan was unthinkable. In order for the Gentiles now to enjoy the promises that were made in the first place to Israel, those promises had to have found fulfillment within Israel and been extended in a continuous line to the Gentiles.[1] The Gentile Church, in a word, was not seen by Luke as the replacement of Israel, but as an extension of the true and believing Israel. God could only form a "People for His Name" among the Gentiles on the basis of the People which was the believing Israel.[2] Luke found the expression of that believing Israel in the first community in Jerusalem.

Yet Luke had to express as well the fact of rejection, and in this the figure of the Prophet served him well. In itself

---

[1] It is entirely consistent for Luke, when speaking of the first preaching of the Gospel to the Gentiles, to call it "God's visitation," thereby establishing one more link to the mission for Israel: ὁ θεὸς ἐπεσκέψατο λαβεῖν ἐξ ἐθνῶν λαὸν τῷ ὀνόματι αὐτοῦ. Cf. Dupont, Etudes, 361-364, especially the clarifying note added after the appearance of "A People for His Name" by Dahl.

[2] Cf. Dahl, "A People for His Name," 324, 326. A. George, "Israël," 525, comments at the end of a fine treatment of this question in Luke-Acts, "Surtout, il n'est pas Juif. Il est moins préoccupé du sort d'Israël que ne l'etait Paul (Rom. 9:1-5); il s'interesse davantage à la mission auprès des païens, à laquelle il à pris part. Il n'en est que le plus remarquable qu'il ait donné dans son oeuvre une telle place au mystère d'Israël." But if our suggestion is correct, Israel held such a place in Luke's thought because he was of the Gentile Church and was a reader of the Scriptures. Israel's fate is important precisely for the Gentiles. Not that Luke had hopes, like Paul, for Israel's conversion; we have no real evidence for that. Luke's major focus is in fact on showing how the Gentiles received salvation. To deny this would be to go against the obvious sense of the text, and in this we agree with the position of Haenchen, Wilson and Dupont. But what these authors neglect is that essential fidelity of at least a part of Israel is important to Luke precisely for the sake of the Gentiles. For the Gentiles now to be among God's people, there had to have been a realization of that people among the historic Israel. Otherwise God's promises even to the Gentiles would be worthless. Wilson, The Gentiles, 244, disputes this and says that the promises of God would have been fulfilled simply by the offer of the Gospel to Israel, for their rejection too had been foretold. But if Luke thought this, he would not have taken such obvious pains to show that all of Israel had not rejected the Gospel, that there was in fact also a "People for His Name" among the Jews.

the prophetic model was an element of continuity with the
Scriptures. And in the understanding of that model which Luke
expressed in the description of Moses in Acts seven, there was
contained a pattern of double rejection which corresponded
perfectly with the plan of his book. Thus he was able to
elaborate the pattern we have seen: Jesus as the Prophet like
Moses, raised up by God from among his brothers to be the
instrument of God's visitation, to bring the good news of
peace and redemption to Israel, but rejected by his brothers,
only to be accepted by God and established in power by the
resurrection; and the Apostles possessing the prophetic Spirit
of Jesus, offering to Israel in the Word about Jesus a second
chance for conversion and inclusion within the people, but they
too finding rejection. So far, the demands of the pattern.
But the rejection cannot be complete. Therefore Luke effects
a most significant alteration in the pattern. Instead of
having all the people reject Jesus, he as much as possible
pictures the ordinary people as positive and accepting both of
Jesus and the Apostles. The rejection is carried out by the
leaders. This division holds good for the whole of the
Jerusalem narrative; once in the diaspora with Paul, although
Luke tries to emphasize the numbers of Jewish believers, the
fact of rejection is dominant. But that did not matter. Once
a faithful Israel was secured in Jerusalem, Luke saw as secured
as well the essential continuity of the spread of the promises
to the Gentiles.

By portraying the leaders as the ones who rejected Jesus
and the Apostles and thereby found themselves rejected from
God's People, Luke created, deliberately it would seem, a
leadership vacuum. This he filled with the Twelve. The
rejected leaders represent the point of discontinuity, of
rejection. The Twelve represent a new continuity, based on
appointment by God through Jesus, and based on the reception
of the power of Jesus in the Spirit.

The Twelve are the point of continuity with the fulfillment of the promises to Israel through Jesus and with the
extension of those promises to the Gentiles. Therefore it is
necessary for Luke to express emphatically and by every
available image that the Gentile mission originates and is

guided by the Twelve. More than this, we shall see by what
means he also expresses the transfer (and thereby the continuity) of authority to the hellenistic missionaries, so that
there is a continuity of leadership to express the continuity
of the Gentile community with Israel.

We begin to see, therefore, the critical role played by
the Jerusalem narrative of Acts in the whole story of Luke-
Acts. Within the bounds of this narrative, Luke must show that
there is a faithful Israel within which God's promises have
found realization. He must show that there is a new leadership
over this Israel and express this as forcefully as possible,
for it is the key to the next concern, which is that he must
show how from this faithful Israel and from this new leadership
the Gentile world came to share in the promises which belonged
to Israel.

The Gospel narrative prepares for the Jerusalem section by
establishing (within the limits we have mentioned): a) the
readiness of the people to listen to the Prophet; b) the rejection of the Prophet by the erstwhile leaders; c) the promise of
authority over Israel given to the Twelve. The part of Acts
which follows the Jerusalem narrative builds on that critical
juncture by a) ensuring that all the spread of the Gospel
derives ultimately from the Twelve, and b) ensuring that the
Gentile community was in every way obedient to the authority of
the Twelve.

We have returned full circle, then, to the importance of
the description of the Apostles in the first part of Acts.

It may appear by now that Acts 4:32ff and the problem of
community possessions have completely been lost sight of. But
all of the analysis we have so far carried out has had the
single goal of defining more accurately the context within
which that problem can be understood. The second part of this
study will be an attempt to show that Luke employs the
materials on possessions to express forcefully the major
aspects of the literary pattern we have discussed in this
first part of the study. We will suggest that just as there
is a literary pattern which shapes the narrative as a whole,
so is there a distinct literary function played by the motif
of possessions within that literary pattern. To be as direct

as possible, we will try to show that Luke uses the language of
possessions symbolically. We shall try to demonstrate that he
employs the language about possessions to express symbolically:
a) the identity of God's People; b) acceptance and rejection in
relation to God's People; c) authority over God's People;
d) the transmission of authority within God's People.

We cannot make such assertions about the passages in Acts,
however, without first considering Luke's way of speaking about
possessions in the Gospel. Indeed, the Gospel provides both
the sternest test to our thesis and the surest entry into the
argumentation concerning Acts. For if it can be shown that in
the Gospel, where Luke was handling material far more refractory than in Acts, he was able to use the possessions motif in
the way we are suggesting, the case for Acts will appear more
plausible.

CHAPTER THREE

Introduction:

In the first two chapters of this study we have delineated
a literary pattern in Luke-Acts which structures the telling of
the story. The question we address in the present chapter is
the relationship of the materials dealing with possessions in
the Gospel part of the story to that literary pattern. There
are really only three possibilities: a) The materials on
possessions in the Gospel cannot be related to any literary
pattern, much less that of the Prophet and the People; they do
not perform any literary function at all, but are simply
included within the framework of the Gospel as an independent
body of teaching on a subject of interest and pertinence to the
author and his readers. b) There is a literary pattern to be
discerned in the materials dealing with possessions, but this
pattern is so different from the one suggested in this study
that it must be questioned whether the proposed literary
pattern of the Prophet and the People is as dominant as has
been argued. c) There is a literary pattern to be discerned
in the materials dealing with possessions, and it is one which
expresses by means of concrete imagery the dominant literary
pattern of the Prophet and the People. We are suggesting that
the third possibility is correct. It will be helpful to
clarify our procedure by the following introductory remarks.

Materials to be Considered:

The use of the expression "materials dealing with
possessions" is deliberately nebulous. We want to include in
this investigation as wide a range of passages as possible, for
Luke is not only extraordinarily rich in passages which talk
about possessions explicitly, he also contains many redactional
or literary touches in passages which at first sight do not
appear to be about possessions. The following types of
passages will therefore be examined in this chapter:
1. passages in which explicit terms designating economic
states are used (e.g., 1:46ff; 4:14; 6:20ff; 7:22; 14:7-24),

127

2. statements explicitly presenting an ideal or a demand
regarding attitudes toward or use of possessions (e.g., 6:29-
30; 37-38; 12:32-34; 9:57-62; 14:25-35), 3. stories in which
possessions or the use of possessions appear to be the point of
the story (e.g., 16:19-31; 16:1-13; 19:11-27), 4. statements
or stories which do not have as their main point of reference
the use of possessions but within which possessions play a role
(e.g., 15:11-32; 11:21-22), 5. sayings or statements about
authority in which possessions or property are involved (e.g.,
20:9-19; 12:41-48).

Studies which have focussed on possessions in Luke have
tended to emphasize the first three categories of passages in
attempting to construct a "Lukan teaching" on possessions and
the use of possessions,[1] to account for the personal[2] or
Scriptural[3] influences which may have shaped that teaching, or
to place this teaching within the redactional outlook (theological and ecclesial) of Luke, by specifying what paraenetic or
polemic purpose might be served by this teaching.[4] The work

---

[1]Cf. e.g., R. Koch, "Die Wertung des Besitzes im Lukas-
evangelium," Bib 38 (1957) 151-169; C. Campbell, Critical
Studies in St. Luke's Gospel (Edinburgh: William Blackwood and
Sons, 1891) 171-308; R. Schnackenburg, The Moral Teaching of
the New Testament 2nd rev. ed., trans. by J. Holland-Smith and
W. O'Hare (New York: Herder and Herder, 1965) 127-131; I. H.
Marshall, Luke: Historian and Theologian, 141-144.

[2]Many have commented on the so-called "ebionitism" of
Luke. In addition to the authors listed in Dupont, Beatitudes
III, 150, n. 4, cf. E. Percy, Die Botschaft Jesu (Lunds
Universitets Arsskrift, n.f. Avd. 1, Bd.49, Nr.5; Lund: C. W. K.
Gleerup, 1953) 106; Campbell, Critical Studies, 171ff;
Schnackenburg, Moral Teaching, 131; Marshall, Luke, 142; L.
Keck, "The Poor among the Saints in the N.T.," ZNW 56 (1965)
108-109; Cadbury, The Making of Luke-Acts, 262-263. Among the
more ludicrous judgments concerning Luke's motivation for
writing the way he did about possessions, cf. A. Ehrhard, The
Acts of the Apostles (Manchester: University Press, 1969) 22:
"It is my opinion that St. Luke who, as a doctor, belonged to
the more affluent classes, was constantly troubled in his con-
science as to whether he had any right to suffer less hardship
than the poor."

[3]Percy, Die Botschaft Jesu, 45-89; A. Gelin, Les Pauvres
de Yahvé (Paris: Éditions du Cerf, 1953) 121ff; Dupont,
Beatitudes II, 19-142.

[4]Cf. H.-J. Degenhardt, Lukas Evangelist der Armen; Dupont,
Beatitudes III, 19-206; considerable attention is paid to the

that has been done at this level contains much that is worthwhile. It must be pointed out that in interpreting these
passages at a different level (that of the story) we are not
suggesting that Luke's purpose was purely aesthetic. Clearly,
the content of the materials on possessions had a significance
for the author and his readers not exhausted by their literary
function. But what has been lacking till now is a sustained
attempt to discover if these materials do make sense at the
literary level as integral parts of the story.

Moreover, the attempt to establish a consistent Lukan
teaching on possessions itself runs into difficulties. In the
introduction to this study we have mentioned the tension exist-
ing between the ideal of almsgiving and the ideal of goods held
in common; this is a tension which should not be too hastily
resolved by harmonization. In our second chapter we also
alluded to the problem presented by the description of the use
of possessions by missionaries in 9:1ff; 10:1ff; 22:35 and the
picture of Paul in Acts. If Luke wants to present an ideal for
his community to follow, which ideal emerges as his own: the
one in which missionaries travel with nothing at all? the one
in which the missionary supports himself by his labor? the one
in which leaders of communities likewise work to supply the
needs of those poorer than they? or the one in which the
leaders, like the Apostles in Jerusalem, preside over a
community of goods? It has frequently been noted that Luke
expresses a predilection for the poor and a hostility toward
the rich. But apart from his thematic statements, where does
this outlook emerge? And how does the rich tax-collector
Zaccheus fit into that outlook? The way in which certain
studies have tried to deal with these problems reveals their
complexity,[1] and the most thorough study of possessions within

role of possessions in S. Brown, Apostasy and Perseverence in
the Theology of Luke, 82ff.

[1]H. Flender, St. Luke, Theologian of Redemptive History,
75-78, sees the tension between the command to renounce all
possessions (14:33) and the implication that possessions should
be dealt with creatively in the parable of the pounds (19:11-
27) as an example of the dialectic tension throughout Luke's
work between the eschatological call of Jesus and the
Christian's responsibility to the world. Brown, Apostasy and

the redaction of Luke moves in many respects in the direction
of the sort of literary analysis we are doing.[1]

The problem we face is that although Luke consistently
talks about possessions, he does not talk about possessions
consistently.

A study which tries to find a literary pattern in
materials about possessions, therefore, must recognize that
Luke frequently speaks about possessions even when he is not
"teaching" about possessions, and that precisely these
instances of implicit non-thematic use may be especially helpful in discerning the nature of Luke's understanding of
possessions which leads to their being employed metaphorically.[2]

Method of Analysis:

Our obvious frame of reference in this examination of

Perseverence, 100-105, invokes different norms for the time of
Jesus and the time of the Church. The demand to leave all
possessions was normative only for Jesus' earthly followers;
for members of the Church, the willingness to part with
possessions expressed by the community of goods was the norm.
Degenhardt, Lukas, dissolves the difficulties by regarding
Luke's use of μαθητής and λαός as code for members of the
Lukan community. The words of the Gospel directed to disciples
(= later spiritual leaders) demand radical poverty; the words
addressed to the people (= simple believers in later Church)
demand only almsgiving. This is a clever solution, but it does
not hold up under close examination. Cf. Marshall, Luke, 207,
n. 1.

[1]The third volume of Dupont's massive study of the beatitudes, a complete reworking of his single-volume, 1954 work,
was published in 1973, and anticipates many points made in the
first part of this chapter. Our conclusions were reached
independently. Dupont's work is especially valuable in stressing the prophetic character of the beatitudes in Luke and in
relating that prophetic proclamation to the Gospel's special
concern for the lost and outcast in Israel. Our major divergence from Dupont comes in our use of the Magnificat, which,
while he treats it separately (III, 186-193), he does not consider sufficiently similar to the overall Lukan view to be
included within the main redactional study. After analyzing
the terms for rich and poor in Luke (Beatitudes III 47-64)
Dupont concludes, "Dans toutes ces antithèses, le rôle des
riches est tenu par les dirigeants d'Israël dans leur refus de
l'Evangile. En arrière-plan de la manière dont Luc présente
les riches on voit se profiler le problème de l'incredulité
d'Israel."

[2]Despite its obvious tendentious character, Campbell's
Critical Studies has the merit of considering a wider range of

possessions as a literary motif is the pattern of the Prophet and the People which we have analyzed in the first part of this study. We will try to show that Luke has used possessions language as a motif within that pattern, with the result that the literary pattern of the Prophet and the People is strengthened by the language about possessions, and that the language about possessions gains a certain clarity when seen as performing this literary function.

As in the first part of this study, both content and structure will be considered pertinent. This sort of analysis is closer to art than science, and there are no absolute criteria for determining whether a text "functions" in a certain way or not, and in the final analysis it is only the convincing quality of the connection once made which validates the method. The criteria for making judgments are basically those of any literary analysis. Thus we shall be particularly concerned about what we call thematic statements, in their relationship to each other, to other thematic statements not concerning possessions which we have analyzed earlier, and to the narrative. In those stories and sayings unique to Luke, we will be interested both in the content of the passages and their redactional or literary placement within the narrative. In the case of materials Luke has taken over unaltered or only minimally altered from the tradition, we will be interested primarily in the placement of the passages within the pattern of the Prophet and the People.

Within this study, this chapter has the function of preparing for our return to the passages about possessions in Acts. Two main interests therefore shape our investigation: 1) We want to find out how Luke uses materials about possessions within the telling of the story, so that the story itself is illuminated and advanced by this language. 2) We want to discover as much as we can about the shape of Luke's understanding of possessions which would cause him to see their metaphoric or symbolic possibilities.

---

passages than many other studies.

A.   The Rich and the Poor

In a number of passages[1] Luke uses the designation of rich and poor not to describe the economic condition of an individual, but as a classification for a group of people. The first thing that should be said about these instances is that they really do not speak about the use of possessions so much as a certain condition of being in the world. We shall consider in turn the poor and the rich.

1.   Three of these statements are clearly related to the beginning of Jesus' prophetic ministry. We have seen in the previous chapter that the Isaiah 61:1 citation in 4:18f functioned as the scriptural legitimation and fundamental premise for the ministry of Jesus as the prophetic Christ. That mission is stated succinctly as εὐαγγελίσασθαι πτωχοῖς. We have also seen that ch. 7 can be seen as the fulfillment within the narrative of the programmatic presentation of Jesus in ch. 4. In response to John's question whether He was the expected one, Jesus answers by listing deeds which partially paraphrase the Isaiah citation, and which climax with πτωχοί εὐαγγελίζονται. As we have suggested, this recalling of the Isaiah citation has the effect of emphasizing that what was prophesied as the mission of the prophet is actually being achieved in the words and deeds of Jesus. The first beatitude in Luke's version must be regarded as possessing this same prophetic character.[2] Framed by the two other statements, the proclamation μακάριοι οἱ πτωχοί ὅτι ὑμετέρα ἐστὶν ἡ βασιλεία τοῦ θεοῦ (6:20) places the fulfillment of the Isaiah citation in Jesus' own mouth. As the prophetic Christ, therefore, Jesus proclaims the Good News to the poor. The poor are those who receive the Kingdom.

The poor appear twice in ch. 14, in the sayings of Jesus to Pharisees who were testing him (14:1). In the lesson on hospitality (14:12), that man is declared blessed (μακάριος) who invites those who cannot repay him, including the πτωχοί (14:13). This lesson is taken up by the parable of the Great

---

[1]Lk 1:48; 1:51-53; 4:18; 6:20ff; 7:22; 14:13, 21.

[2]Cf. Dupont, Beatitudes II, 123-142; H. Schürmann, Das Lukasevangelium, 326-327.

Banquet, in which, after those first called to the banquet
refuse, the poor (πτωχοί) are invited to come. We are clearly
to understand this as the eschatological or Messianic banquet
(cf. 14:15).[1] The call of God to the poor functions here as
the basis for human hospitality. More than that, told to a
hostile audience, the call of God to the poor is a reflection
and defense of Jesus' own prophetic mission to proclaim the
Good News to the poor.[2]

    2. In four of these passages, the poor take a promi-
nent place[3] among others to whom the Good News, God's Visitation, comes. The citation of 4:18 lists with the poor the
captives (αἰχμάλωτοι), the blind (τυφλοί) and downtrodden
(τεθραυσμένοι). The list of 7:22 includes the blind (τυφλοί),
the lame (χωλοί), lepers (λεπροί), deaf (κωφοί) and the dead
(νεκροί). The lists of 14:13 and 21 are identical: called
with the poor are the crippled (ἀνάπειροι), the lame (χωλοί)
and the blind (τυφλοί). Certainly these lists form a compen-
dium of human misery. But are the categories of hardship
simply random? The lists of 14:13 and 21 in particular appear
to have a more precise significance. These categories, viz.
the crippled, lame and blind (excluding the poor), are the
types of "blemish" found in Lev 21:18 as prohibiting participation in the cult of Israel.[4] We also know from Qumran that
men with such blemishes were considered unworthy of and
therefore excluded from the eschatological war and Messianic
Banquet.[5] The unfortunates listed here by Luke are therefore

[1] J. Jeremias, The Parables of Jesus, 69.

[2] Jeremias, Parables, 176-180.

[3] In the Isaiah citation of 4:18, in 14:13 and 14:21, the
πτωχοί appear first; in 7:22, they appear last on the list,
clearly as a climax.

[4] Cf. also II Sam 5:8: τυφλοὶ καὶ χωλοὶ οὐκ εἰσελεύσονται
εἰς οἰκίαν κυρίου. E. Klostermann, Das Lukasevangelium, 513,
and J.-M. Lagrange, Evangile selon St. Luc, 402, cite the terms
found in Plato's Crito, 53A, to show that the list is typical
for the poor of any city street, but in the light of the
Isaiah citation in 4:18 and 7:22, the scriptural background
to the list here seems sure.

[5] Cf. 1QSa 2:5-6 and 1QM 7:4-5.

not only weighted with misery; they are rejected from full
participation in the life of the people. They are, in a word,
the outcast. But the poor were not considered to be ritually
blemished. What is striking is that Luke has included the poor
so prominently in each of these lists, as though to assert that
in the eyes of men, the poor were just as much in an outcast
position, just as rejected from the people, as those with
ritual blemish. He shows by this means the radical nature of
the prophet's proclamation: the Good News is addressed, the
Kingdom is given not only to those recognized as belonging to
the people but also, and indeed especially, to those on the
fringes of the people, the outcasts.

   3. The blessing directed to the poor in 6:20 is also
combined with two other descriptive categories. The literary
problems involved in the analysis of the beatitudes are
multiple and complex,[1] but the following points can be made
with some certainty.

    a) The poor are blessed together with those who
hunger now (πεινῶντες νῦν) and weep now (κλαίοντες νῦν) (6:21).
The fourth beatitude is far more specific; they are blessed who
are rejected by men (6:22). It should be noted that this
rejection is connected to their allegiance to the Son of Man
and is seen as following the pattern of the rejection of the
prophets by "their fathers."[2] This beatitude explicitly
connects the rejection of the poor, therefore, to the rejection
of the prophet Jesus. This beatitude specifies the listeners
as the disciples of Jesus.[3] The poor, therefore, are once more
included among those who are rejected, those outcast by men,
and this rejection is associated with the rejection of the

---

[1]Cf. Dupont, Beatitudes I, 207ff; Percy, Die Botschaft
Jesu, 40-45 and 82-84.

[2]Dupont, Beatitudes, II, 294-318; III, 38ff.

[3]Schürmann, Lukas, 335. The judgment that the audience
for the discourse as a whole is made up of the disciples must
be made cautiously, for the woes, too, are spoken in the
second person. The fourth beatitude, however, definitely
points to a paraenetic concern for the Christian disciples
who would undergo persecution for the sake of the Christ.
For the literary problems, cf. Dupont, Beatitudes III, 21-97;
Schürmann, 337ff.

prophets.

    b) There is a double pattern of reversal in the
beatitudes and woes: a) The present situation of the poor and
rejected will be reversed by God (6:23). b) The blessings
given to the poor are contrasted to the woes levelled at the
rich (6:24-26). What sort of description is here given of the
rich? They are those who enjoy their παράκλησις now. The
παράκλησις stands in direct contrast to the Kingdom of God.
The reader cannot resist thinking of Simeon, who awaited and
received in the person of Jesus the παράκλησιν of Israel
(2:25ff). The rich are those who do not await such a consolation, because they have one of their own. In contrast to the
hunger and sorrow of the poor, they are filled and laugh
haughtily.[1] But they too will experience the divine reversal.
Their present good fortune will be turned to hunger and weeping
(6:25). As the fourth beatitude was helpful in discerning the
"outcast" character of the poor, so is the fourth woe in
specifying the good favor enjoyed by the rich before men.
They are spoken well of by men (6:26); they are accepted.
They are like the false prophets who received honor from the
fathers of old.

    c) Now if we remember that these words are
spoken by the one who is the Prophet announcing the time of
God's Visitation, who is Himself to experience both acceptance
and rejection within the people, the beatitudes and woes appear
as words of prophetic judgment. These are not sapiential
utterings, but prophetic blessings and curses. Among the crowd
he addresses are those who are the outcasts from the people; by
accepting from the prophet the Good News, by accepting Him as
the Prophet, they will be rejected still more by men; but they
will have found acceptance in the Kingdom and will receive a
reward in heaven (6:23). But also among Jesus' listeners
(ideally if not actually) are those who are rich, self-
confident, accepted by men, who have no need of the comfort
extended by the Good News. They are to reject the Prophet

---

[1]γελῶντες is not an expression used neutrally; it generally denotes the laughter of derision by a superior over an
inferior. Cf. K. Rengstorf, "γελάω," TDNT 1 (1964) 660;
Dupont, Beatitudes III, 66-69.

136

and those who accept the Prophet. Jesus does not say that they
will themselves be rejected because of this. Why? Because the
prophetic word of woe itself expresses their rejection.[1] By
refusing the prophetic word, they are identified as "rich" and
are rejected by God.

In Jesus' own proclamation of the beatitudes, the quality
of prophetic proclamation of the Good News probably was the
dominant element, with little or no emphasis upon "poverty" as
a quality of spiritual responsiveness.[2] Luke retains this
perspective more than Matthew, in whose version of the beatitudes there is evident an obvious moralistic tendency. Is
there to be found in Luke's designation of the "poor," then,
any hint of such responsiveness? It seems to be present in
14:21ff, where the poor respond to the invitation to the
banquet. And we find it again in the passage to be considered
next.

4. The Magnificat does not use πτωχοί for the poor,
but ταπεινοί, a term with nuances which emphasize the "lowly"
or "humble" aspects of poverty,[3] and used in the LXX together
with πτωχοί to describe the oppressed and downtrodden.[4] That
the meaning of "poor" and not simply "humble" is present in
this passage is clear from the contrast in vv. 1:52 and 53:
the ταπεινοί and πεινῶντες stand over against the δυνάσται and
πλουτοῦντες. The Is 61:1 citation influenced Luke's other uses
of "poor." The literary influence here seems to come primarily
from the Song of Hannah in I Sam 2:1-10.[5] As the prophecy of
Simeon in 2:34 cast the narrative about Jesus in a pattern of
rising and falling within Israel, so the Magnificat casts the
fate of the rich and poor within Israel.

---

[1]Cf. Dupont, Beatitudes III, 28ff.

[2]Cf. Dupont, Beatitudes II, 139-142.

[3]Cf. W. Grundmann, "ταπεινός," TDNT 8 (1972) 1-5;
Schürmann, Lukas, 74-75.

[4]Grundmann, "ταπεινός," 6-11.

[5]Cf. I Sam 2:7: κύριος πτωχίζει καὶ πλουτίζει ταπεινοῖ
καὶ ἀνυψοῖ. R. Laurentin, Structure et Théologie de Luc I-II,
82-85, sees the Magnificat as following the "procédé anthologi-
que" of composition, and relates it to a number of O.T.
passages.

a) God's visitation to the lowliness (ταπείνωσις) of Mary stands as an example or as a realization of God's visitation to Israel to fulfill the promises made to Abraham (1:55). The "raising up" of Mary from lowliness (so that all will call her μακαρία, cf. 6:20) reflects the raising up of the poor in Israel.

b) Here the poor are specified as those who fear God (τοῖς φοβουμένοις αὐτόν), indicating a responsiveness to His Word. Thus Mary also is blessed because she believed the things said to her by the Lord (1:45), and in a uniquely Lukan passage, Jesus proclaims as μακάριοι those who hear the Word of God and keep it (11:28). As in the beatitudes, the poor are described as those who hunger (πεινῶντας, 1:53). These God has "raised up" (1:52), and, as in the beatitudes, "filled" (1:53).

c) In the Magnificat, the rich (πλουτοῦντες) are those who are proud of heart (ὑπερηφάνους διανοίᾳ καρδίας αὐτῶν, 1:51) and are powerful, among the rulers (δυνάστας, 1:52). As in the beatitudes, they are seen as those who enjoy acceptance and power within the people.[1] Their fate is to be scattered (1:51) and pulled down from their thrones (1:53), that is, rejected by the God who raises up the lowly.

d) The raising of the lowly and the lowering of the mighty is found elsewhere in Luke, and in interesting places. There may be an allusion to it in the Isaiah 40:3-5 citation of 3:4-6, again in connection with the revelation of the σωτήριον τοῦ θεοῦ (3:3) as in 1:47. More explicitly, Luke twice employs the saying found also in Matt 23:12: πᾶς ὁ ὑψῶν ἑαυτὸν ταπεινωθήσεται καὶ ὁ ταπεινῶν ἑαυτὸν ὑψωθήσεται. The placement of these sayings in Luke is illuminating. In 14:11, it is said by Jesus as a rebuke to the Pharisees, whom Jesus observed seeking the best places at table (14:7), and immediately precedes the sayings on the invitation of the poor in 14:13 and 21. The second instance (18:14) is again addressed to the Pharisees at the end of the parable of the Pharisee and tax-collector, which as we recall, has a significance beyond the simple moral lesson, but points to the acceptance of the tax-collectors by God and the rejection of the Pharisees. In

[1]Schürmann, Lukas, 76-77.

138

the parable the one who "trusted in himself because he considered himself just" and "scorned others" is lowered, whereas the τελώνης is raised, justified by God (δεδικαιωμένος).[1]

　　　5.　The passages we have been considering all have a certain thematic character, that is, they are general in form and placed in contexts which announce, summarize or defend the prophetic ministry without explicit connection to the story. By looking at these passages in isolation, we have found them to have a formal pattern of acceptance and rejection, and in one instance, of rising and falling. At the very least, the thematic statements on the rich and the poor form a parallel to the pattern of the prophet and the people. But can we go further? A hint that we might was provided by the placement of the beatitudes, and by the persistence of the image of the raising of the lowly throughout the Gospel. Let us now see if the content of the thematic statements can be related to the narrative of the story.

　　　We have found the dominant element uniting the various references to the poor has been that they are rejected by men, are among the outcasts of the people. The rich are characterized as men enjoying acceptance and power. In the working out of the narrative, Luke scarcely uses the designations rich and poor (where he does, we will examine below). But what we do find in his story, and in the thematic statements analyzed in the last chapter, is the pattern of acceptance and rejection involving the division between the leaders and the people. Luke does not mention the poverty of those who respond to Jesus, but he consistently emphasizes their outcast status, and this under his favorite rubric of "sinners and tax-collectors."[2] Thus it is the people and tax-collectors who justify God by receiving the baptism of John (7:29) and are

---

[1] Jeremias, Parables, 142; A. Descamps, Les Justes et la Justice dans les evangiles et le christianisme primitif, 98.

[2] The same concern for the outcasts is reflected in Luke's treatment of the Samaritans (Lk 10:25-37; 17:11-19; Acts 8). Cf. J. Jervell, Luke and the People of God, 113-132. It has been suggested by Ehrhardt, Acts of the Apostles, 47, that the same is true of the baptism of the Ethiopian Eunuch in Acts 8:26, for "no eunuch, no man sexually mutilated shall enter into the gathering," (Deut 23:1).

the friends of Jesus (7:35; 15:1-3). Peter the sinner (5:8)
leaves all things to follow Jesus, as does the tax-collector
Levi (5:27). The sinful woman accepts Jesus as Prophet
(7:36ff), and the exorcized women follow Jesus and support
Him (8:3). The rich tax-collector Zaccheus receives Jesus into
his house and is called a son of Abraham (19:9). The thematic
statements designating the poor specify them as outcasts; the
narrative shows us that this poverty is not an economic designation, but a designation of spiritual status. The tax-
collectors could certainly be called "rich" in economic terms,
but though they had money, they did not have acceptance. It is
at this level that the thematic statements and the narrative
mesh. Because of their outcast status, the sinners and tax-
collectors were among the "poor" to whom the Good News was
proclaimed. Because they accepted this prophetic proclamation,
they were among the blessed poor to whom the Kingdom belonged.

In the narrative, too, we find that aspect of the "rich"
consisting of acceptance by men and power exemplified by the
Pharisees. They are the leaders of the people who justify
themselves and are well spoken of by men (16:15), and who scorn
the others, especially the sinners and tax-collectors (15:1-3,
18:9). In contrast to the sinners and tax-collectors, they
have refused the word and baptism of John, rejecting thereby
God's plan for them (7:30), and are now rejecting the prophet
Jesus (7:36ff, 13:31ff, 19:39). It is this context of the
rejection of the prophet which makes intelligible the otherwise
obscure characterization of the Pharisees as φιλάργυροι
(16:14),[1] a description which historically was more applicable
to the tax-collectors than to the Pharisees.[2] Just as the
tax-collectors are among the "poor" because they are outcasts
and accept the prophet, so are the Pharisees money-lovers

[1]Cf. above, p. 109, and Dupont, Beatitudes III, 62-63.

[2]This is not to suggest that there were no covetous
scribes and Pharisees. Cf. the references in Str-B IV, 336ff,
and J. Jeremias, Jerusalem in the Time of Jesus 3rd rev. ed.
Trans. by F. H. and C. H. Cave (Philadelphia: Fortress Press,
1967) 114-115. But the rapacity of tax-collectors was notorious (Jeremias, Jerusalem, 310-311), and the charge against the
Pharisees appears motivated by more than historical reminiscence.

because they are accepted by men and reject the prophet.

      6. Our analysis leads to the following conclusions:
1) The use of the terms rich and poor in Luke's Gospel go
beyond the designation of economic circumstances to express
conditions of powerlessness and power, being outcast by men or
accepted by men. 2) The preaching of the Gospel to the poor
and the proclamation of woes to the rich signify that by God's
visitation in the Prophet Jesus, these conditions are reversed,
that the outcast are called to salvation and the men who enjoy
present acceptance are to be rejected. 3) In the working out
of the narrative, the poor are to be found in those who respond
to the prophet, particularly the sinners and tax-collectors.
4) In the narrative, the rich are found in those who reject the
prophet, the leaders and particularly the Pharisees and Scribes.
5) We conclude therefore that there is not only a formal
parallel between the thematic statements concerning rich and
poor and the literary pattern of the prophet and the people,
but also a meshing at the level of content. The expressions
rich and poor function within the story as metaphorical expressions for those rejected and accepted because of their response
to the prophet.

      7. We will now test these conclusions by an analysis
of the Lukan parable of Lazarus and the Rich Man (16:19-31).
As with the other parables to be considered later in this
chapter, our considerations here must exclude any peripheral
questions[1] and focus upon the distinctively Lukan handling of
the passage, which means in effect, to see how he uses this
parable within his story.[2] Our study of Luke 9-19 in the last

---

[1]For the discussion of whether an earlier Egyptian tale
(found also in Rabbinic versions) was used, cf. Percy, Die
Botschaft Jesu, 93ff; Jeremias, Parables, 183ff; C. Evans,
"Uncomfortable Words--V," ExpT 81 (1969-70), 229-230. The
Lukan language and style in the story have been analyzed by
Dupont, Beatitudes III, 173ff.

[2]Among recent attempts to deal with the redactional framework of chapter 16 as a whole, cf. Dupont, Beatitudes III,
162ff; Degenhardt, Lukas, 113ff; F. Danker, "Luke 16:16--An
Opposition Logion," JBL 77 (1958) 231-243; J. Derrett, "Fresh
Light on St. Luke XVI. I. The Parable of the Unjust Steward,"
and "II. Dives and Lazarus and the Preceding Sayings," NTS 7
(1960-1) 198-219 and 364-380.

chapter revealed that from 15:1 to 17:1 the literary pattern of
contrast between the disciples and the opponents was drawn
particularly sharp.[1] In response to the attacks of the Pharisees because he welcomes tax-collectors and sinners (15:1-3)
Jesus tells the three parables of "the lost." He then turns to
the disciples (16:1) and tells the story of the unjust steward
(16:1-8), to which are appended a series of sayings (16:9-13)
concerning the use of possessions. The mocking of the money-
loving Pharisees (16:14) is directed against all these sayings,
but in particular the final one, in which Jesus states emphatically the impossibility of serving both God and Mammon (16:13).
As we have pointed out, this rejection is not only of the
prophet's words; the Pharisees reject Him (ἐξεμυκτήριζον αὐτόν,
16:14). Jesus' response to this mocking follows the typical
Lukan pattern: those who reject the prophet are themselves
rejected by God. The self-justifying Pharisees are known by
God, and they are βδέλυγμα ἐνώπιον τοῦ θεοῦ (16:15).[2]

In this context, the suggestion that Jesus in v. 16 mouths
what was originally a protest of the Pharisees is appealing,
but ultimately unproveable.[3] The talk about Law in these
verses remains puzzling.[4] Its function appears to be, however,
to point forward to the next parable. The true introduction
to the story of Lazarus and the Rich Man is this dispute about
the keeping of the Law between Jesus and the Pharisees. The
Pharisees claim to be the keepers and defenders of the Law.
Jesus characterizes their attitude as that of hypocrisy (16:15).
They do not observe the Law and the Prophets, for as the
following story will make clear, they do not observe the laws
of almsgiving. The parable of Lazarus and the Rich Man has as
its focus this dispute. When the parable ends, the dispute is
over, and Jesus once more turns to the disciples (17:1).

---

[1]Cf. above, pp. 109-110.

[2]Cf. Degenhardt, Lukas, 132; W. Foerster, "βδελύσσομαι,"
TDNT 1 (1964) 598-600.

[3]Cf. Danker, "Opposition Logion," 236. The opinion of
Degenhardt, Lukas, 132, that Luke had in mind contemporary
opponents of the Church lacks any foundation.

[4]Dupont, Beatitudes III, 167.

142

The characters of the parable correspond to the categories of the thematic statements. They are simply τις πλούσιος and τις πτωχός, the name of the latter not having any particular significance for the story.[1] No moral attributes are given to either directly. In every respect they appear as examples, as types.[2] The movement of the first part of the story is that of a dramatic reversal of fortunes, and in that respect reaches a satisfying conclusion in vv. 25-26. The man who enjoyed τά ἀγαθά in his earthly life is now tormented; the man who had only τά κακά, ὧδε παρακαλεῖται in the Bosom of Abraham (v. 25). To this point, the parable is a perfect illustration of the first beatitude and woe. The man who had his παράκλησις in this life is deprived (cf. 6:24), and the poor man enjoys the metaphoric expression for the Kingdom (6:20), being in the bosom of Abraham. There is no moralism here; simply the Divine reversal.

The situation becomes more complicated when the rich man pleads for his brothers (v. 27ff). Now there is found the implication that there is a reason for the reversal. The man had not only been rich during his life, but also hard of heart. His wealth had made him insensitive to the demands of the Law and the Prophets that he give alms to the poor. The concrete expression of this rejection of the Law and Prophets was his ignoring of the poor man sitting at his gate. This implication is expressed by v. 29, ἔχουσι Μωϋσέα καί τούς προφήτας. ἀκουσάτωσαν αὐτῶν (the rich man also had these guides the

---

[1]Jeremias, Parables, 183, and Derrett, "Dives and Lazarus," 371, claim that the etymology of Lazarus' name, "God helps," is of special significance in the story, but it is doubtful Luke knew of that significance.

[2]The description of the poor man is interesting, however, in that he is not only poor, but also apparently a cripple (ἐβέβλητο) a leper (εἱλκωμένος) and hungry (ἐπιθυμῶν χορτασθῆναι). His being licked by dogs is not a sentimental touch, but a sign of his outcast condition. Luke has combined in this description elements from his lists of 6:21; 7:22; 14:13 and 21. Dupont, Beatitudes III, 174, notes that these elements contrast point by point the description of the rich man, so that there is here a miniature reflection of the contrast found in the beatitudes. Percy, Die Botschaft Jesu, 94-95, considers that already in the description of both is found a moral judgment against the rich man, for by the logic of the story, he could not have failed to notice the needy man.

heeding of whom, we understand, would have saved him from his fate) and by the expression in the beginning of the story that the poor man ἐπιθυμῶν χορτασθῆναι ἀπὸ τῶν πιπτόντων ἀπὸ τῆς τραπέζης τοῦ πλουσίου ἀλλὰ καὶ οἱ κύνες ἐρχόμενοι ἐπέλειχον τὰ ἕλκη αὐτοῦ (16:21). By rejecting the poor man, the rich man rejected as well the Law and the Prophets. Luke pictures his situation and that of his brothers as hopeless. The rich man himself admits that his brothers are so locked in their attitude that they cannot heed the Scriptures and convert (16:30), and the final words of the parable seal their rejection: even if someone should come back from the dead to warn them, they would not listen (16:31).

The parable therefore is one of rejection. By having Jesus tell this parable to the Pharisees whom he has characterized as φιλάργυροι, Luke makes the parable pertain immediately to their rejection. As the rich man had scorned the demands of the Law and the Prophets to give alms, so the Pharisees reject the teaching of the living Prophet Jesus on almsgiving (16:9-13).[1] In spite of their claim to hold to the literal demands of the Law, they reject the outcasts (15:1-3), just as the rich man rejected the outcast Lazarus. As the rich man was rejected from a place in the Kingdom, so are the Pharisees. The utter hopelessness of their situation is intended in the saying about one rising from the dead. The reader cannot miss here the reference to the resurrection of Jesus,[2] who would be rejected by the leaders once again in their rejection of the words of the Apostles.

---

[1] In the light of this, it is perhaps significant that in 11:39-40, Luke inserts into the attack on the Pharisees a charge not shared by Matt 23:25f. To the Pharisees' concern with ritual purity, Jesus contrasts the need to give alms with the clear implication that they do not: ἄφρονες οὐχ ὁ ποιήσας τὸ ἔξωθεν καὶ τὸ ἔσωθεν ἐποίησεν; πλὴν τὰ ἐνόντα δότε ἐλεημοσύνην καὶ ἰδοὺ πάντα καθαρὰ ὑμῖν ἐστιν (11:40). Luke uses ἄφρων only here and in the story of the rich fool. We should note also that this verse contains an element we shall find elsewhere in Luke's thought: the implied relationship between the internal disposition of the heart and the external disposition of possessions. Luke 20:47 also shares with Mk 12:40 the charge that the Scribes devoured the houses of widows.

[2] Evans, "Uncomfortable Words," 230.

The Lukan placement of the parable of Lazarus and the Rich
Man therefore brings into sharp focus how he uses the motif of
the rich and the poor to symbolize the pattern of the Prophet
and the People. He has made this story about the rejection of
the rich apply directly and unmistakeably to the rejection of
those leaders who reject the Prophet Jesus.

B. The Role of Possessions in Response to God's Visitation

Luke speaks about possessions most frequently in contexts
that are intrinsically dramatic, those of crisis and response.
The forms of the crisis vary (calls to discipleship, invita-
tions, eschatological dangers, the death of an individual), and
we are admittedly coloring the situation by calling all of them
"visitations" of God. Yet this expression, which is so
characteristic for the pattern of the Prophet and the People,
does not distort the picture, for although all these crises are
not directly attached to the response to Jesus, many of them
are, and those that are not are found to exhibit the same
pattern. From the frequency with which Luke uses the language
of possessions to describe what is happening in such situations,
we can only conclude that he found it a particularly congenial
imagery. In analyzing these passages, we are interested both
in the way Luke uses possessions to express the dynamic of
acceptance and rejection, and how the language of possessions
expresses the interior disposition of the one who responds
either positively or negatively. We shall begin by considering
two sets of passages which continue the pattern developed above,
that is, where the language about possessions is directly
connected with the literary pattern of the Prophet and the
People.

1. The Call of the Rich Man to Discipleship
(18:18-30) is found also in Matt 19:16-30 and Mk 10:17-30, and
Luke's account is substantially the same as the parallels.
Even the Lukan placement of the story after the blessing of
the children (18:15-17) appears to follow Matt and Mk so that
the story of the Rich Man appears as a contrast to the reception of the Kingdom ὡς παιδίον (18:17).[1] Two factors, however,

---

[1]Cf. Dupont, Beatitudes II, 161-181.

make Luke's story perform a much sharper literary function, a
small but important redactional change within the account and
the wider context in which it is placed.

a) In Luke's account the rich man is not a
youth, as in Matt 19:20, nor is there a positive response of
Jesus to the man, as in Mk 10:21. Rather, Luke identifies the
man explicitly as an ἄρχων, that is, as a ruler of the people.[1]
Further, his initial question and his response to Jesus' first
demand show that he considers himself among the just, one of
the pious.

b) Within the pattern of contrasts employed by
Luke in the journey to Jerusalem, therefore, the encounter with
the rich man is a confrontation with an opponent, a leader of
the people. The leader who has proven himself pious by the
keeping of the commandments, but who is so wealthy that he
cannot respond to Jesus' call to sell all that he has and give
to the poor and follow Him, is therefore pictured consistently
with Luke's presentation of the leaders elsewhere as being
φιλάργυροι and not givers of alms, that is, among the rich.
It is furthermore a direct example of the rejection of the
prophet by a rich leader of the people.

c) Jesus' concluding words τὰ ἀδύνατα παρὰ
ἀνθρώποις δυνατὰ παρὰ τῷ θεῷ (v. 27) lead to the positive
contrast provided by the disciples. Possessions in themselves
do not fatally hinder a response to God's call, for Peter and
those with him have left τὰ ἴδια to follow Jesus. This particular contrast to the rich man has already been provided by
the parallels (Matt 19:27ff, Mk 10:28ff). Within Luke's overall pattern in this section of the Gospel, of course, it
appears as one more contrast between leaders and disciples.
But Luke has placed another story in 19:1-10 which presents
an even stronger contrast. The ἀρχιτελώνης Zaccheus was like
the ἄρχων, πλούσιος. But he received the Prophet into his
house, and with a spontaneous gesture of conversion gave half
his possessions to the poor and repaid those he had cheated
fourfold. He who was, like Peter, a sinner, one of the "lost,"

---

[1] Contra Cadbury, The Style and Literary Method of Luke,
79, the change is deliberate and significant. Cf. Dupont,
Beatitudes III, 155.

was able to respond to the prophet's visitation positively
whereas the rich, pious leader could not.

2. The Parable of the Great Banquet (14:15-24) is,
in spite of the obvious similarities, a story with quite a
different point than Matt 22:1-10.[1] In Luke the story hinges
around the refusal of the first invited to respond, and the
calling of the poor and outcast, who do respond. Besides providing a basis for the lesson on hospitality in 14:12ff,
therefore, the parable functions as a defense of the prophetic
mission of calling the poor, spoken before a hostile audience
(we recall that it is addressed to the Pharisees who were
testing Him, 14:1). In effect, the parable is one of rejection,
spoken to those who were rejecting Jesus (cf. 14:24).[2]

In both Matthew and Luke, the excuses for not attending
the banquet were involvements with the cares of life. But Luke
elaborates these excuses more than Matthew. The first man
bought a field and had to go see to it (14:18); a second had
purchased five yoke of oxen (a wealthy man, indeed!), and had
to go test them (14:19); the third had just married, and so
could not come. It seems clear that these excuses are modelled
on the causes for exemption from the Holy War listed in Deut
20:5-7,[3] but the characteristic aspect of the Lukan treatment
of the excuses is their involving quality. Those invited are
so entangled by, so preoccupied with their acquisitions
(property and wife) that they are deaf to the call.

Following the pattern of contrasts in this section of his
work, Luke then has Jesus turn immediately to the crowd (14:25)
and address to them the demands of discipleship. The parable

---

[1]Jeremias, Parables, 64-65, 67-68; also the version in the
Gospel of Thomas, 64.

[2]Jeremias, Parables, 179-180; also O. Glombitza, "Das
Grosse Abendmahl:Lk. XIV 12-24," NovT 5 (1962) 10-16.

[3]These were excused from the Holy War: ὁ ἄνθρωπος ὁ
οἰκοδομήσας οἰκίαν καινήν; ὁ ἄνθρωπος ὅστις ἐφύτευσεν ἀμπελῶνα;
ὁ ἄνθρωπος ὅστις μεμνήστευται γυναῖκα (Deut 20:5-7); in addition, those who were fearful or cowardly (20:8). Cf. J.
Derrett, Law in the New Testament (London: Darton, Longman and
Todd, 1970) 126-153, who regards the parable as a midrash on
Zeph 1:16 in the light of these Deuteronomic prescriptions.

of the banquet pictured the rejection of those too involved
with possessions to heed God's call and was addressed to those
Luke has termed money-lovers, the Pharisees. But for the crowd
there is still a chance for repentance, still a call to discipleship, which is no less a manifestation of God's visitation.
It is interesting that the first and third demands of discipleship correspond to the excuses for not answering the call to
the banquet. Corresponding to the excuse of marriage, v. 26
demands that a man "hate" all those close to him, renounce all
significant human relationships, including τὴν γυναῖκα to
follow Jesus. The third demands the renunciation of possessions: whoever οὐκ ἀποτάσσεται πᾶσιν τοῖς ἑαυτοῦ ὑπάρχουσιν οὐ
δύναται εἶναί μου μαθητής (14:33).[1]

By attaching these sayings to the parable of the banquet,
Luke has not only established a literary connection between
them; he has again effectively symbolized the pattern of the
acceptance and rejection of the Prophet through the language
of possessions. Involvement with possessions and relationships
caused the rejection of the invitation and led to the rejection
of those invited; this is addressed to the Pharisees who are
rejecting Jesus even as he sits at table with them (14:1). To
those still able to follow Him, Jesus gives the demands of
rejecting relationships and possessions. The dramatic impact
of this is evident. Jesus' call to discipleship is thereby
colored by the call of God to the eschatological banquet; it
too is a visitation of God. And behind the call to discipleship looms the threat of rejection for those who like the
Pharisees are too involved with possessions to acknowledge the
invitation.[2]

_____

[1]The οὕτως resumes the whole passage, including the two
small parables of the tower, and the king who goes to war
(14:28-32), the point of each being the need to respond
adequately to the demand of the call, which in this case
leads to the cross (v. 27). Cf. Degenhardt, Lukas, 109-112.

[2]A similar pattern might be found in the calling of the
would-be disciples (9:57-62), if the excuse offered in the
last, uniquely Lukan encounter could be seen as referring to
possessions (reading the τοῖς of ἀποτάξασθαι τοῖς εἰς τὴν
οἶκόν μου as neuter). Most commentators, however (Easton,
Luke, 155; Grundmann, Lukas, 206; Loisy, Luc, 289; Klostermann,
Lukas, 475), regard it as referring to family relationships,

148

3. In a series of passages not as immediately
related to the pattern of the Prophet and the People, but
demonstrating the same literary dynamic of acceptance and
rejection, Luke's penchant for using language about possessions
to symbolize those responses remains constant. These passages
share two features. They all are about a crisis situation
which demands a response, and in all of them possessions
symbolize either the negative or positive responses to that
crisis. Negatively, possessions function as a sign of alienation; a man is so preoccupied with them and with trying to
secure his life by their means, that his response to the
crisis is inhibited. Positively, possessions are a sign of
conversion; by selling possessions and giving alms, a man
shows that he is responding to God's visitation. In both
cases, Luke sees the way a man handles possessions as an indication, a symbol, of his interior disposition.

           a) The Days of Noah and Lot (17:22ff). This
eschatological discourse is addressed to the disciples after
the rejection of the Pharisees' question about the coming of
the Kingdom (17:20-21). Luke 17:26-27 shares with Matt 24:37-
41 a comparison of the days of the Son of Man to the days of
Noah. As things were in the time of that cataclysm, so will
they be when the Son of Man comes. The activities of men in
the days of Noah are said to be eating and drinking and
marrying and being given in marriage, up to the final moment.
When the cataclysm came, ἀπώλεσεν πάντας (17:27).[1] The visitation caught them by surprise. They were so involved with the
affairs of life that they were deaf to their impending doom,
and so were destroyed together with all their activities.

___

on analogy with Mk 6:46, and this would fit better the allusion
to the call of Elisha in I Kings 19:20. In either case, the
candidate's problem is involvement, which inhibits his response.
Luke's view of riches as stifling is reflected in his version
of the explanation of the parable of the sower (8:11-15), in
which riches are not described as deceitful (as in Matt 13:22
and Mk 4:19), but are included among the μεριμνῶν καὶ ἡδονῶν
τοῦ βίου. The use of the passive συμπνίγονται may also enhance
somewhat the impression of riches as smothering.

[1]The ἀπώλεσεν πάντας in both similes is Lukan. Matt 24:39
has ἦρεν ἅπαντας.

But Luke adds another comparison (17:28ff) not found in Matt. The coming of the Son of Man will be like the situation in Sodom in the days of Lot, when men ἤσθιον ἔπινον ἠγόραζον ἐπώλουν ἐφύτευον ᾠκοδόμουν. The distinctively Lukan preoccupation is evident here. To the involving activities of the previous simile, Luke has added four activities dealing with possessions, buying, selling, planting, building.[1] When the cataclysm came, ἀπώλεσεν πάντας. The repetition of this phrase effectively sets the stage for the following presentation of the attitudes proper for those who are faced with the crisis of the coming of the Son of Man. They are not to come down from the roof to save a vessel, nor if they are in the field are they to turn back to the house for things left behind.[2] This instruction is found in Matt 24:17-18 and Mk 13:15-16, but Luke has placed it in a unique context, for he explicitly attaches this command to the example he alone has cited: μνημονεύετε τῆς γυναικὸς Λώτ (17:32). She was the one who "turned back" and so lost her very life. By the placement of this reminder, Luke apparently intends us to understand that her "looking back" was to save the things she had left behind in her flight. Trying to save those possessions, she lost her life. The point is brought out explicitly in the following saying (17:33) which is a variant of Lk 9:24 peculiarly suited to this context:[3] ὃς ἐὰν ζητήσῃ τὴν ψυχὴν αὐτοῦ περιποιήσασθαι ἀπολέσει αὐτὴν ὃς δ᾿ ἂν ἀπολέσῃ ζωογονήσει αὐτήν. Luke's use of περιποιέω here is particularly intriguing. It can mean simply "preserve" or "save," but the word has such strong associations with acquiring, grasping and hoarding possessions,[4] that we are led, especially in the context established by Luke, to understand the phrase as "whoever seeks to 'possess' his life" precisely

---

[1]Thereby rounding out again as in 14:18-20 and 14:26-33 the pattern of involving activities: relationships and possessions.

[2]The μὴ ἐπιστρέψατο εἰς τὰ ὀπίσω recalls the ἐπιστρέψον μοι . . . βλέπων εἰς τὰ ὀπίσω of 9:61-62.

[3]Cf. also Matt 16:25; Mk 8:35.

[4]Cf. the references under περιποιέω in Liddell-Scott, Greek-English Lexicon (Oxford: Clarendon Press, 1925); also Lagrange, Luc, 466.

in the sense of securing by means of possessions, or to hold as a possession. This passage shows, first, how congenial Luke found the language of possessions for expressing response to a crisis. The possessions imagery in this passage is entirely due to his redaction. Second, the passage highlights dramatically the negative function of possessions as inhibiting a response to God's visitation. Third, we see established a correlation between the "self" and "possessions." In this case, the hoarding or seeking of possessions is equated with trying to preserve the self. The result is the loss of both possessions and the self.[1]

   b) The Strong Man (11:21-22). This very short simile adds another small touch to the Lukan preoccupation with possessions. The story (cf. also Matt 12:29-30, Mk 3:37) is part of Jesus' response to his critics who charged He was casting out demons in the name of Beelzebul,[2] and is meant to demonstrate that if the power of the demon is being destroyed, then a still stronger force, that of God Himself, is at work in the ministry of Jesus.[3] Matt and Mk make the comparison swiftly: if anyone wishes to plunder the goods of a strong man, he must himself be strong enough to overcome him before he can go about his business. But Luke's version tells the story from the point of view of the man guarding the house, and shows a marked interest in the relationship of this strong man

---

[1]The entangling or burdening effect of possessions is also intimated in the three verses Luke adds to another eschatological discourse, 21:34-36. Those who must confront the terrors to come must not let their hearts be burdened either by pleasures or μερίμναις βιωτικαῖς, lest they be caught unaware. Rather, they are to be watchful and praying, with enough freedom of movement to flee (ἐκφυγεῖν), and to stand erect before the Son of Man.

[2]It must be admitted that Luke does not specify the identity of Jesus' opponents here as sharply as either Matt 12:24 (Pharisees) or Mk 3:22 (Scribes from Jerusalem). In Luke they are simply some from the crowd (v. 25 together with v. 14). This is a case, therefore, in which the pattern of opposition described in chapter two of this study is less evident. It is, however, a context of hostility toward Jesus.

[3]Cf. C. H. Dodd, The Parables of the Kingdom (London: Nisbet, 1935), 123f; cf. also W. Grundmann, "ἰσχύω," TDNT 3 (1965) 399-401, who sees in the parable an allusion to Is 53:12.

to his possessions.[1] Here we see the strong man, armed to the
hilt (καθωπλισμένος), guarding not just a house but a palace
(αὐλήν); he is therefore a wealthy man. Because he is armed,
because he is guarding them, he considers his possessions to
be ἐν εἰρήνῃ. The possessions being "at peace" stands as a
symbol of the man's control over his situation; he is "at
peace." But when the stronger one breaks in he strips the man
of the armour on which he had depended, and disperses his
treasure (11:22). The scattering of the possessions symbolizes
the man's loss of control, the scattering of his own power over
his house. The ἐφ' ᾗ ἐπεποίθει is a subtle touch. The strong
man did not really have the intrinsic strength to withstand the
attack. He and his possessions were from the beginning vulner-
able. He had to rely on something outside himself (his armour)
to protect what was outside himself (his riches). Too much
weight should not be placed on this lively little story, but it
demonstrates how in a story which is not really about possessions but about power, Luke not only shows interest in possessions, but expresses the dynamic of the story by having the
fate of the possessions at each stage reflect the condition of
the possessor.

        c) An atmosphere of crisis and fear also colors
the extended treatment of possessions in chapter 12:22ff.
These sayings are addressed to the disciples and are introduced
by the saying on avarice (12:15) and the parable of the Rich
Fool (12:16-21), both addressed to the crowd. Once more, the
content of the sayings is to be understood in the light of the
story within which Luke has placed them. Luke has placed these
sayings in a context of conflict and division, in which the
distinction between the followers of Jesus and the opponents is
particularly clear.

    In 11:37-52, Luke has Jesus denounce the Pharisees and the
Lawyers. His attacks on them result in their actively seeking

---

[1]In Matt 12:29 and Mk 3:27 the fate of the σκεύη is
incidental; the taking of the house is essential. So, too,
the Gospel of Thomas, 35. An excellent analysis of the Lukan
treatment of this passage can be found in S. Legasse, "'L'Homme
Fort' de Luc XI 21-22," NovT 5 (1962) 5-9.

152

to entrap him (11:53).[1] Once more, the Lukan pattern: the
prophetic word stimulates latent hostility toward the prophet
into active rejection.   Luke notes in 12:1 that a huge crowd
thronged around Jesus, but his words are addressed to the
disciples.   The disciples are to avoid the leaven of the
Pharisees which is hypocrisy.   Thus the completion of the
pattern: those who reject the prophet are to be rejected from
the people that is being formed around Him.

The note of threat and active persecution directed at
Jesus introduced by 11:53 color the subsequent sayings addressed to the disciples (12:4-12).   Jesus' fate of being rejected
by men will be shared by them, and he instructs them in the
proper attitudes for this crisis.   We notice the elements of
fear and anxiety which permeate these sayings.   The disciples
are not to fear (μὴ φοβηθῆτε) the men who can only kill them
(12:4) but to fear God (12:5).   When they are brought before
synagogues in judgment, they are not to be anxious (μὴ
μεριμνήσητε) about what to say, for the Spirit will instruct
them (12:11-12).[2]   Now if we look at the sayings which follow
the instructions on possessions, we see the element of crisis
and division continuing.   Jesus is to be the cause of division,
turning even members of the same family against each other
(12:49-53).

Luke has therefore effectively placed the paraenesis on
possessions within the context of crisis dominating this part
of the story.   From 11:53, the Pharisees are actively seeking
to do away with Jesus.   The instructions given to the disciples
serve to emphasize their share in the rejection of Jesus, to

---

[1]The dramatic coloration this verse gives to the following
passages and in particular the subsequent encounters with the
Pharisees (especially 13:31ff, and 14:1ff), is important.
After this open rupture Jesus' meetings with the Pharisees are
not neutral, but hostile.   Gaston, No Stone on Another, 324,
correctly notes the eschatological tone given to the possessions sayings of ch. 12 by this context.

[2]The promise of 12:12 is fulfilled in Acts 4:8 and 5:32.
The saying on blasphemy against the Holy Spirit is particularly
important for understanding the implications of the rejection
of the Apostles' word.   In the time of the second rejection,
the refusal to hear the voice of the Prophet (through whom the
Spirit speaks) leads to final and definitive rejection.   Cf.
Brown, Apostasy and Perseverence, 107ff.

separate them from the opponents, and to prepare them for the
crisis. We shall note that in the sayings on possessions, the
same concerns are manifested: how to deal with fear and
anxiety and how to view possessions in a context of threat to
one's very life.

The instructions of Jesus to the disciples are interrupted
by a question from the crowd (12:13). In the context of tribu-
lation and rejection which Luke has established, the request
made to Jesus that he be an arbiter in a land dispute[1] appears
trivial and offensive,[2] and effectively sets the stage for
instructing the disciples on the proper attitude towards
possessions. The saying: ὁρᾶτε καὶ φυλάσσεσθε ἀπὸ πάσης
πλεονεξίας ὅτι οὐκ ἐν τῷ περισσεύειν τινὶ ἡ ζωὴ αὐτοῦ ἐστιν
ἐκ τῶν ὑπαρχόντων αὐτῷ acts as a thematic statement for the
whole subsequent development. Possessions are what men use to
preserve their life, to gain security against threat. But
Jesus rejects this. The "self" is not secured by possessions,
and there is no correspondence between an increase in possessions and the state of a man's life. The parable of the Rich
Fool illustrates this dramatically.

The story of the Rich Fool is straightforward.[3] The man
is rich because he has so many ἀγαθά he doesn't have room to
store everything. He is a fool (ἄφρων)[4] because he thinks that
once he has all his goods tidily stored away (like those of the
strong man, ἐν εἰρήνῃ), his ψυχή will be secured and he can
live the good life. But for all his planning, he has not
reckoned on the cataclysm; that very night he will lose his
life (12:20). The question ἃ δὲ ἡτοίμασας τίνι ἔσται; is
delicately phrased, but forceful. The loss of the ψυχή is the
loss of everything. This story reminds us in several ways of

[1]The question, and the first part of Jesus' answer, but
not the second, are found detached from the parable of the rich
fool in the Gospel of Thomas, 72.

[2]Jeremias, Parables, 165.

[3]It is present in an even starker form in the Gospel of
Thomas, 72.

[4]Jeremias, Parables, 165, regards the use of "fool" here
as the same as in Ps 14:1, that is, as a description of a man
who by his way of living denies the existence of God.

that of the strong man, particularly in the view of possessions
as fragile, as arousing false security and requiring constant
preoccupation. As in that story, too, we find here the disposition of the possessions signifying the condition of the
possessor at each stage of the story. The man at first is
concerned about securing his life: the possessions are stored
in barns. The man at the end is "lost"; the possessions are
scattered, who knows where? The moral appended to the story in
12:21: οὕτως ὁ θησαυρίζων ἑαυτῷ καὶ μὴ εἰς θεὸν πλουτῶν
suggests that the Rich Fool's is not the only way, that
possessions can be used in order to "secure one's place"
before God.[1]

Jesus now turns to the disciples (12:22) with positive
instructions concerning possessions. The sayings are paralleled by Matt 6:25-34, 19-21, but have in Luke a particular
emphasis because of their placement within the story. The
essence of the teaching is found in 22-23: μὴ μεριμνᾶτε τῇ
ψυχῇ τί φάγητε μηδὲ τῷ σώματι τί ἐνδύσησθε. ἡ γὰρ ψυχὴ πλεῖόν
ἐστιν τῆς τροφῆς καὶ τὸ σῶμα τοῦ ἐνδύματος. The reader cannot
fail to see the connection between the "Don't worry" here and
in the context of persecution in 12:11, nor the strength given
to the distinction between possessions and the "self" by Jesus'
saying in 12:15. The self is not only superior to whatever can
be used to support or nourish it, but as the following verses
show, the attempt to secure more of life by possessions is in
any case futile (25-26). How then is the self secured? πλὴν
ζητεῖτε τὴν βασιλείαν αὐτοῦ καὶ ταῦτα προστεθήσεται ὑμῖν (v.
31). It is by the response of seeking God's Kingdom that one's
life is secured and all that is needful for life is gained.

Luke now adds a saying not found in Matthew, which is
clearly related to the earlier sayings in ch. 12 (cf. 12:4):
μὴ φοβοῦ, τὸ μικρὸν ποίμνιον, ὅτι εὐδόκησεν ὁ πατὴρ ὑμῶν
δοῦναι ὑμῖν τὴν βασιλείαν (v. 32). This is an advance over
the previous statement about the Kingdom. They are not only
to seek it; it has in fact been given to them. The relation
to 6:20 here is clear. The reason why Jesus' disciples need
not fear (need not therefore cling to possessions in the

---

[1]Cf. Degenhardt, Lukas, 78-79; Lagrange, Luc, 360.

tribulations coming as a result of their association with
Jesus) is that they already possess the Kingdom. Their lives
are already secure. Indeed, because of this most fundamental
security, they are able to give away their possessions. Again
in a uniquely Lukan saying: πωλήσατε τὰ ὑπάρχοντα ὑμῶν καὶ
δότε ἐλεημοσύνην (v. 33). Luke here introduces the positive
use of possessions as a sign of response to the gift of the
Kingdom. It has two movements: separation from possessions
and the bestowal of them on others.[1] In contrast to the fool
who stored up treasure for himself but lost his life, this
giving of alms is the way of being rich towards God, of
establishing a sure treasure in heaven (v. 33). The next
verse, though found also in Matt 6:21, corresponds so well
with what we have seen in Luke's own presentation that we can
accept it unhesitatingly as representing his own view: "where
your treasure is, there also your heart will be," (v. 34). If
a man's heart is centered on his earthly possessions, he will
be incapable of responding to God's visitation; if his heart is
centered on the Kingdom, he will give away his possessions and
find his treasure with God. In both responses, the disposition
of possessions is a sign of the response of the heart to God.

The following section (12:35-38) should not be seen as
introducing a new development but as a continuation of the same
argument. Found only in Luke, the verses give an explicit
eschatological coloration to the teachings on possessions we
have just considered. Being free from the preoccupations and
false security associated with possessions and expressing his
response to the Kingdom by the giving of alms, a man is ready
for the coming of his Lord (v. 35). As in the eschatological
discourse of ch. 21, we see that the proper attitude is one of
alertness, watching, which is made possible by a freedom from
possessions: μακάριοι οἱ δοῦλοι ἐκεῖνοι οὓς ἐλθὼν ὁ κύριος
εὑρήσει γρηγοροῦντας (12:37). Again a macarism applied to
those whose stance is that of the poor, those responsive to

---

[1]Apart from some general statements on giving (Lk 6:29-30,
37-38 = Matt 5:40; 7:38), Luke presents almsgiving as a
response to conversion in the Gospel. Thus, the commands of
John to those who asked him τί οὖν ποιήσωμεν (3:10-11), the
demand made of the rich ruler (18:22), and the spontaneous
response of Zaccheus (19:8).

God's visitation. The passage pictures the Lord ministering to
his servants; we shall return to this striking image and the
peculiar Lukan redaction of vv. 41-48 later in this chapter.

        d) The role of possessions in responding to a
crisis also characterizes the third and most difficult of the
uniquely Lukan parables dealing directly with possessions, the
parable of the Dishonest Steward (16:1-8). The difficulty of
interpreting this parable, especially in relation to the sayings appended to it (16:9-13) is notorious, and has given rise
to the most divergent opinions regarding the true significance
of the parable.[1] The following remarks can be offered, while
acknowledging their necessarily tentative nature.

    The Steward's trouble began by the way he used possessions;
the goods which belonged to his master, and over which he had
charge, he scattered, wasted (16:1). When his master finds
out, the crisis begins. He is called to account (16:2). It is
important to stress the crisis character of the story, for it
is the Steward's ability to respond to this crisis (literally a
visitation of his lord) which forms the point of the story, the
reason for the master's admiration and the example for the
disciples. The steward is praised for being so φρονίμως (16:8)
in a bad situation. His cleverness consisted in continuing to
disperse possessions (by the reduction of the amounts owed).
But this time the dispersal does not effect his rejection (the
loss of his position) as it had in the first instance but his
acceptance by those new friends from which he can expect a quid
pro quo (16:4).

    There are two morals directly attached to the story. The
first centers on the cleverness of the response itself; the
Sons of Light should be as adept in their response to God's

---

[1]A representative sampling: G. Krüger, "Die geistesgeschichtlichen Grundlagen des Gleichnisses vom ungerechten
Verwalter," BZ 21 (1933) 170-181; A. Feuillet, "Les riches
intendents du Christ," RSR 34 (1947) 30-54; P. Gächter, "The
Parable of the Dishonest Steward after Oriental Conceptions,"
CBQ 12 (1950) 121-131; A. Descamps, "La composition littéraire
de Luc XVI 9-13," NovT 1 (1956) 47-53; J. Derrett, "Fresh Light
on Luke XVI. I: The Parable of the Unjust Steward," NTS 7
(1960) 198-219; J. Topel, "On the Injustice of the Unjust
Steward," CBQ 37 (1975) 216-227; Jeremias, Parables, 45-48;
Degenhardt, Lukas, 114-131; further references can be found in
Dupont, Beatitudes I, 107, n. 2.

visitation. The point of the comparison is clearly not the morality of the man's action, but the aptness of it.[1] The second moral flows from the first, but now picks up the use of possessions. As the steward used possessions to secure a place for himself, so should the disciples: ἑαυτοῖς ποιήσατε φίλους ἐκ τοῦ μαμωνᾶ τῆς ἀδικίας ἵνα ὅταν ἐκλίπη δέξωνται ὑμᾶς εἰς τὰς αἰωνίους σκηνάς (16:9).[2] (We might mention in passing that in the light of Acts 4:32ff, the idea of making "friends" through the sharing of possessions is an interesting combination.) The connection of v. 9 to v. 4 in any case, cannot be missed.[3] In the light of Luke's use of language elsewhere about laying up treasure in heaven (12:33), there can be no doubt that this saying refers to almsgiving.[4]

The precise understanding of the three sayings contained in vv. 10-12, in themselves, in relation to each other, and in relation to the story, is most difficult, even though their general import seems clear enough. In each of the sayings there is a contrast between the lesser and the greater. V. 11 specifies this in terms of possessions, and we are able to understand the lesser reality in each of the statements to refer to possessions and the greater to the disposition of the self before God.[5] Thus, possessions as such are lesser, though faithfulness in their handling indicates faithfulness in what is more important (v. 10). The failure to dispose of "wicked mammon" faithfully will lead to one's not being entrusted with what is genuine. If there is infidelity in regard to what is

---

[1]Cf. Feuillet, "Les riches intendents," 33; Jeremias, Parables, 46, n. 89.

[2]For the "eternal tabernacles," cf. Degenhardt, Lukas, 124; Feuillet, "Les riches intendents," 36-37; Jeremias, Parables, 46, nn. 85, 88. Descamps, "composition littéraire," 49, suggests that in the Lukan redaction (regarding v. 9 as composed by Luke) the "eternal tabernacles" look forward to the story of Lazarus.

[3]Dupont, Beatitudes I, 109; Jeremias, Parables, 46; Descamps, "composition littéraire," 49.

[4]Degenhardt, Lukas, 120ff.

[5]Cf. Feuillet, "Les riches intendents," 43-44. Krüger, "geistesgeschichtlichen Grundlagen," 181, has some good observations on the gl w 'mr mode of argumentation here.

essentially alien to the self--another's--what really belongs
to the self will not be given (v. 12). These sayings are
complex and even paradoxical. What emerges from them is the
sense that the disposition of possessions, while in some way
exterior to the self, less important than the self, even in
some degree unworthy of the self, is nevertheless of critical
importance for expressing the disposition of the self.

Luke concludes this teaching with a saying shared by Matt
6:24, that no man can serve two masters and that the disciples
must choose between service to God and service to Mammon
(16:13). This last saying reveals the profound seriousness
with which Luke regarded the use of possessions. "Mammon"
here becomes personified as an idol, the service of whom is
the rejection of God.[1] The way a man handles possessions, the
attitude he assumes towards possessions, is not irrelevant to
his inner response to God but expresses in the most vivid and
concrete manner the quality of that response. By giving away
his possessions in alms (v. 9), a man can use possessions to
express and indeed effect the saving of what is real and his
own, that is, his very self. But by clinging to possessions
which are themselves only transitory and unworthy of being the
center of a man's life, a man makes them an idol and shows himself to be rejecting the call of the Living God. As we have
pointed out earlier, it is this series of sayings, which in a
real sense penetrate to the heart of Luke's understanding of
the significance of possessions for the revelation of a man's
heart, that the money-loving Pharisees mock and reject.

C. Possessions as Metaphor for Human Relations

In the previous section, we found that Luke uses the
language of possessions with great frequency to express man's
response to God's Visitation. How a man disposes of his
possessions indicates the quality of that response, whether
it is one of accepting or rejecting God's presence in his life.
We have suggested that Luke's understanding of possessions is

---

[1]Cf. Dupont, Beatitudes III, 172; Degenhardt, Lukas, 128-
129. The personification of Mammon as an idol opposed to God
renders the characterization of the Pharisees as a βδέλυγμα in
16:15 all the sharper.

such that they can stand as a symbol of the state of a man's
heart before God.

We should note here emphatically, however, that we are not
suggesting that Luke has chosen possessions as a symbol simply
as an aesthetic device, or that the significance of possessions
for him is exhausted by their symbolic function. The opposite
would appear to be true. Luke takes with great seriousness
both the literal problem and opportunity presented by men's
actual use of and attitude towards possessions. He grasps the
literal power possessions exert in centering and dominating
men's lives. It is precisely this profound appreciation of the
literal role of possessions that enables Luke to perceive the
rich metaphoric possibilities to be found in the language of
possessions for expressing the conditions of men's hearts.

But have we yet shown that Luke uses this language metaphorically? We have shown that this is the case in the way the
thematic statements about rich and poor are expressed in the
narrative and in the way Luke has expressed the fate of the
protagonist in passages concerning the wife of Lot, the strong
man, the rich fool, and the dishonest steward by means of the
language of possessions. It still may be objected that these
instances reveal nothing more than a concern for possessions in
the literal sense, and that the patterns we have suggested are
simply coincidental.

For this reason, a consideration of the Story of the Lost
Son (15:11-32) is particularly important. The Lukan composition of the story as we now read it is clear.[1] We have already
pointed out in the last chapter the significance of the story
in its literary context.[2] At the most direct level of a human

---

[1]The studies of E. Schweizer, "Zur Frage der Lukasquellen,
Analyze von Luk. 15,11-32," TZ 4 (1948) 460-471, and J.
Jeremias, "Zum Gleichnis vom verlorenen Sohn," TZ 5 (1949)
228-231, show, as so many studies of Lukan passages have done,
that the pericope contains a mix of semitisms and "good Greek."
Jeremias sees semitisms throughout, but Schweizer only in a few
verses; Schweizer sees the non-semitic verses as Lukan composition, Jeremias the whole pericope from a source. The passage
is, in a word, typically Lukan, and as we shall see, at least
in one particular, the thought and language can be attributed
to Luke without much doubt.

[2]Cf. above, pp. 109-110.

story, the passage is "about" the departure and return of a son
to his father and the jealousy of the older son. Through the
story the attitudes of both sons, and more importantly, the
father, are revealed.[1] At the level of "Gospel," the story is
about the merciful love of God toward those who are lost, and
stands as a defense of the Good News against those who would
restrict God's mercy to the just.[2] At the level of Luke's
Gospel, the story also functions to criticize the opponents of
Jesus, the Scribes and Pharisees, who had attacked his accessi-
bility for sinners and tax-collectors.[3] No one would claim
that the story is "about" possessions, or that Luke intended to
convey a particular lesson about possessions through the
story.[4] It is likely therefore that whatever is said about
possessions in the story flows not from any paraenetic intent,
but from the spontaneous understanding and instinctive literary
art of the author. There might have been any number of ways
for Luke to tell this story; that he did so in the way he did
shows something of his appreciation of the metaphorical
strength of possessions language.

We find that each stage of the story, that is to say, each
development in the relationship between father and sons, is
expressed through the imagery of possessions. In the beginning
the father and both sons were on the property together. The
first dramatic impulse in the story occurs when the younger son
asks for his μέρος τῆς οὐσίας (15:11), and the Father divides
the property (διεῖλεν αὐτοῖς τὸν βίον). The process of separation begins with the division of the property. The separation

---

[1]Cf. L. Cerfaux, "Trois réhabilitations dans l'Evangile,"
Recueil 2, 51-59.

[2]Cf. Dupont, Beatitudes II, 237ff.

[3]Jeremias, Parables, 131-132; K. Bornhäuser, Studien zum
Sondergut des Lukas (Gütersloh: C. Bertelsmann, 1934) 119ff.

[4]J. Derrett, "The Parable of the Prodigal Son," NTS 14
(1967) 56-74, discusses the legal aspects of the property
motif, but misses completely its symbolic significance within
the story. Cf. also K. Rengstorf, Die Re-Investitur des
Verlorenen Sohnes in der Gleichniserzählung Jesu Luk.15, 11-32
(Arbeitsgemeinschaft für Forschung des Landes Nordrheim-
Westfalen. Geisteswissenschaften 137; Köln: Westdeutscher
Verlag, 1967).

is further accentuated by the younger son's συναγαγὼν ἅπαντα
and going to another place (15:13). The dissoluteness of the
son, the beginning of his being "lost," is expressed by the way
he used his possessions: διεσκόρπισεν τὴν οὐσίαν αὐτοῦ ζῶν
ἀσώτως (15:13). And the beginning of his conversion comes with
his feeling need, poverty: καὶ αὐτὸς ἤρξατο ὑστερεῖσθαι . . .
καὶ οὐδεὶς ἐδίδου αὐτῷ (15:14-16), and he recognizes his condition as that of being "lost" ὧδε ἀπόλλυμαι (15:17). The taking
of possessions for oneself therefore expresses alienation, and
the dissipation of possessions expresses personal diminishment.
We note further that the son's return to the father is expressed by the father's bestowing on him the family's most precious
possessions (15:22-23). Alienation, conversion and return are
all expressed by possessions.

The most interesting line of all, however, is placed in
the mouth of the father in his response to the elder son's
complaint that such gifts had never been given to him, even
though he had always been faithful: τέκνον σὺ πάντοτε μετ᾿
ἐμοῦ εἶ καὶ πάντα τὰ ἐμὰ σά ἐστιν (15:31). Here in a completely unstudied and spontaneous fashion, Luke has expressed
an understanding of possessions which reveals how they can be
a symbol of human relationships. When people are together in
unity ("You are with me always") they share all possessions
("All that is mine is yours"), and the sharing of possessions
signifies that unity. When persons are alienated, the property
is divided, and the separation of persons is expressed by each
holding "what is his own." It cannot go unnoticed how
strikingly 15:31 anticipates the language and thought of Acts
4:32ff, particularly in the note that those who are together
in unity share all with each other.

Luke 15:11-32 therefore shows that Luke is quite capable
of using the language of possessions to symbolize the movement
of a story which is not about possessions, but about human
relations in a dynamic of separation and unity. This clear
metaphoric usage strengthens the probability that the literary
connections we have suggested earlier in this chapter are not
arbitrary, but represent what is actually in the text.

D. Possessions and the Twelve

Our analysis in chapter two indicated that Luke specifies
the division in the People caused by the Prophet Jesus as a
split between the people and the leaders of the people. We saw
that as the erstwhile leaders fell away from their place of
authority, Luke (already in the Gospel) prepared for the
assumption of authority over Israel by the Twelve. In Acts,
that authority is clearly bound up with the distribution of
goods. It is interesting therefore to see how Luke uses the
language of possessions in regard to the Twelve in the Gospel.

1. Community of Goods before Pentecost?: It must be
said at once that Luke does not explicitly picture the disciples and Jesus as holding goods in common during Jesus'
ministry in the way suggested by Jn 12:6 and 13:29 where it
is stated that Judas held the common purse (γλωσσόκομον).
There are however some small touches in his presentation which
may indicate that he so thought of the situation, or that he
anticipated the picture of the sharing of goods in Acts. We
have already seen that the disciples of Jesus came from among
the ἁμαρτωλοί and τελῶναι, and that Peter, James and John
responded to Jesus' call by leaving all things, doing what the
rich ruler could not. In the case of the three disciples,
there are two small touches which are interesting. The fellow
workers of Peter are called μέτοχοι (5:7), and James and John
are called κοινωνοί τῷ Σίμωνι (5:10). In Peter's response to
Jesus' statement on the difficulty of the rich entering the
Kingdom (18:28), Luke has changed the ἀφέντες τὰ πάντα of Matt
19:27 and Mk 10:28 to ἀφέντες τὰ ἴδια, a small change indeed,
but one which anticipates the language about possessions in
Acts 4:32ff.[1] We can note as well that Jesus' promise to Peter
that they would receive πολλαπλασίονα ἐν τῷ καιρῷ τούτῳ (18:30)
finds a concrete fulfillment in the narrative of Acts. Finally
in 8:1-3, Luke describes Jesus accompanied by the Twelve and by
the women, who διηκόνουν αὐτοῖς ἐκ τῶν ὑπαρχόντων αὐταῖς (8:3).

---

[1]This has also been noticed by Brown, Apostasy and
Perseverence, 101, and Dupont, Beatitudes III, 157. Dupont
(III, 156) also sees the διάδος of 18:22 as anticipating the
language of Acts 4:35. Legasse, "'L'Homme Fort'," 8-9, sees
the use of διαδιδόναι in Lk 11:22 as a foreshadowing of Acts
4:35.

Jesus and the Twelve are at the center of a sharing of goods.[1]
Particularly in the light of Luke's insistence that the core of
the first Jerusalem community consisted of Galileans (Acts
1:11; 2:7; 10:37ff; 13:31) these small touches are suggestive,
but remain only that.

2. Possessions and the Sending of the Twelve and Seventy
(-Two): We have spoken already about the difficulties presented by 9:1ff, 10:1ff and 22:35-36 when seen from the point of
view of Luke's paraenetic intention.[2] If we see the language
of possessions in these passages as expressing the literary
pattern of acceptance and rejection, however, these problems
do not arise. In 9:3, Jesus tells the Twelve: μηδὲν αἴρετε
εἰς τὴν ὁδὸν μήτε ῥάβδον μήτε πήραν μήτε ἄρτον μήτε ἀργύριον
μήτε [ανα] δύο χιτῶνας ἔχειν. The command to the Seventy
(-Two) is very similar: μὴ βαστάζετε βαλλάντιον μὴ πήραν μὴ
ὑποδήματα καὶ μηδένα κατὰ τὴν ὁδὸν ἀσπάσησθε (10:4). It is
obviously futile to pick apart the elements of these commands
to determine which possessions the Twelve could use and which
the Seventy (-Two). That Luke himself was less than careful
about these particulars is indicated by the remarkable fact
that when he revokes his command to the Twelve in 22:35, he
uses the elements of the command to the Seventy (-Two): ὅτε
ἀπέστειλα ὑμᾶς ἄτερ βαλλαντίου καὶ πήρας καὶ ὑποδημάτων μὴ
τινος ὑστερήσατε! Nor can we find any particular attitude
towards possessions themselves stressed in these passages,
much less an ideal of asceticism. Certainly there is a note
of urgency to be found in the commissions as a whole, which is
heightened by the injunction in 10:4 to "greet no one on the
road." Is there here an image of the eschatological readiness,
of being freed from possessions for the visitation of the Lord,
such as we saw in chs. 17 and 21? If this were so, the revocation at the last supper, when Jesus was entering into his time
of rejection, would be even more puzzling.

The significance of the use of possessions in these
passages must be seen in their context within the story.[3]

_____

[1]Cf. Brown, Apostasy and Perseverence, 103.

[2]Cf. above, pp. 81, 128-129.

[3]Conzelmann, Theology of St. Luke, 82, places the

When we look at the commands to the missionaries, we see that
the focus is not on their lack of possessions, but rather on
the problem of their acceptance or rejection by those to whom
they preached, the households they entered (9:4-5, 10:5-8).
It is in relation to their acceptance or rejection by the
people that their lack of possessions is significant. We see
further in 10:7-8 that the missionaries could expect food and
shelter from the households which received them. Now, the
Apostles' answer to Jesus in 22:35 indicates that during their
missionary journey, in spite of their lack of possessions, they
did not experience need, with the clear implication that they
were accepted by the households and were supported by them.
Their being able to travel without possessions of their own
was a sign of the acceptance of their message and themselves
during Jesus' lifetime.

It is to this situation of acceptance that the words of
22:36 provide a direct contrast. The Apostles will now need
the support of possessions because like Jesus they are entering
a situation of rejection and persecution. Thus Jesus says of
Himself τοῦτο τὸ γεγραμμένον δεῖ τελεσθῆναι ἐν ἐμοί τὸ καὶ μετὰ
ἀνόμων ἐλογίσθη . . .,[1] and as He experiences rejection, so too
will they who are with Him in His testing (22:28). Their
needing possessions now is a sign of their rejection by men.

In view of the problems connected with trying to construct
a "missionary ideal" out of these passages, it is likely that
the literary function we have suggested is not only an additional, but the essential significance of the possessions
language in these passages.

---

passages within the context of the narrative, but mistakenly
applies the distinction between the age of Jesus and the age
of the Church. Cf. Brown, Apostasy and Perseverence, 103, n.
426a. P. Minear, "A Note on Luke 22:36," NovT 7 (1964-5),
128-134, correctly sees that the sayings must be analyzed not
in terms of some overriding chronological division, but in the
immediate story.

[1]Is 53:12, a prophecy which in Luke finds literal fulfillment (as Wilckens, Die Missionsreden der Apostelgeschichte,
124, points out) in Jesus' crucifixion between two κακοῦργοι
(23:32). Lindars, New Testament Apologetic, 85, sees the
citation as part of a passion apologetic. Minear, "A Note,"
132, suggests that the ἄνομοι are the Apostles, but this runs
contrary to the whole tone of the passage.

3. <u>The Authority of the Twelve and the Overseeing of
Property</u>: The way in which Luke connects the authority of the
Twelve to the overseeing of property or the distribution of
goods is of course directly pertinent to our examination of
Acts. As in the previous passages, the connection is not made
blatantly in the Gospel, but none the less surely.

a) We saw in the last chapter that Luke alone establishes such a close literary connection between the power
bestowed on the Twelve in their sending and the feeding of the
five thousand.[1] Although, as we mentioned in that place,
Luke's terminology is not consistent in the passage (shifting
from Apostles to the Twelve to the Disciples), it is he who has
explicitly inserted the δώδεκα into the account at 9:12 (cf.
Matt 14:13-21, Mk 6:30-44). This insertion not only strengthens the symbolism of the twelve baskets of food (9:17), it
draws the closest connection between the <u>authority</u> of the
Twelve and their distributing food to the multitude. The only
plausible answer to the question why Luke has drawn this
connection is that he wished to associate the authority of the
Twelve with the διακονία τραπέζαις, as in Acts.

b) This anticipation of the Apostles' role is pro-
jected even more strongly by 12:41ff. We already considered
in some detail the passages leading up to 12:38, but did not
proceed further because of the way Luke has arranged the
following verses.[2] The saying of v. 39, which is again about
readiness for the visitation, is no longer applied to the
δοῦλοι of the household as in the previous simile (12:37-38),
but to the οἰκοδεσπότης. The saying concludes: καὶ ὑμεῖς
γίνεσθε ἕτοιμοι (12:40). But who are the ὑμεῖς in this
instance? The simile spoke of the master of the household,
the one in authority. Luke uses this shift to interpose an
interesting question: εἶπεν δὲ ὁ πέτρος κύριε πρὸς ἡμᾶς τὴν
παραβολὴν ταύτην λέγεις ἢ καὶ πρὸς πάντας (12:41). Jesus does

---

[1] Cf. above, p. 113. Brown, <u>Apostasy</u> and <u>Perseverence</u>,
59f, notes Luke's elimination of the sharp rebuke of the
Apostles found in Mk, but does not see the impression made by
having the Apostles distributing food immediately after their
reception of power.

[2] Cf. above, p. 155.

not answer his question directly, but continues with the
sayings about the faithful and unfaithful stewards of households (12:42-48), that is, again about those in authority.

By inserting Peter's question in this place Luke has
established a separation between the rest of the disciples to
whom these sayings have been addressed and those whom Peter
calls "us" which in context can only mean the Twelve.[1] This
simple redactional touch has transformed the following parable
(found also in Matt 24:45-51 in a different context) into a
lesson on authority for the Twelve.

The content of the parable is the more interesting because
of this redactional placement. a) We see that authority again
is expressed in the image of a steward placed over a household,
one who oversees the other servants that handle the goods of
the household. b) Instead of Matt's aorist κατέστησεν, Luke
uses the future καταστήσει. The Twelve will hold this place of
authority. c) Faithfulness in the office is rewarded by being
placed over still more possessions (12:44), whereas unfaith-
fulness, expressed by beating the servants (the opposite
behaviour to that of the Lord in 12:37) and the typical Lukan
description of dissoluteness (cf. 12:19; 17:27, 28), is
punished by dismemberment and complete rejection. d) That the
rejected servant will have τὸ μέρος αὐτοῦ with the unbelievers
is reminiscent of the description of the fate of Judas in Acts
1:25. By being rejected, the steward no longer has a "share"
in the property, much less authority over it, but "his share"
is rejected along with him. e) The sayings which follow,
particularly v. 48 "to whom much has been given, more will be
asked," favor the interpretation that this parable has been
addressed to those who would assume authority over Israel, the
Twelve.

c) When the dispute arose among the Twelve at the
Last Supper over who was greatest (22:24ff), Jesus rebukes them
and contrasts the way rulers of the nations act with the way
their authority should be exercised: ὁ ἡγούμενος ὡς ὁ διακονῶν
(22:26), and bases this upon His own example: ἐγὼ δὲ ἐν μέσῳ

---

[1]Jeremias, Parables, 50. Gaston, No Stone on Another,
325, sees the change as effecting an address to the Church,
in contrast to outsiders.

ὑμῶν εἰμι ὡς ὁ διακονῶν (22:27). Jesus serves them as they sit
at table, and this is to be the expression of their own authority. The image of the master waiting on the servants reminds
us of the parable of 12:37 and of the Twelve distributing food
to the five thousand (9:10ff). The authority of the Twelve
over Israel is to be expressed in their διακονεῖν τραπέζαις
(Acts 6:2), in the distribution of goods to the community.
Theirs is an authority of service, as was that of Jesus. But
their authority is not less real, for as Jesus received from
the Father (καθὼς διέθετό μοι ὁ πατήρ μου) He gives to them
βασιλείαν over the twelve tribes of Israel. The authority of
the Twelve possesses a certain paradoxical character. It is
the full prophetic power of Jesus for judgment, but it is
expressed through the mundane symbol of handling the community
goods, of "waiting on tables." For Luke, the βασιλεία of the
Twelve is not a distant end-time reality, but an actual
governance expressed concretely in the life of the Jerusalem
community.[1]

   4. Two Parables of Power and Property: It remains to
consider two parables which Luke shares with parallels, but
which take on a particular significance within his overall
redaction. In both cases, there is found a relationship of
authority to property.

      a) The Parable of the Vineyard (20:9-19): We saw in
the last chapter that although Luke's basic story is shared by
Matt 21:33-46 and Mk 12:1-12, Luke has sharpened the element of
the rejection of the leaders of Israel.[2] He only slightly
accentuates the possessions language in the parable, undoubtedly because the version which came to him represented his own
outlook perfectly.[3] As in 13:1-8 and 12:41ff, authority is
once again expressed as the overseeing of property. In this
instance the "property" is understood as the people Israel, and

_____

[1]Cf. Brown, Apostasy and Perseverence, 64.

[2]Cf. above, pp. 119f; also Dodd, Parables, 131.

[3]J. Derrett's elaborate discussion of the legal aspects
of the parable (Law in the New Testament, 286-312) sheds little
light on the meaning of the parable in context. Cf. also
Jeremias, Parables, 70-77.

the authority, that of the leaders of the people. Their abuse
of authority is expressed by their refusal to let go any of the
property to its rightful owner, to give him the produce that is
due him. Luke sharpens this aspect slightly by twice adding
"They sent him away emptyhanded" (20:10-11). The climax of
their rebellion comes when they try to seize not only the
profits, but the property itself. By killing the heir, they
wish to have the κληρονομία for themselves. For this usurpa-
tion, they are cut off in the most literal fashion: ἀπολέσει
τοὺς γεωργοὺς τούτους (20:16). And the property? δώσει τὸν
ἀμπελῶνα ἄλλοις. We have seen already with the wife of Lot,
the rich fool and the strong man that the loss of self was
expressed by the loss of possessions. We shall see it again
in the story of Judas. The "others" to whom the vineyard is
given in Luke's understanding are the Twelve. It is they who
will oversee the vineyard of the Lord that is Israel, they who
will assume the authority lost by the leaders of the people.

        b) The Parable of the Pounds (19:11-27): The Lukan
treatment of this parable is particularly interesting, and
provides a final example of the way the possessions motif
functions within the telling of the story. In Matt 25:14-30,
the story is one in a series of eschatological parables, with
no direct reference to the story line of the Gospel; the
meaning of the story is self-contained. The parable is one of
a master going off on a journey, and leaving money with his
servants for them to make a profit, as a test of their ingenu-
ity and fidelity. The distribution of the money ἑκάστω κατὰ
τὴν ἰδίαν δύναμιν (v. 15) reveals the moralistic tone of the
story. Those who used the money profitably were placed over
still more property (vv. 21, 23), and the fearful servant who
gained no profit was cast out, rejected from the "joy of His
Lord" (v. 30).

        Luke on the other hand has given the parable a dramatic
placement within the story of the Prophet and the People. The
time and place of Jesus' progress to Jerusalem are noted, and
the parable is told specifically to those who thought ὅτι
παραχρῆμα μέλλει ἡ βασιλεία τοῦ θεοῦ ἀναφαίνεσθαι (19:11).[1]

_____

[1]It is sometimes asserted that the peculiar Lukan

By this touch alone, we would be justified in seeking a relationship between the parable and the situation in the story it
is intended to illuminate. Luke has, in addition, fitted the
parable of the pounds within another story, that of a Nobleman
who went off to receive a kingdom (19:12). The elements of the
two stories are inextricably mixed. The result is that there
are two groups with whom the King must deal when he returns:
the servants to whom he gave money for profit during his
absence (9:13), and those fellow-citizens (πολῖται) of his who
did not want him as king and tried to foil his accession to
power (19:14). The "politicization" of the parable is indicated by the rewards given to the servants who dealt profitably
with the Nobleman's possessions. According to the measure of
their gain, they are given authority over cities (9:17, 19),
that is, they are given power and authority within the new
kingdom, βασιλεία. The profitless servant is not cut off, as
in Matt; he is simply divested of his possessions and given no
further authority. His lack of imagination in dealing with
possessions, we understand, showed him unfit for rule. In
Luke's version, it is rather the ἐχθροί of the King who are
utterly rejected; they are slaughtered before his eyes (19:27).
Because they rejected him as king, they have no part at all in
his kingdom.

Luke has therefore combined a severe rejection story with
a story about the bestowal of authority, expressed by

redaction of this parable has the purpose of teaching the delay
of the coming of the Kingdom. Cf. J. Dupont, "La Parabole des
Talents (Mat.25:14-30) ou des Mines (Luc 19:12-27)," RTP ser.3
19 (1969) 382-383; Conzelmann, Theology, 113; Jeremias,
Parables, 59; Dodd, Parables, 146ff. Gaston, No Stone on
Another, 354-355, thinks the parable presents a warning against
political revolution. Brown, Apostasy and Perseverance, 104,
and Flender, Luke, 60, treat the parable within the context of
schemas of two ages, or the dialectic tension of Luke's
theology. Little attention is given to the obvious meaning of
the parable as interpreting the events of the story which
follows. It is difficult to see how Luke could have been
teaching the delay of the kingdom, when he immediately has
Jesus proclaimed as King in the entry to Jerusalem, and bestowing βασιλεία on the Apostles. Nor is there, in the Lukan
version, any hint of a long delay between the Nobleman's departure and return, such as we find in Matt 25:19. It is
probably the case here again that the paraenetic interest is
less pronounced than the dramatic.

possessions. Luke does not leave the reader in any doubt about what situation this story was meant to illustrate. Immediately upon finishing the story, Luke notes: καὶ εἰπὼν ταῦτα ἐπορεύετο ἔμπροσθεν ἀναβαίνων εἰς Ἱεροσόλυμα (19:28). He has just told a story about a king going to get a kingdom and the rejection he experienced. He follows with the account of Jesus entering Jerusalem, surrounded by the throngs of his disciples proclaiming him as King (ὁ βασιλεύς) (19:38). And who are those who reject this acclamation of Jesus as King? As we saw in the last chapter, it is the Pharisees, who demand of Jesus that his disciples be silent (19:39). We are clearly to infer from the parable that those leaders who did not accept Jesus as King were to be cut off, to have no place in the Kingdom. Who then are the servants who would be placed in authority within the Kingdom? Can we not understand them to be the Twelve, upon whom Jesus is shortly to bestow βασιλεία over Israel?

Luke is clearly using the story of the pounds to illustrate the story of the Prophet and the People. At this point again, the language of possessions and the literary pattern of the Prophet and the People merge.

E. Conclusions to Chapter Three

We began this chapter by listing three possibilities of relationship between possessions and the literary pattern of the Prophet and the People. In the course of the chapter we have shown: a) that there is a discernible literary pattern to be found in these materials, b) that at the very least this pattern parallels that of the Prophet and the People, and that c) in a large number of instances the materials on possessions are used by the author to directly express the pattern of the Prophet and the People. We have further found that by so using these materials, Luke employed the language about possessions not only literally, but also metaphorically, or symbolically. The metaphoric possibilities of this language were exploited to express a) the inner response of men's hearts to God's Visitation and b) authority. The fact that we have been able to find as extensive a literary use of these materials as we have is the more impressive given the fact that a) Luke was using materials which frequently were shared to some extent by the tradition, and therefore less capable of free adaptation, and b) Luke's purpose in using these materials was not purely aesthetic, but also paraenetic.

At the end of chapter two, we termed this examination of the possessions material in the Gospel a test case for the analysis of Acts. We have found that Luke is not only capable of using possessions language metaphorically, in order to express through concrete imagery the movement of his story, but that in fact he has a pronounced tendency so to use it.

CHAPTER FOUR

Introduction:

    We have returned full circle to our exegetical starting
point. In the previous chapters we have established that there
is a discernible literary pattern dominating the narrative of
Luke-Acts, a pattern which can be called "The Prophet and the
People." We have also seen the extent to which Luke in the
Gospel expressed this pattern by use of possessions language.
We are now able to analyze in detail the passages concerning
possessions in the Jerusalem narrative of Acts, to establish
with some precision their literary function.

    Our examination of the pattern of the Prophet and the
People showed the critical place of the Jerusalem narrative
within Luke's work as a whole. Because of his appreciation of
the continuity of God's action among His people, of his fulfillment of the promises made to Abraham, and of the spread of the
Gospel to the Gentiles as an extension of these promises, Luke
must within this narrative establish first that there was a
believing people within the historic Israel to whom the blessings came. Second, he must secure the place of the Twelve as
the prophetic successors to Jesus around whom the faithful
people forms; to do this, he must also show how the old leaders
of Israel are definitively rejected from their place over the
people. Third, he must prepare for the spread of the Gospel to
the Gentiles by showing how those who carried out that mission
derived their authority from and maintained submission to the
Twelve, the essential authority over the people.

    We are trying to find out whether Luke uses the motif of
possessions here as he did in the Gospel, to express metaphorically the main lines of his story; whether, in other words, the
language about possessions is not simply "about" possessions,
but forms an integral part and plays a symbolic role in the
telling of the story of the Prophet and the People.

    We will consider in sequence the election of Matthias
(1:12-26), the first description of community life (2:41-47),

173

174

the healing of the lame man (3:1-10), the second description of
community life (4:32-37), the story of Ananias and Sapphira
(5:1-11), the appointment of the Seven (6:1-7), the story of
Simon Magus (8:14-25), and the relief sent to Jerusalem (11:27-
30; 12:25). In each case, we will try to place the passage
within the story line. In effect, we are filling in the gaps
left by our examination of chapter one of this study. We
examined there the pattern of the Prophet and the People without explicit reference to the possessions language. Now we'll
see how Luke has fitted that language within the story. A
certain amount of repetition and overlapping is inevitable in
this kind of procedure. To keep that repetition to a minimum,
there will be no attempt to support again our special use of
terms like "prophet" when applied to the Apostles, or "Men of
the Spirit," or "the People" when speaking of the believing
part of Israel.

A. The Election of Matthias (1:12-26).

From the beginning of the second volume, Luke centers the
reader's attention on those who will be the main characters of
this part of the story. By many small touches, Luke reminds us
of the special relationship of the Twelve to Jesus and the role
they are to play. They had been chosen by Jesus and been
instructed by Him before the Ascension (1:2); it was to them
that Jesus appeared over the space of forty days (1:3) and with
them that He ate (1:4); and in response to their questions
about the restoration of the Kingdom to Israel, Jesus resumes
His promise of Lk 24:49 that they are to receive the power of
the Spirit and be witnesses to Him (1:6-8). These "Men of
Galilee" watch Him depart and hear the promise that Jesus will
return in the same way (1:11).[1]

The logic of the story and Luke's own penchant for following promise by fulfillment would indicate that the story of

---

[1]S. Brown, Apostasy and Perseverence in the Theology of
Luke, 53, emphasizes the way Luke shows the continuity of the
Apostles' physical presence with Jesus from Galilee to Jerusalem. Coming to the passages from the perspective of the
problem of perseverence, Brown has treated in some detail many
of the issues concerning possessions we are considering.
Though in agreement on many points, our difference lies in the
precise function assigned to the language of possessions.

Pentecost should follow Jesus' departure. Why does Luke
interrupt this natural flow? Because he must first deal with
a problem of the first magnitude.[1] The circle of the Twelve
has been broken. One of those chosen by Jesus, who received
the power to preach and to heal (Lk 9:1ff), who was to exercise
βασιλείαν over the twelve tribes of Israel (Lk 22:30),[2] was a
traitor, with a heart possessed by Satan (Lk 22:3), and he led
Jesus' enemies to Him (22:47). The attention Luke gives to the
fate of Judas and the election of his replacement shows the
importance of the Twelve in his understanding of Israel.[3] We
have seen in the Gospel how Luke pictured the people forming
around the core group of the Twelve on the way to Jerusalem.
The number twelve is itself of symbolic importance because of
their role within Israel. We saw this adumbrated in the feeding of the five thousand and in the promise made to the Twelve
at the last supper.[4] In Acts, Luke will picture the faithful

---

[1]The literary placement of the election itself indicates
the importance of the problem it must resolve. The whole movement of the story presses toward the fulfillment of Jesus'
promise. The election brings the reader up short. The need
to replace Judas before Pentecost shows a great deal both about
the significance of the Twelve and of the bestowal of the
Spirit in Luke's thinking.

[2]Brown, Apostasy and Perseverence, 84; Jervell, Luke and
People of God, 85; and K. Lüthi, "Das Problem des Judas
Iskariot -- neu untersucht," EvT 16 (1956) 98-114, argue that
whereas Luke has Judas present at the last supper he so alters
the "twelve thrones" saying to exclude him from the reception
of authority from Jesus. This may be too fine. The problem
presented by Judas was his full inclusion in the apostolic
circle. If Jesus had promised authority only to the eleven,
the crisis created by Judas' apostasy would not have been
nearly as great.

[3]Cf. Brown, Apostasy and Perseverence, 94-97; A. Ehrhardt,
The Acts of the Apostles, 14; H. Flender, Luke, Theologian of
Redemptive History, 121; C. Masson, "La Reconstitution du
Collège des Douze," RTP ser.3 5 (1955) 193-201; Ph.-H. Menoud,
"Les Additions au Groupe des douze Apôtres d'après le Livre des
Actes," RHPR 37 (1957) 71-80; K. Rengstorf, "Die Zuwahl des
Matthias," ST 15 (1961) 35-67; Jervell, Luke and the People of
God, 75-112.

[4]Jervell, Luke and the People of God, 85, correctly notes,
". . . the circle of the Twelve is linked explicitly to the
concept 'Israel', primarily as it is seen in the eucharistic
discourse (Luke 22:30)." Cf. also Masson, "Reconstitution,"
198.

people as forming around and under the authority of the Twelve.
In a real sense, the Twelve are Israel, in nuce.

The betrayal of Judas was not simply the failing of an
individual; it splintered the numerical and therefore symbolic
integrity of that group which constituted the beginning and
essential authority of the believing Israel. Peter also
betrayed Jesus, but Peter's falling away was one of weakness,
and his fall and restoration was predicted by Jesus; he would
return to strengthen his brothers (Lk 22:32). But Judas' sin
was an apostasy from his apostolic office,[1] a threat to the
fulfillment of Jesus' promise and the whole plan of God. The
defection of Judas posed a unique problem and the election of
his replacement was a unique solution. As the others of the
Twelve died there would be no need to replace them, for once
the Twelve had been definitively constituted and the Spirit
bestowed, the faithful Israel would have come into existence,
and have fulfilled its role in God's plan.[2] That is why Judas'
successor must be elected before Pentecost. Luke's use of
possessions language in this passage is particularly interesting.

1. Vv. 12-14 set the stage for the discourse. The
place is the upper room.[3] The participants are listed. First,
the remaining eleven Apostles, listed here (with some variation
in order) as they were in Lk 6:14-16. The repetition of the
whole list makes the absence of Judas glaringly apparent, and
anticipates the subject of the discourse. With the eleven are
Mary and the women and Jesus' brothers, in short the members of
the group that came up with Jesus from Galilee (cf. Lk 8:1-3,
19-20, 23:49). This listing and the mention of the "men of
Galilee" in 1:11 emphasize the Galilean provenance of the first

---

[1]Cf. Brown, Apostasy and Perseverence, 70.

[2]Jervell, Luke and the People of God, 95; Rengstorf,
"Zuwahl," 58-59; Menoud, "Additions," 75.

[3]In spite of the different words employed, Luke may have
intended us to understand this as the ἀνάγαιον of Lk 22:12.
Cf. Lake-Cadbury, 10; Haenchen, 153. It would make excellent
dramatic sense to have the restoration occur where the promise
of authority was first given.

Jerusalem community.[1] The group that formed around Jesus in
his ministry would be the foundation of the people.[2] Now it
should be carefully noted that Luke has already prepared us to
see in this group a sharing of possessions, and most importantly, to see the Apostles as those who have left τὰ ἴδια in
their following of Jesus. The group in the upper room ἦσαν
προσκαρτεροῦντες ὁμοθυμαδὸν τῇ προσευχῇ (1:14). With this
phrase, and the ἐπὶ τὸ αὐτὸ of 1:15, Luke introduces the
stereotyped language which he will use of the community through
this first part of Acts.[3] Prayer is the preparation for any
decisive event.[4]

2. Vv. 15-20: In fulfillment of Jesus' prediction
in Lk 22:32, Peter emerges as the spokesman, strengthening his
brothers.[5] Remarkably, he does this by authoritatively interpreting the Scriptures, just as Jesus did.[6] He places the
death of Judas and the election of his successor under the δεῖ
of divine necessity. The double use of δεῖ (1:16, 21) indicates the importance of this situation in Luke's eyes. The

---

[1]Cf. Conzelmann, Theology of St. Luke, 38, n. 1.

[2]The number 120 does not appear accidental. M. Sanhedrin
1:6 states that the smallest village that can legitimately have
a sanhedrin must number 120. Cf. Lake-Cadbury, 12. It may be
doubted, however, that Luke intended a reference to the "men
of the Great Assembly," as suggested by E. Stauffer, "Jüdisches
Erbe im urchristlichen Kirchenrecht," TLZ 77 (1952) 202.

[3]Cf. Haenchen, 154.

[4]The suggestion of Lake-Cadbury, 10, that τῇ προσευχῇ
refers to place of prayer, is unnecessary. Luke pictures the
believers as remaining in the upper room. Luke typically
precedes any important business with prayer; cf. Lk 3:21; 6:12;
9:28; 22:41; Acts 4:24ff; 13:2.

[5]Cf. Brown, Apostasy and Perseverence, 73. For the Lukan
vocabulary and style in the passage, cf. J. Renie, "L'Election
de Matthias (Actes 1, 15-26); Authenticité du Recit," RB 55
(1948) 43-53. E. Haenchen, "Judentum und Christentum in der
Apostelgeschichte," ZNW 54 (1963) 161, says this passage is
"ein Testfall . . . für die Art, wie Lukas in der Apostelgeschichte arbeitet." Cf. also Menoud, "Additions," 74.

[6]The significance of this should not be lightly passed
over. There is no more telling indication of how Luke saw the
Apostles possessing the power of Jesus than in his having them
authoritatively interpret the Scriptures as He did.

splintering and healing of the Twelve fall as much within the
divine plan as the death and resurrection of the Prophet Jesus.

The two uses of δεῖ also structure the discourse into two
parts. The first section deals with the death of Judas, the
second with his replacement; the two parts are joined by the
two elements of the composite scriptural citation.[1] The
betrayal of Judas was such a scandal and required this kind
of scriptural interpretation precisely because of the position
he had held among the Twelve: ὅτι κατηριθμημένος ἦν ἐν ἡμῖν
καὶ ἔλαχεν τὸν κλῆρον τῆς διακονίας ταύτης, v. 17. The use of
"numbered among us," like the verb used in 1:26, stresses the
importance of the number of the Twelve.[2] The number, in turn,
can only be significant if the Apostles are defined in terms of
Israel. Judas had received "the share of this ministry." We
note first that the Apostolic role is described as a διακονία
as in Lk 22:24ff, here and in 1:25. The "share" is also echoed
in 1:26. We will reflect later over the implications of this
language. V. 17 makes very clear, however, that Judas' position before his betrayal was that of full inclusion in the
Twelve, and there can be no avoiding the crisis his apostasy
caused. The Prophet had been rejected even by one among those
He had chosen as "His own."

3. Peter describes the fate of Judas in vv. 18ff.
We are able to distinguish the distinctive aspects of Luke's
account more clearly because we have for comparison Matt
27:3-10.[3] Though both are about the death of Judas, the
accounts are so different that we must conclude either that
Luke was using an independent tradition, or as is more likely,

---

[1]Cf. the analysis of the structure of the pericope in
relation to the Scriptural citations in Dupont, Etudes, 309-
320.

[2]Cf. the incisive remarks of Jervell, Luke and the People
of God, 84-85.

[3]We leave aside the account of Papias. For a discussion
of all three versions, cf. K. Lake, "The Death of Judas,"
Beginnings V, 22-30. An attempt to harmonize Luke and Matthew
can be found in J. Sickenberger, "Judas als Stifter des
Blutackers; Apg.1,18f.," BZ 18 (1929) 69-71. For the structural similarities in the Acts and Matt account, cf. P. Benoit,
"La Mort de Judas," Synoptische Studien, 1-19.

considerably shaped the story himself.[1] Luke says nothing
about Judas' fate in the Gospel. In his account of the
betrayal, however, three small points are worth noting: First,
Luke says that Judas was ἐκ τοῦ ἀριθμοῦ τῶν δώδεκα (Lk 22:3)
again stressing as in Acts 1:17, the place of Judas among a
particular number.[2] Second, Luke (as John 13:27) sees Judas'
betrayal as resulting from a possession by Satan (Lk 22:3), a
connection we will meet again in ch. 5.[3] Third, Luke portrays
Judas' action as a conspiracy; he enters into conference with
the High Priests (συνελάλησεν) and they strike an agreement on
the price of betrayal (συνέθεντο αὐτῷ).

We can note the following points in the Matthean presentation. First, when Judas saw that Jesus had been condemned to
death, he repented his action, and sought to undo it precisely
by returning the money of betrayal to the High Priests and
Elders, confessing that he had sinned (Matt 27:3-4). When they
refused the money, he flung it on the Temple floor, went out
and hanged himself. His repentance was late and ineffectual,
but it happened, and was expressed by his return of the money.
Second, the Priests take the money but because it is unclean
decide to use it for the purchase of a burying field for
foreigners (Matt 27:7). Third, Matthew notes that the reason
the field got its name ἀγρος αἵματος was because of the use of
the betrayal money to buy it (27:8). Fourth, Matthew concludes
with a free composite scriptural citation (using Zech 11:12-13
and Jer 32:8-9), the point of the citation being the price of
the field, and not the fate of Judas.[4]

In Luke's version everything, including the scriptural
citation, is centered on the defection of Judas as one of the
Twelve. The most interesting difference in the accounts concerns the use of money. In Luke's story Judas does not return
the money as a sign of repentance, but takes the μισθὸς τῆς

[1]Cf. Benoit, "La Mort de Judas," 1.

[2]Jervell, Luke and the People of God, 84.

[3]Brown, Apostasy and Perseverence, 85-86, and Lüthi, "Das
Problem," 100, emphasize Judas' use of money as being motivated
by a demonic force.

[4]Cf. B. Lindars, New Testament Apologetic, 116-122.

ἀδικίας (the betrayal money)[1] and ἐκτήσατο χωρίον (1:18).   In
the light of what follows, we are justified in understanding
χωρίον as a farm.[2]   This action of Judas is placed in immediate
contrast to his holding the κλῆρος τῆς διακονίας. We notice
further that his buying a farm for himself is the exact opposite of the way the believers in 4:32ff sold their farms and
fields to share possessions with all. We are suggesting that
the buying of a farm is a symbol of his apostasy from the
community of the Twelve, who we already know, have left τὰ
ἴδια.

Judas' death also takes place on this same property in
Luke's version. The description is vague, but seems to imply
that Judas fell off a building.[3]   There is no mention of
suicide here; rather his death appears as a divine punishment,
executed, ironically, on the property he had bought for himself.
It is because Judas died there that the field became known as
"the field of blood" according to Luke, and not, as in Matthew,
because of the "blood money" used to purchase it.

All that happened to Judas was in fulfillment of the
Scripture (1:16). Like Matthew, Luke has brought together
disparate verses from the O.T. Luke's combination here has
no precedent,[4] and is intriguing. Ps 68:26 (LXX) by itself
refers to the state of the property, and is a curse: γενηθήτω
ἡ ἔπαυλις (the field or farm) αὐτοῦ ἔρημος καὶ μὴ ἔστω ὁ
κατοικῶν ἐν αὐτῇ. Luke has changed the persons of the verse
from plural to singular to fit it to the case of Judas' farm.[5]

_____

[1]τῆς ἀδικίας can be seen as an objective genitive = the
reward for his unrighteousness. Brown, Apostasy and Perseverance, 86; Conzelmann, Die Apostelgeschichte, 29; and Lake-
Cadbury, 13, suggest the genitive has the strength of an adjec-
tive = unrighteous reward. Brown, however, too hastily assumes
a parallel to Lk 16:9, 11. The "unrighteous reward" does not
necessarily characterize the money itself as "unrighteous
mammon." It is Judas' use of the money which is decisive.

[2]Cf. Haenchen, 160.

[3]Haenchen, 160; Lake-Cadbury, 13; cf. also A. Knox, "The
Death of Judas," JTS 25 (1923-4) 289-290.

[4]Cf. T. Holtz, Untersuchungen über die Alttestamentlichen
Zitate bei Lukas, 46.

[5]Lindars, New Testament Apologetic, 103. For the use of

But it is here we must ask the fundamental question. It is not
surprising, in the light of his offense that Judas should be
cursed; but why should his property be cursed by being doomed
to desertion--unless, just as the purchasing of the field was
a sign of Judas' defection, so the desolation of the field
stands as a sign of his perdition?

The verse from Ps 109:8 on the other hand, applies not to
the property, but to the position of authority which Judas had
held: τὴν ἐπισκοπὴν αὐτοῦ λαβέτω ἕτερος, which opens the way
for the election of his successor. Why has Luke brought these
verses together in this way? Let us note the progression in
the passage to this point: a) Judas is numbered among the
Apostles and has a share in the ministry; b) Judas buys a field
and is struck dead on the field; c) his property is cursed
to perpetual desolation; d) another is to assume his office.
There is in this arrangement an evident and powerful penetra-
tion of the notion of apostolic authority by the metaphor of
property. Judas' apostasy from the Twelve is expressed by the
buying of a field, his perdition is expressed by the emptiness
of that field, and that empty property in turn expresses the
vacancy of the apostolic office which can now be assumed by
another.[1]

4. That Luke is here using property as a metaphor is
suggested as well by v. 25. The community prays God to show
which of the two candidates He has chosen λαβεῖν τὸν τόπον τῆς
διακονίας ταύτης καὶ ἀποστολῆς ἀφ' ἧς παρέβη Ἰούδας πορευθῆναι
εἰς τὸν τόπον τὸν ἴδιον.[2] The one chosen is to take the place
of the ministry which Judas abandoned by going to his own
place. Only a strictly literal rendering here does justice to
the metaphorical nuance.[3] Seeing Judas' going to his own place

Ps 68 in passion apologetic, cf. Lindars, 99ff, and Dupont,
Etudes, 300.

[1]"The deserted building is not simply the due punishment
of the traitor, but the technical grounds for electing a new
Apostle," Lindars, New Testament Apologetic, 103.

[2]The reading τόπον τὸν ἴδιον is much stronger than κλῆρον.
Cf. Ropes, 10.

[3]Masson, "Reconstitution," 196, sees in 1:25 "un jeu de
mots assez subtil. τόπος = 'place' étant pris dans la première
membre de phrase dans son sense figuré et dans la second dans

as his death, or damnation, or the like[1] misses the allusion of
τὸν τόπον τὸν ἴδιον which again presents a strong contrast to
the believers who called nothing "their own." We also see that
the "going" of Judas is not subsequent to his betrayal, but is
the act of betrayal itself. The image of Judas' apostasy was
"going to his own place," that is, buying the field. By this
action of acquiring property, Judas expressed his falling away
from the τόπος of the Twelve and his apostasy from the κλῆρος
of the ministry.[2] And the one elected is now able to take this
τόπος.

The major point of vv. 21-26 is that the circle of the
Twelve is again full. Matthias is chosen by lot,[3] and
συγκατεψηφίσθη μετὰ τῶν ἕνδεκα ἀποστόλων.[4] The crisis caused
by the betrayal of Judas has been resolved, and the prayerful
nucleus of the people is now prepared to receive the promised
gift of the Holy Spirit.

5. We have found in this passage that the motif of
possessions has been used by Luke with particular effectiveness
to express the pattern of acceptance and rejection in regard to
the apostolic office. The story is not "about" possessions; on
the contrary, the passage stands as a prime example of the way

---

son sense propre." L. Thornton, "The Choice of Matthias," JTS
46 (1945) 58, notes the play on words between κλῆρος and τόπος,
and concludes that by going to the χωρίον he had bought, Judas
did not go to the 'place' (Gethsemane) to which his κλῆρος
called him. Thornton does not notice the play on τόπος at
1:25b.

[1]Cf. Haenchen, 162; J. O'Neill, The Theology of Acts, 8;
A. Tricot, "Sur Actes 1,15 et 25," RSR 15 (1925) 166-167;
Dupont, Beatitudes III, 136 (with bibliography).

[2]Brown, Apostasy and Perseverence, 84, sees the "going" of
Judas as the act of betrayal, and sees "his own place" as his
"partnership with religious and military authorities." This is
certainly how Judas apostasized. But the connection Luke draws
between the τόπος here and the buying of a field functions as a
metaphoric expression of that apostasy.

[3]On the casting of lots, with its apparent relation to the
Qumran practice (Trocmé, Le "Livre des Actes" et Histoire, 200),
cf. J. Fitzmyer, "Jewish Christianity in Acts in Light of the
Qumran Scrolls," SLA, 250-251, and W. Beardslee, "The Casting of
Lots at Qumran and in the Book of Acts," NovT 4 (1960) 245-252.

[4]Cf. Acts 19:19, and Jervell, Luke and the People of God,
84-85.

in which Luke uses possessions symbolically. We must remember
that Luke had no need to use the possessions aspect of the
story in the way he did--our comparison with Matthew shows that
clearly. The possessions motif is not intrusive; indeed it is
so subtle and natural that it takes some examination to see
that Luke is using the image of property as a symbol. But once
we grasp this, we are able to make sense of the diverse aspects
of the account.

B. The First Description of Community Life (2:41-47).

This passage forms the climax of the first stage of the
Acts narrative, a section which might fairly by characterized
more as an expression of what Luke thought had to have happened
at the beginning, than as a chronicle of historic events.[1]
With the election of Matthias the essential authority of the
people was restored, and by the outpouring of the Spirit the
faithful Israel was itself definitively established.[2] Peter's
speech makes clear (as we saw in chapter one) that this
bestowal of the Spirit is an eschatological event, an outpouring of the spirit of prophecy and the fulfillment of the
promises made to Abraham that in his seed his descendants would
be blessed. By having present at Peter's speech representatives of Judaism from all over the world (2:9-11), by having
Peter extend the promises to all those far and near who call on
the name of the Lord (2:39), and by having three thousand of
those who hear respond in faith to Peter's message (2:41), Luke
has already in principle established that the believing people
which formed around the core of Galilean disciples was a people

---

[1]Ehrhardt, The Acts of the Apostles, 12-13, speaks of the
Lukan infancy narratives and the ascension as "mythological."
If the term is understood properly (that is, non-pejoratively)
as the symbolic expression of essentially ineffable experiences, the characterization is fair and accurate, not only for
those narratives, but particularly for the Pentecost account.

[2]Cf. J. Schmitt, "L'église de Jérusalem, ou la 'restauration' d'Israël," RevScRel 27 (1953) 209-218, who analyzes the
Jerusalem narrative from the perspective of the Deuteronomic
promises, and sees the self-understanding of the "restored
Israel" as that of the first believers, rather than the
theological perspective of Luke.

184

drawn from all the historic Israel, including the diaspora.[1]

Luke now has the opportunity to describe the life of this community created by the Spirit. The placement of the passage, the generalized nature of the description (the imperfect verbs indicating continued action), and the careful balancing of elements all indicate that this is his purpose. The passage therefore deserves our careful attention. The most important thing about possessions in this passage can be said at once, and that is the fact that they appear here at all. It is, after all, not to be taken for granted that the way the first Christians handled their possessions should be included among the essential characteristics of their life; that Luke saw fit to remark on this here shows the importance he gave to possessions as the expression of the inner life.

We saw in the Gospel how Luke speaks of possessions as a sign of conversion. Thus the crowd responded to the Baptist's preaching by asking τί οὖν ποιήσωμεν, and John told them they should share their food and clothing with others (Lk 3:11). We have a similar pattern here (Acts 2:37). Struck to the heart by the words of Peter,[2] the crowd asks τί ποιήσωμεν ἄνδρες ἀδελφοί; Peter tells them they should repent and be baptized so that they will receive the Holy Spirit (2:38). Their repentance is an act of separation from "this wayward generation" (2:40), the part of the historic Israel which rejected the Prophet. As in the Gospel, therefore, what Luke has to say about possessions in the following verses falls within the context of conversion.

1. V. 41 sketches the essential nature of the faithful Israel. They are those who have "accepted the Word" who have come to believe in the word spoken about the risen Prophet by His witnesses. The cultic sealing of their acceptance is baptism, which with two exceptions in Acts (8:15, 10:47) is understood as the occasion for the reception of the Spirit, and

---

[1]Cf. A. Wikenhauser, Die Apostelgeschichte, 41; S. Wilson, The Gentiles and the Gentile Mission, 121-124.

[2]A possible allusion to Ps 109:16, κατανενευγμένον τῇ καρδία; Haenchen, 183. Lindars, New Testament Apologetic, 109, suggests its use may have been prompted by the citation of Ps 109 at 1:20.

is so intended here (cf. 2:38 above). The life of the first
believers, then, is the life of the Spirit. V. 42 specifies
four activities through which this life is manifested.[1] Those
who were baptized were sedulous, προσκαρτεροῦντες (cf. 1:14,
2:46), in their attention to the teaching of the Apostles, the
common life (κοινωνία), the breaking of bread, and prayer.
These four elements are then elaborated by vv. 43-47.[2] The
structure of the passage indicates that in using κοινωνία in
v. 42 Luke intends us to understand that spiritual sharing
which was manifested by the community of possessions.[3]

----

[1]With Haenchen, 191, and L. Thornton, The Common Life in
the Body of Christ (London: Dacre Press, 1941), 5, we see v.
42 as specifying four elements of the first believers' lives,
and not, as J. Jeremias, Die Abendmahlsworte Jesu 3rd ed.
(Göttingen: Vandenhoeck and Ruprecht, 1960), 111, as four
elements of the primitive liturgy. Cf. also B. Reicke, Glaube
und Leben der Urgemeinde, 57, who notes on the other hand that
the distribution of goods is given a cultic coloration by the
other elements of v. 42. However v. 42 was composed (cf. H.
Zimmermann, "Die Sammelberichte der Apostelgeschichte," BZ n.f.
5 [1961] 75f), it is clear that it stands in the closest relation with vv. 43-47, and should not be interpreted apart from
the perspective offered by those verses. Thus the conclusion
of F. Mussner, "Die Una Sancta nach Apg.2,42," Praesentia
Salutis (Düsseldorf: Patmos-Verlag, 1967) 212-222, that the
κοινωνία of 2:42 qualifies the adherence of the believers to
the teaching of the Apostles as an "Idealbild" of a heresy-less
primitive community, does not take into account the clear
reference to the "common life" through the sharing of possessions in vv. 44-45.

[2]The structure of the passage as a whole shows a careful
balance of elements. 41b and 47b form an inclusio by their
references to the growth of the community. The teaching of the
Apostles is picked up by v. 43 (and not by v. 46, which speaks
of all being in the Temple). The κοινωνία is amplified by the
description of community possessions in vv. 44-45; the breaking
of bread by v. 46, and the prayers by v. 47a, which also refers
back to the "fear" of v. 43. The development of vv. 43-47,
therefore, forms a rough but consistent correspondence to the
four elements of v. 42.

[3]Cf. Haenchen, 191; Reicke, Glaube und Leben, 57; Dupont,
Etudes, 518; J. Campbell, "κοινωνία and its cognates in the New
Testament," JBL 51 (1932) 374; H. Seesemann, Der Begriff
KOINΩNIA im Neuen Testament, 87-89. F. Hauck, "κοινός," TDNT
3 (1965) 809, says that κοινωνία here does not signify a concrete practice, but "it is rather an abstract and spiritual
term for the fellowship of brotherly concord established and
manifested by the life of the community." That is precisely
the point: the sharing of possessions is the external manifestation of this spiritual fellowship, and for Luke the reality
and symbol are inseparable.

2. It should not be surprising that the elaboration of the teaching of the Apostles in v. 43 focuses on their working of τέρατα καὶ σημεῖα and arousing fear among the people, for the Gospel has prepared us to see the teaching of Jesus and the Apostles as a demonstration of power.[1] What is more striking is the way in which Luke has so naturally and immediately transferred to the Apostles the stereotyped language associated with Moses and the Prophet like Moses, Jesus, so that the Apostles are at once seen to stand in that prophetic tradition.[2] The authority of the Apostles in this passage is sketched only briefly, but we see that it has both an inward and outward reference: the believers adhere to their teaching, and those outside are filled with awe. This is stated in a matter of fact way. We shall see that as the Apostles' authority is threatened, Luke will progressively emphasize it.

3. Luke devotes vv. 44-45 to an elaboration of the κοινωνία, first with a general statement of principle, then with a recounting of the practice. In v. 44, the expression "all the believers" together with the verb in the imperfect denote a universal, continuing practice, and not the occasional spontaneous generosity of individuals. Luke has brought together two correlative phrases. First, all the believers were ἐπὶ τὸ αὐτό.[3] Although there have been attempts at defining this expression along the lines of the technical (?) Qumran designation for community,[4] the LXX provides adequate precedent for its use[5] and more significantly, the phrase appears quite at home in the topos on friendship.[6] The way Luke has already

---

[1] Cf. above, pp. 112f.

[2] Cf. Cerfaux, Recueil 2, 147ff.

[3] For the textual difficulties, cf. Ropes, 24, and Dupont, "L'Union entre les premières Chrétiens dans les Actes des Apôtres," NRT 91 (1969) 906.

[4] Cf. Fitzmyer, "Jewish Christianity," 241-242; H. Braun, Qumran und das Neue Testament I, 143.

[5] Cf. Cerfaux, Recueil 2, 153; Dupont, "L'Union," 907. Cf. also the use in I Cor 7:5; 11:20; 14:23.

[6] Cerfaux, Recueil 2, 150-151.

used the phrase in 1:15 and 2:1 suggests that we understand it
simply as "together." In the light of the other characteristic
expression ὁμοθυμαδόν (1:14, 2:46), however, ἐπὶ τὸ αὐτό
bespeaks more than physical contiguity; it implies a unity of
heart among the believers.[1] The second phrase, εἶχον ἅπαντα
κοινά, is an obvious reminiscence of the hellenistic _topos_ on
friendship, τοῖς φίλοις πάντα κοινά.[2] What Luke has done,
therefore, is to make οἱ πιστεύσαντες [ἦσαν] ἐπὶ τὸ αὐτό stand
for τοῖς φίλοις in the proverb. From all that we have seen of
Luke's use of language about possessions, it is clear that his
use of the proverb is not artificial, but functions as a profound expression of his own understanding. As we have seen in
our analysis of the story of the Lost Son and the death of
Judas, Luke sees the sharing of all possessions as the natural
and inevitable corollary of life together. In the perfect
unity of mind and heart established by the Spirit, only a full
sharing of goods could function as an adequate expression of
that interior oneness.

V. 45 spells out the practice, with two notable differences from the description of chapter four. First, the terms
for possessions are vague and generalized: κτήματα and
ὑπάρξεις lack any specificity.[3] Second, there are only two
stages to the process. The believers sell their possessions
and distribute them to all as each had need. There is no role
assigned here to the Apostles, and in particular there is not
the intermediate stage of laying possessions at the Apostles'
feet. This difference is an important clue to the literary
function of each passage. As we shall see in chapter four,
where the emphasis is on the question of the Apostles' authority and the issue of inclusion/exclusion from the people,
possessions dominate the description. Here, where the purpose
is to describe the essential aspects of the life of the
believers, the use of possessions stands among other elements
as a straightforward symbolization of the believers' spiritual
unity.

---

[1]Dupont, "L'Union," 903-908.

[2]Cf. above, pp. 2-3.

[3]Cf. Haenchen, 195.

4. Vv. 46-47 complete the elaboration of v. 42.
The mention of the believers προσκαρτεροῦντες ὁμοθυμαδὸν ἐν
τῷ ἱερῷ allows us to allude to another aspect of the pattern
of the Prophet and the People in Luke-Acts.[1] There is no doubt
that not only Jerusalem is important for the structuring of
Luke's work, but Jerusalem as the place of the Temple: the
infancy narratives reach their climax with the entry of Jesus
into the Temple; the Temple temptation holds climactic position
in the Lukan temptation narrative. Particularly interesting is
the way Luke speaks of the Temple from ch. 19 of the Gospel.
From the time Jesus chases out the money changers who made the
house of prayer a den of thieves, the Temple becomes the locus
of Jesus' teaching before his death and the place of the
Apostles' preaching all during the Jerusalem narrative of Acts.
This connection is made so insistently (Lk 19:47-8; 20:1; 21:1-
5; 24:53; Acts 2:46; 3:1ff; 5:12, 25, 42) that we must wonder
if Luke may not have in mind some text like Mal 3:1-4, in which
the Lord appears in the Temple and purifies the people so that
they can offer acceptable sacrifices.[2] It appears that by
placing the Christians so emphatically within the Temple
environs, Luke is making a statement about the true Israel;
the real possessors of the Temple are the faithful members of
the people.[3] Luke also knows the Temple has been destroyed,
so that the Temple appears as a sign of the rejection of the
unfaithful part of Israel (cf. Lk 19:44 with 21:6; Acts 7:48-9)
and as the place of the climactic rejection of Paul (Acts
22:27ff). The role of the Temple within the pattern of the
Prophet and the People is therefore a complex one[4] and cannot
be analyzed here. We can suggest, however, that by placing the
first believers in the Temple, Luke may be expressing the

---

[1] Immediately, of course, v. 46 sets the stage for the next
incident, the healing of the lame man at the gate of the Temple.

[2] This suggestion has already been made by R. Laurentin,
Structure et Théologie de Luc I-II, 56f, in regard to the
entrance of Jesus into the Temple at the climax of the infancy
narrative.

[3] Cf. Conzelmann, Theology, 147.

[4] Cf. Flender, Luke, 107-109; Gaston, No Stone on Another,
365-369.

conviction that the last authentic role of the Temple was
played when it was taken over by the believers and became the
place where the Word about Jesus was preached.

Concerning the breaking of bread in the households, we
need only note that Luke describes the practice as an occasion
for messianic joy (ἐν ἀγαλλιάσει, cf. Lk 1:14, 44), and
probably saw it as a cultic act which involved the presence
of the risen Lord (cf. Lk 22:14; 24:30, 35, 43; Acts 1:4;
10:41; 18:11).[1] The account closes with mention of the favor
(χάρις) enjoyed by the believers with the people of Jerusalem,[2]
thus qualifying the φόβος of v. 43 as the fear of religious awe
so familiar in Luke. We need only remark in passing that the
awkward ἐπὶ τὸ αὐτό at the end of v. 47, which has generated so
many textual variants, and stimulated such discussion,[3] may
properly be seen as a final emphasis upon the unity of the
first community.[4]

5. The literary function of possessions in this
passage is remarkable only for its lack of complexity. Luke
has obviously described the life of the first believers in
idyllic terms.[5] But the very atmosphere of peace which per-
vades this first description raises important questions about
the subsequent narrative. Having so beautifully expressed the
ideal of life together in this passage, why must Luke return
to it again in chapter four, and with such a different emphasis? Or, if his purpose was to treat here of the community's

[1]Cf. Reicke, Glaube und Leben, 61; Ph.-H. Menoud, "Les
Actes des Apôtres et l'Eucharistie," RHPR 33 (1953) 21-36;
W. Dowd, "Breaking Bread, Acts 2:46," CBQ 1 (1939) 358-362.

[2]D reads πρὸς ὅλον τὸν κόσμον. J. Epp, The Theological
Tendancy of Codex Bezae Cantabrigiensis in Acts, 77, considers
this an instance of D's tendency to bypass the Jews in stressing the universality of salvation.

[3]Cf. C. Torrey, The Composition and Date of Acts, 10-14;
M. Wilcox, The Semitisms of Acts, 93-97; H. Sparks, "The
Semitisms of the Acts," JTS n.s. 1-2 (1950-1) 17-19; D. Payne,
"Semitisms in the Book of Acts," Apostolic History and the
Gospel, 142.

[4]Cf. Wilcox, Semitisms, 98-100; Haenchen, 193.

[5]Schmitt, "L'église," 217, calls the mood of this description one of a "paix paradisiaque."

190

use of possessions, why didn't he follow with the story of
Barnabas, Ananias and Sapphira? The answer is found in the
turn the story takes after this passage. We have noted that
2:41-47 is the climax of the first period. It is a narration
which contains no sour notes, no hint of division. The number
of converts is large, all are united, the authority of the
Twelve is undisputed. But with this description, the completely halcyon days of the first community are ended. By placing
the believers in the Temple, Luke has provided a smooth transition to the next section, which opens with Peter and John on
their way to the Temple for prayer (3:1). But after the healing of the lame man a new element enters the story, an element
of conflict and rejection, centering around the Twelve and
their authority.

C. The Healing of the Lame Man (3:1-10).

Our treatment here will be very brief, for this is the one
passage in the first part of Acts where the role of possessions
is minor. In v. 6, Peter responds to the lame man who had
sought alms from the two Apostles: ἀργύριον καὶ χρυσίον οὐχ
ὑπάρχει μοι ὃ δὲ ἔχω τοῦτό σοι δίδωμι. ἐν τῷ ὀνόματι ᾽Ιησοῦ
χριστοῦ τοῦ Ναζωραίου περιπάτει. The statement clearly contrasts what the Apostle lacked to what he had. The man sought
alms and got healing. The whole passage, as we have seen, sets
up the first encounter with the Council and enables Luke to
clarify the nature and derivation of the apostolic power.[1]
Peter's remark does remind us that Luke has not yet placed the
Apostles at the center of the community goods, when, presumably,
they would have the purse and be able to give alms. Or, we
could suggest that Peter's lack of funds resulted from the
community's goods being shared out among the members, so that
there was none left over for alms to outsiders. But these
remarks are simply attempts at harmonization and do not get to
the heart of the matter. It is obvious that in this passage,
possessions are being used simply as a negative foil, to point

---

[1]For a full discussion of this healing story within the
Lukan theology and from a perspective similar to our own, cf.
the unpublished dissertation of D. Hamm, This Sign of Healing,
Acts 3:1-10 (St. Louis University, 1975).

up the enormity of what the Apostles did possess, the power to
heal in the Name of Jesus.

D. The Second Description of Community Life/Ananias and
    Sapphria (4:32-5:11).

The progress of Luke's narrative from the healing of the
lame man to the appointment of the Seven hinges on the conflict
created by the authority of the Twelve over the people. The
story moves from a first challenge to that authority to an
unconscious and ironic vindication of it by the opposition.
This context is critical for the understanding of the literary
function of 4:32-5:11. We shall therefore begin with a fairly
extended discussion of the movement of the story in these
chapters, then analyze the function of 4:32-5:11 within that
context.

1. The Context:

    a) Peter's Speech (3:12-26): We devoted considerable
attention to this speech in chapter one of this study and saw
how, starting from the clarification of the Apostles' power
(3:13) as the power of God glorifying His servant Jesus, the
discourse moves into a presentation of the rejection and vindication of the Prophet Jesus. We also saw how the opportunity
to accept or reject the Prophet whom God raised up was renewed,
made contemporary for the hearers of the speech.[1] We now take
note of the way the call to conversion at the conclusion of the
speech serves as a literary prophecy for the following narrative.

If vv. 20-21 are read apart from the context of the speech
and its place in the story, they are difficult. But read within the story-line, they are clear enough. Peter promises first
that a certain result will follow upon conversion which will
occur in two stages. For those who convert, there will come
the "times of refreshment" which will last until (ἄχρι) the
sending of the Christ to accomplish the restoration of all
things. This passage should not be understood apart from Acts
1:11 (Jesus will return in the same way the disciples saw him
going), and Jesus' response to the Apostles' question about the

---

[1] Cf. above, pp. 65-67.

restoration of the Kingdom to Israel in Acts 1:6, a response
which answers the question about restoration in terms of their
witness and, primarily, the gift of the Holy Spirit (1:8). It
would be perfectly in keeping with Luke's understanding, therefore, to see the promised "times of refreshment" precisely as
the enjoyment of the Abrahamic blessings by the believers among
Israel, their possession of the Holy Spirit.[1] The strong
emphasis in 3:24ff on the opportunity presented to the present
generation (all the prophets talked about these days, 3:24
. . . you are sons of the prophets and the covenant, 3:25 . . .
to you first God has sent His son blessing you, 3:26) makes
this even more likely. Furthermore, as we have seen so frequently, it is entirely typical of Luke's literary method to
follow such programmatic statements by their fulfillment in the
narrative. Where then are we to find those enjoying the "times
of refreshment"? In the description of community life in
4:32ff. When we look at that passage, we will find another
reason to support this suggestion.

We have also seen that vv. 22-23 make contemporary the
threat of extermination from the people for those who do not
heed the Prophet. For this threat, too, there is an immediate
fulfillment in the narrative in the way Luke describes the
progressive alienation of the leaders from the people, and most
directly in the story of Ananias and Sapphira, where the
failure to heed the prophetic authority of the Apostles leads
to the ultimate extermination from the people, death.[2]

b) The First Trial (4:1-22): The response to Peter's
Pentecost speech had been entirely positive. But here the
response of faith by many (4:4) is sharply contrasted to the
leaders' anger at the Apostles' teaching of the people (4:1).
Their rejection is expressed by putting the Apostles in prison,

---

[1]Cf. F. Mussner, "Die Idee der Apokatastasis in der
Apostelgeschichte," Praesentia Salutis, 223-234.

[2]Cf. Schmitt, "L'église," 214. Brown, Apostasy and
Perseverence, 106, contests this by claiming that the punishment spoken of in 3:23 is directed not at sinful Christians,
but unbelieving Jews. He does not support this contention.
It is doubtful that Luke had this distinction in mind, and the
wording of the threat itself makes clear that πᾶσα ψυχή would
be cut off for not heeding the prophet's words.

thus setting up the first direct confrontation between the old
leaders and the new, and posing the question which dominates
this part of the narrative: who are the true leaders of the
restored Israel?

The encounter opens with the question, "By what power or
in what name have you done this?" (4:7). Peter's response
makes clear, as had the opening of his speech in 3:12, that it
is the power of the rejected but risen Prophet Jesus who is at
work in the Apostles. He goes further, however, and places the
blame for the death of Jesus directly on the leaders (4:10-
11).[1] The boldness of the Apostles' defense shows indeed that
they speak with Jesus' own power (4:12), and that, together
with the indisputable presence of the healed man, reduces the
leaders to issuing nothing more than a rebuke. We notice that
they would have liked to have done more, but already their
grasp on the people was slipping: μηδὲν εὑρίσκοντες τὸ πῶς
κολάσωνται αὐτοὺς διὰ τὸν λαὸν ὅτι πάντες ἐδόξαζον τὸν θεὸν
ἐπὶ τῷ γεγονότι (4:21). This first skirmish is indecisive,
but sets off a chain of important consequences. The Apostles
had won favor among the people, it is true, and the erstwhile
leaders were beginning to lose control, but the success of the
mission was nevertheless threatened. For the first time the
Apostles had, like Moses, like Jesus, experienced rejection.
Would they now, like Moses, like Jesus, be filled with new
power to assert their full authority over the people? And
would they be rejected a second time, like Moses and Jesus?
And would those who rejected them this second time be themselves rejected from the people definitively?

c) The Prayer for Power (4:23-31): The Apostles
return πρὸς τοὺς ἰδίους, that is to the other Apostles,[2] and
relate the threats of the Sanhedrin. In response, the Apostles
pray that they might receive the power to carry on their

---

[1] Cf. above, pp. 68f.

[2] Against the opinion of most commentators (e.g., Haenchen,
226; Bauernfeind, Die Apostelgeschichte, 79; Lake-Cadbury, 45;
Flender, Luke, 141), Dupont, Études, 521, correctly identifies
the ἰδίους to whom Peter and John return as the Apostles.
"Pierre et Jean rejoignent les autres membres du collège
apostolique, et, tous ensemble, les Apôtres prient Dieu de les
secourir dans l'exercice de leur ministère."

194

mission. It is undoubtedly true that this scene stands as an
example of the piety of the believers, and showed how they
turned to prayer in times of crisis,[1] but much more is involved
here. First, we notice that in the prayer (vv. 25-28), the
trials of the Apostles are not mentioned at all, but only the
rejection of Jesus,[2] followed by the petition on behalf of the
Apostles. This strengthens the bonds of identification between
Jesus and the Apostles by implying that the rejection of the
Apostles is based on and is the continuation of the rejection
of Jesus. Second, as we have noted before,[3] the power asked
for τοῖς δούλοις σου is the power associated with the Prophet
Jesus, the power to proclaim the Word boldly, to work signs and
wonders, to heal. This also clearly emphasizes the prophetic
authority of the Apostles. Third, the violent manifestation of
the Spirit signifies that this power is in fact being bestowed,
which is manifested immediately by their speaking the Word of
God μετὰ παρρησίας (4:31).[4]

If it had not been obvious to the reader before, Luke here
makes it plain that the words and deeds of the Apostles from
here on in the story will be the powerful words and deeds of
men filled with the Spirit of God, possessed with the same
prophetic authority as Jesus. In the story of Acts, this
second bestowal of the Spirit is far from being a doublet of
the Pentecost account; it is a watershed in the story. From
now until the end of the Jerusalem narrative the authority of
the Apostles will be continually emphasized and heightened, so
that even their subsequent trials and experiences of rejection
will appear as triumphs and as vindications of their authority.

d) The Power of the Apostles (5:12-16): If we move
over the two passages of central interest to us and pick up the

[1]Haenchen, 229.

[2]It has been frequently noted that the citation from Ps 2
here appears to have had an influence on the Lukan passion
narrative. Cf. Haenchen, 226-227; Wilckens, Die Missionsreden
der Apostelgeschichte, 132, n. 1; M. Rese, Alttestamentliche
Motive in der Christologie des Lukas, 95; Dupont, Etudes, 265.

[3]Cf. above, p. 60.

[4]Dupont, Etudes, 522.

narrative after the story of Ananias and Sapphira, we see that
the power of the Apostles is portrayed in almost superhuman
terms. Again they are said to work σημεῖα καὶ τέρατα among the
people (5:12). They ignore the injunction of the leaders by
preaching once more in the portico of Solomon.[1] Vv. 13-14 have
caused commentators problems, since they appear at first sight
to be contradictory. Luke mentions first that although the
people magnified the Apostles, none dared join them; then he
adds that a great number of believers was converted to the
Lord.[2] But if we translate κολλᾶσθαι as "associating with" in
the physical sense, there is no real problem.[3] Indeed, the
verse further emphasizes the majesty of the Apostles, lending
them an aura of the numinous. Such is the awe they inspire
(5:11) that none dare approach them; they are set apart. Yet
their power is compelling and attractive,[4] and many are drawn
to belief. So great is the force radiating from the Apostles
that people bring the sick out into the streets so that the
shadow of Peter might fall on them, and they are all cured
(5:15-16).

---

[1]Much of the confusion created by this passage can be
eliminated if we simply understand the Apostles as the subjects
of v. 12b and those referred to by αὐτοῖς in v. 13. Against
Haenchen, 241, 245, there is no reason why the ἅπαντες of v.
12b should refer to all the believers and not just the Apostles.
From 4:1, the whole focus of the story has been on the Apostles,
and it continues to be here. Further, as we learn from 5:26
and 5:42, the Temple is the place where the Apostles teach.

[2]Cf. Torrey, Composition and Date, 32. Dibelius, 91,
suggested that an early scribal error replaced τῶν δὲ ἀρχόντων
with τῶν δὲ λοιπῶν. Brown, Apostasy and Perseverence, 144-145,
thinks that the use of κολλᾶσθαι in 5:13 ". . . evidently
signifies the absence of the definitive commitment of faith,
despite the popularity which the Apostles enjoyed." This is
hardly likely.

[3]Against Haenchen, 243, n. 5, all the uses of κολλάω in
Acts (8:29; 9:26; 10:28; 17:34) make perfectly good sense when
understood as indicating physical proximity. The element of
"spiritual allegiance" discerned in 17:34 is supplied by
πιστεύω. Luke's use of κολλάω in the story of the Lost Son
(Lk 15:15) indicates physical attachment but hardly an allegiance of mind and heart.

[4]Haenchen's allusion (244) to the Mysterium Tremendum
here is apposite.

196

Luke pictures the power of the Apostles here as an almost abstract and impersonal force. Not even Jesus was said to cure by the mere shadow of his presence.[1] The effect of all this is to make the reader wonder whether there is any power at all that can resist this movement, for those who proclaim it have the power to strike dead (Ananias and Sapphira) and to heal the sick by a word, by their mere presence.

     e) The Second Trial (5:17-42): The crisis of the Apostles' authority over the people reaches its climax and resolution in the second confrontation with the leaders, a confrontation which makes clear that the old leaders of Israel have totally lost their hold over the people and are powerless to impede the movement of the Gospel. The second imprisonment of the Apostles comes about because the leaders are jealous of their success (5:17). But no sooner are they put in prison, than an angel of the Lord frees them and orders them back to the Temple to preach the Word of this life, which the Apostles do (5:19-21).[2] By this _deus ex machina_ Luke has pulled out every literary stop to show how invincible the progress of the Word and the authority of the Apostles is. If the whole cosmic paraphernalia is ready to post bail, being clapped in prison by the leaders appears as no more than a minor irritation, a temporary setback. The opposition of men is an exercise in futility.

    The following scene, drawn with great irony,[3] reduces the pretensions of the erstwhile leaders to absurdity. The whole power structure of Israel meets in solemn assembly (5:21) to pass judgment on these upstarts who had the temerity to challenge their power. But the prisoners have disappeared. The leaders are left to dither about how this could have happened (5:24), and while they argue, a messenger arrives with the news that the men they had imprisoned are at that very moment standing in the Temple διδάσκοντες τὸν λαόν (5:25).

---

[1]The nearest thing in the Gospel narrative is the healing of the woman who touched Jesus' garment, Lk 8:43ff.

[2]The story of Peter's release in 12:7ff has obvious similarities.

[3]Cf. J. Jonsson, _Humor and Irony in the New Testament_ (Reykjavik: Bókaútgáfa Menningarsjóds, 1965), 209.

The Council is reduced to persuasion in their attempt to get the Apostles back for trial. If they try to use force, they run the risk of being stoned by the people (5:26; cf. Lk 20:6). With deftness and even humor, Luke has subtly but surely established his point: the effective leadership over Israel has passed from the old leaders to the new. The old leaders are so alienated from the people that they risk suffering the punishment for blasphemy (cf. Acts 6:11, 7:58) if they openly oppose the Twelve.

As we noted in chapter one of this study, the confrontation between Peter and the Council is considerably sharper than at the first trial.[1] The leaders accuse the Apostles of bringing the blame for Jesus' death on them (5:28), and in Peter's response there is no denial of this charge, but by implication (5:30-31), its affirmation. We also saw how the witness of the Apostles is linked to that of the Holy Spirit in 5:32, so that the rejection of that witness becomes tantamount to disobedience to God and a sign of not possessing the Holy Spirit. Luke proceeds to show that this is true of the leaders by having them become enraged at Peter's words and seeking to kill the Apostles (5:33).

The intervention of the Pharisee Gamaliel at this juncture appears to save the Apostles' lives. More importantly, it provides Luke with an opportunity for expressing through the mouth of Gamaliel what surely must be his own view of matters. The advice of Gamaliel makes perfectly good sense at one level, that of theology. If a movement is from God, nothing can stop it anyway; if it is from men, it will wither away of its own accord. The policy of hands-off is not only prudent, but in this case necessary, unless they wish to run the risk of becoming θεομάχοι (5:39). But although this view of things makes perfectly good sense from Luke's standpoint, in the mouth of Gamaliel the words are filled with a tragic irony. Luke knows, and the reader by this time surely knows, that the Apostles' witness is from God, impelled and validated by the Spirit. The reader also knows that the leaders have already done what they could to stop the Apostles, and that they will

---

[1]Cf. above, p. 69.

right after Gamaliel's advice proceed to beat the Apostles and
command them to stop preaching in the Name of Jesus. The
leaders are therefore already convicted of being θεομάχοι.
But the irony is still deeper. By what right does Gamaliel
take such an Olympian view of things? His words are words of
hypocrisy, for the witness of the Apostles and the Spirit
called for conversion. Gamaliel and the leaders had been
confronted by this witness. For them to take a stance of
hands-off was itself hypocritical and showed that they did
not possess the Spirit of obedience to God.[1] Gamaliel in this
scene is not the "good Pharisee" he is often seen as; his words
(which are true for Luke, and clearly have an apologetic motivation as understood by Luke) carry for him self-condemnation.

In any case, whatever action the leaders might take would
be useless. The position of the Twelve has been too firmly
established. After their beating we find them triumphant:
πᾶσάν τε ἡμέραν ἐν τῷ ἱερῷ καὶ κατ' οἶκον οὐκ ἐπαύοντο
διδάσκοντες καὶ εὐαγγελιζόμενοι τὸν χριστόν 'Ιησοῦν (5:42).
We see therefore that the story around 4:32-5:11 is that of
the progressive assertion of the authority of the Twelve over
against threat from the outside, and the steady erosion of the
old leaders' authority over Israel.

2. The Passages (4:32-5:11): Within the context we have
established, it is fairly easy to define the literary function
of these passages dealing with possessions. We notice first
that the setting for the passages is within the community
(4:32). Set between the external challenges to the leadership
of the Apostles by the leaders, these passages serve to establish and symbolize their authority within the people. Second,
the passages taken together form a sort of diptych presenting
the positive and negative aspects of the same dynamic, joined
by the common elements of possessions and the authority of the
Apostles.

a) 4:32-37 consists of a generalized statement about
the practice of community goods (32-35) and the donation of
Barnabas (36-37). The generalized description follows this

---

[1]This nuance is caught by Ehrhardt, Acts of the Apostles,
28, who says Gamaliel "missed the bus."

structure: a) a first statement of the ideal (v. 32), b) the
powerful work of the Apostles (v. 33), c) a specification of
the practice of sharing (34), d) now with the Apostles at the
center of the community goods (v. 35). In this progression we
see that v. 33, regarded by some as intrusive,[1] actually flows
consistently from 4:31 and provides Luke with a natural transition to the insertion of the Apostles within the community
sharing.

b) In v. 32 Luke fleshes out the elliptic reference
to the hellenistic proverb found in 2:42. By calling the
believers καρδία καὶ ψυχὴ μία, as we have seen, Luke has combined the classic hellenistic definition of friendship with the
traditional biblical term for the inner man.[2] He has thereby
explicitly identified the community as a community of friends.
As we have already seen from ch. 2, however, it is clear that
the basis of this friendship is their unity in the Holy Spirit.
The proverb is now expanded in its negative and positive forms.
Saying "none of those who had anything called it his own" is
the same thing as saying "they had all things in common." The
negative phrasing of course, points us to the story of Judas,
who manifested his apostasy from the Twelve by seeking a "place
of his own" (1:25). Here as in 2:42, then, the community of
possessions functions in the first place as a manifestation of
spiritual unity; the way the believers disposed of their
possessions showed that they were one heart and soul.

c) Two further things can be said about v. 33. First,
the witness of the Apostles to the resurrection of Jesus is
carried out with δυνάμει μεγάλη, clearly as a result of the
outpouring of the Spirit in 4:31. This mention sets up the
presentation of the Apostles' authority within the community.
Second, corresponding to that "great power," Luke says that
χάρις μεγάλη was upon all of them. We might at first think
that this "grace" meant, as it did in 2:47, the favor the
community enjoyed among the people, but it does not. Luke
does not speak of favor πρὸς anyone, as he did there; rather
the grace or favor is upon (ἐπί) all of them. This slight

---

[1]Cf. above, pp. 7-8, n. 3.

[2]Cf. above, p. 5.

200

divergence is significant, because from what follows immediately in v. 34, it is clear that Luke sees the χάρις which the
community enjoyed as the blessing of God.[1] The connection thus
established with the following verse further strengthens the
position of v. 33 within the context.

      d) V. 34 contains a clear allusion to Deut 15:4-5 in
the phrase οὐδὲ γὰρ ἐνδεής τις ἦν ἐν αὐτοῖς. The passage in
Deuteronomy deals with the legislation for the release of the
land every seven years and with the duty of almsgiving to the
poor. It reads: ὅτι οὐκ ἔσται ἐν σοι ἐνδεής ὅτι εὐλογῶν
εὐλογήσει σε κύριος ὁ θεος σου ἐν τῇ γῇ. "Being without need"
therefore is a <u>sign</u> of God's blessing, a blessing of Israel
"on the Land." Deut 15:5 gives the condition for this blessing: ἐὰν δὲ ἀκοῇ εἰσακούσητε τῆς φωνῆς κυρίου τοῦ θεοῦ ὑμῶν
φυλάσσειν καὶ ποιεῖν πάσας τὰς ἐντολας ταύτας ὅσας ἐγὼ
ἐντέλλομαί σοι σήμερον.[2] The commandments given that day
included, of course, the sharing of the land with the poor and
the giving of alms.

      By means of vv. 33b-34, therefore, Luke portrays the
believing community as the faithful Israel which enjoys the
blessing of God on the land.[3] It is this allusion which adds
support to our contention that Luke is here placing the fulfillment of the promise in 3:20-21 that those who converted
would enjoy the "times of refreshment." It also cautions us
from supposing that, because of his use of the hellenistic
proverb, Luke is simply portraying the Christian community as
a philosophic school. Consistent with his presentation
throughout, Luke sees the community as the authentic Israel,
the receiver of God's blessings.

      e) Vv. 34b-35 elaborate the practice of sharing.
The language of possessions is here more concrete than in 2:45.
Whoever had a χωρίον (field or farm) or οἰκία (house) sold
them. But now we find a new element. They took the profits

---

[1]So Haenchen, 231, n. 4. The change of wording is slight,
but the change of emphasis is considerable. This is not
noticed by Gaston, No Stone on Another, 303.

[2]The similarity of this command to Deut 18:5ff should be
evident.

[3]Schmitt, "L'église," 214.

of these sales καὶ ἐτίθουν παρὰ τοὺς πόδας τῶν ἀποστόλων. The
insertion of the Apostles here at the receiving end would imply
that they also carried out the distribution: διεδίδετο δὲ
ἑκάστῳ καθότι ἄν τις χρείαν εἶχεν (cf. 2:45). The laying of
the possessions at the Apostles' feet so that they might make
distribution is the most significant difference in this account
from 2:44-45. What does the act signify? The fact that Luke
repeats the same expression three times (4:35, 37; 5:2) lends
it a certain ritual quality. Simply as a human gesture, the
action would seem to symbolize a handing over into the power of
another, therefore an act of submission to another.[1] When what
is handed over is property (or the price for property), it
would seem to indicate the giving over to another's disposition
the power of subsistence, that is, life. Can this interpretation be supported?

   We have noted on many occasions that Luke employs consciously "biblical" language. It is interesting to note that
there is a rich precedent for "being at the feet of another" in
the LXX. The consistent reality symbolized by being at the
feet of another is submission; conversely, to have another at
one's feet symbolizes authority, dominion. Thus, Joshua tells
his commanders to place their feet on the necks of the captive
kings, and promises that in like manner will the Lord treat all
Israel's enemies (Josh 10:24). A particularly fascinating
scene is the one in which Abigail goes out to meet David,
carrying with her presents. She falls ἐπὶ τοὺς πόδας αὐτοῦ
(I Sam 25:24). Again in 25:41 she falls at his feet and
declares herself a handmaiden for washing his feet. In this
instance, the possessions brought to David indicate her allegiance to his cause; falling at his feet indicates she is placing
herself in submission to him, disposing herself for his judgment. The enemies of David also fall ὑπὸ τοὺς πόδας αὐτοῦ
(II Sam 22:39). Particularly in the psalms, authority is
signified by having others under the feet. Thus for the Son
of Man, God has placed all things ὑποκάτω τῶν ποδῶν αὐτοῦ
(Ps 8:7; cf. Pss 17:10; 46:4; 98:5; 131:7). And in another

---

[1]The references to extra-biblical literature are scattered.
Cf. Wettstein, Novum Testamentum Graecum II, 481.

text favored by N.T. writers we read that "the Lord said to my Lord κάθου ἐκ δεξιῶν μου ἕως ἄν θῶ τοὺς ἐχθρούς σου ὑποπόδιον τῶν ποδῶν σου" (Ps 110:1).

As in the other gospels, Luke uses the posture of being at another's feet as a gesture of submission. Thus the repeated use in the story of the sinful woman (Lk 7:38, 44, 45, 46). The Gerasene demoniac sits at Jesus' feet after his exorcism and, when Jesus is departing, falls at his feet (8:35, 41). Mary the sister of Martha sits πρὸς τοὺς πόδας τοῦ κυρίου to hear His words (10:39), and the healed Samaritan falls on his face παρὰ τοὺς πόδας αὐτοῦ (17:16). Luke cites Ps 110:1 in Lk 20:43 and Acts 2:35 in reference to the authority of Jesus. Further, he has Cornelius reverence Peter πεσὼν ἐπὶ τοὺς πόδας (Acts 10:25), and during Paul's first defence, he says that he studied παρὰ τοὺς πόδας Γαμαλιὴλ (Acts 22:3).

It is clear from all these passages that the posture of being at another's feet indicates the disposition of the self in submission to another. Why do we suggest that the laying of possessions at the feet of the Apostles symbolizes precisely the same thing? Could it not simply indicate that the believers were willing to let the Apostles handle the possessions? But to say this is to miss the whole significance which Luke gives to the disposition of possessions. Without going outside this passage, we have already learned that the disposition of possessions is a direct symbol of the disposition of the self. This is the meaning of having all things in common as an expression of spiritual unity. When the believers lay their possessions at the Apostles' feet, therefore, they were symbolically laying themselves there, in a gesture of submission to the authority of the Twelve.[1]

By the language of possessions in this passage, Luke has symbolically expressed that the believing community was united in the Spirit and was the faithful Israel enjoying the blessings of God promised to the land, and, most significantly at this point in the story, has shown that by laying their possessions at the feet of the Apostles these believers

---

[1]"Significabant, apostolos, divina gubernante sapientia, arbitrium omne rerum habere," J. Bengel, Gnomon Novi Testamenti 3rd ed. (Berlin: Gustav Schlawitz, 1855), 283.

accepted their authority over Israel. Thus while their
authority was being challenged by persecution from without,
the Apostles' authority over the people was being affirmed
from within.

      f) Vv. 36-37 relate the donation of Barnabas.
Barnabas as we have seen, is himself a prophetic man of the
Spirit and together with Paul will be the great missionary to
the Gentile world. Isn't it intriguing that Luke should intro-
duce him precisely at this point in the story?[1] We will
suggest the precise reason why Luke has introduced him in this
connection later. But for now, we should note that this is
the very first contact between Barnabas and the Twelve. He is
introduced with three biographical details, two of which will
be picked up later and have considerable relevance for the
telling of the story. The first detail is that he was a Levite,
and although membership in the tribe of Levi was certainly
associated in the O.T. with the question of property (the
Levites having had no portion in the Land),[2] there does not
seem to be any particular significance attached to that here.

      Second, Barnabas was not a Jerusalemite but a hellenistic
Jew, a native of Cyprus, and, as we shall see, this is particularly important in view of his role in chapter eleven. The
third biographical detail may at first seem insignificant, but
it is of the first importance. Barnabas' original name was
Joseph. His name Barnabas was given him by the Apostles.[3]
Luke translates this new name Barnabas as "son of consolation"[4]

----

[1]His introduction at this point is no more accidental than
that of Paul at the stoning of Stephen; Luke writes with a purpose. The answer to the question why Barnabas' gift was
singled out (cf. Dupont, "L'Union," 900) may have less to do
with the extraordinary nature of his generosity, than the role
he would play later in the story.

[2]Cf. e.g., Deut 12:12; 14:29; Josh 14:3, 4; 18:7. But
also, Josh 21:1ff.

[3]The textual evidence wavers between ὑπό and ἀπό, but
there is no real difference in meaning. Barnabas is named by
the Apostles, just as Jesus (Acts 2:22) is shown forth by God
(ἀπό) as Prophet. Cf. Haenchen, 231, n. 6.

[4]For the discussion of what Barnabas actually means, cf.
A. Deissmann, Bible Studies Trans. A. Grieve (Edinburgh: T. & T.
Clark, 1901) 307-310, and "Barnabas," ZNW 7 (1906) 91-92; also

and we shall see again how pertinent this is to Barnabas' role
in Acts.[1] What is most significant, however, is the naming
itself. It goes without saying that in the biblical tradition,
the bestowing of a name on another is an act of authority over
the thing or person named.[2] Indeed, there is a real sense in
which naming someone indicates control, effective power over
the other. In Luke-Acts, Peter is the only other to receive a
new name, and he receives it from Jesus (Lk 6:14). By stating
that Barnabas was given a new name by the Apostles, therefore,
Luke has from the beginning placed Barnabas in submission to
their authority.[3]

Luke further symbolizes this position of submission by
describing Barnabas' first action in the Book of Acts. He
sells the field which he owned and ἤνεγκεν τὸ χρῆμα καὶ ἔθηκεν
παρὰ τοὺς πόδας τῶν ἀποστόλων (4:37). By laying his possessions at the feet of the Apostles, Barnabas, like the other
believers, acknowledges their authority over him. Thus by two
symbolic actions, Luke has attached Barnabas to the authority
of the Twelve. This is Luke's first step in using possessions
to symbolize the smooth transition of authority to the Gentile
mission. By having from the beginning one of the two great
leaders of the Gentile mission express his submission to the
Twelve by receiving from them a new name and laying his goods
at their feet, Luke is subtly but effectively creating an image
in the reader's mind: the image of the Gentile mission under
the authority of the Twelve.

g) Ananias and Sapphira (5:1-11):[4] This passage is

H. J. Cadbury, "Some Personal Names in Luke-Acts," _Amicitiae
Corolla_ ed. by H. Wood (London: University of London Press,
1933) 47-48.

[1]Cf. Cerfaux, _Recueil_ 2, 177.

[2]Cf. H. Bietenhard, "ὄνομα," _TDNT_ 5 (1967) 253ff, and K.
Schmidt, "καλέω," _TDNT_ 3 (1965) 496-497.

[3]Bengel's remark is again perceptive: "Novum specimen
majestatis apostolicae, fidelibus cognomina dare," _Gnomon_, 283.

[4]The difficulty of this passage is evident from the lack
of satisfying analyses of it. The suggestion of Ph.-H. Menoud,
"La Mort d'Ananias et de Saphira (Actes 5:1-11)," _Aux Sources
de la Tradition Chrétienne_, 146-154, that the story was

explicitly connected with the last by the third repetition of
the phrase παρὰ τοὺς πόδας τῶν ἀποστόλων (5:2), by the use of
possessions, and by the role of the Apostles. It presents a
negative contrast to the picture of community life in 4:32-37.
That passage showed the fulfillment of the blessing in 3:20-21;
this passage showed the fulfillment of the threat in 3:22-23:
those who do not heed the voice of the Prophet will be cut off
from the people.[1] Together, the passages contain the full
pattern of inclusion/exclusion.

It is probable that Luke is alluding to another OT passage
in this story.[2] Acts 5:2 reads: καὶ ἐνοσφίσατο ἀπὸ τῆς τιμῆς.
In the LXX of the story of Achan (Josh 7:1ff) we read that
after Israel had conquered Jericho and in accordance with
God's command had placed all its goods under the ban,
ἐνοσφίσαντο ἀπὸ τοῦ ἀναθέματος. Achan was the one who kept
something back for himself out of that devoted to God, with
the result that the whole assembly was placed under the ban
and was unable to defeat its enemies (7:13). God tells Joshua
that the one who violated the ban must himself be placed under
the ban, that is, be destroyed. After a ritual process of
elimination, Achan is identified, and confronted by the man of
God with a demand for the truth. Achan confesses (7:19) and
is then stoned by the whole community (7:25).

The Acts story is similar in these respects: there is a
deceitful holding back of goods, a confrontation with God's
spokesman, and the cutting off the miscreants from the people

---

originally aetiological for the first deaths in the community,
is implausible; but even if it were correct, it would tell us
little about Luke's use of the story. Trocmé's suggestion
("Livre des Actes," 197-199), that Ananias and Sapphira were,
on analogy with Qumran, trying to buy their way into the ranks
of the perfect, is even less helpful. J. Derrett, "Ananias,
Sapphira, and the Right of Property," Downside Review 89 (1971)
225-232, offers a strange blend of rabbinic lore and psycholo-
gizing. Sapphira dies, for example, when she realizes that
she will not be able to mourn properly for her husband, who is
deprived of such rites because he has been punished by heaven
(230). Brown, Apostasy and Perseverence, 98ff, sees in this
passage the similarity to the apostasy of Judas, and has
worthwhile remarks.

[1]Cf. Schmitt, "L'église," 214.

[2]Brown, Apostasy and Perseverence, 196; Haenchen, 237.

206

by death. But there are also these important differences:
a) the property of the community itself is not said to be
sacred, as was that under the ban; b) in confrontation with
the man of God, the truth is not told but a lie; c) there is
no suggestion that the community was in danger of suffering
divine retaliation because of the sin of the couple; d) the
couple's death is not accomplished by the people stoning them
but simply by the powerful word of the Apostle.

In the light of these differences, we cannot regard the
story of Ananias and Sapphira as a retelling of the story of
Achan. Nevertheless, the certain verbal allusion of 5:2,[1]
and the major structural similarities enable us to suggest
that Luke was using the Achan story as a rough model for his
own, and that he intended the story to communicate much the
same message: that the misuse of possessions was an offense
against the community and thereby against God and must be
punished by exclusion from the community in the most radical
fashion. In Luke's story, interestingly, the role of Peter is
much greater than Joshua's, and the offense is seen much more
as being against the authority of the Apostles, as we shall now
see.

Vv. 1-2 reveal the counterfeit nature of the couple's
action from the first. For although they imitate the gesture
of the believers by selling their field,[2] they immediately show
that they are not "one heart and soul" with the community, for
they enter into a conspiracy to hold back something for themselves (ἐνοσφίσατο . . . συνειδυίης καὶ τῆς γυναικός), and lay
only a portion (μέρος) at the feet of the Apostles.[3] The
community's practice of sharing all things was a manifestation
of their total spiritual unity. To make the grand gesture of
sharing all things, while holding back something that can be

---

[1] νοσφίζομαι occurs elsewhere in the N.T. only at Tit 2:10,
and in the LXX only at Josh 7:1 and II Macc 4:32.

[2] κτῆμα, 5:1 = χωρίον, 5:3, 8.

[3] It is important to note that it is not simply the holding
back of the goods which constitutes the sin. It is specifically the conspiracy to do so, which disrupts the unity of the
Church. This conspiracy is manifested by the holding back of
possessions.

called "one's own," is a mockery of that Spirit of unity. It
is also a direct challenge to the authority of the Apostles.
For if they are not Men of the Spirit, if they are merely human
administrators, the conspiracy would work: Ananias and
Sapphira could enjoy the benefits of being among the people,
and still maintain their independence from it and from the
authority of the Twelve.

Peter shows immediately in vv. 3-4 that he is indeed a
Prophet, for he knows at once the nature of their conspiracy
and confronts Ananias with it. He knows that Ananias has not
acted out of the Spirit of God, for that Spirit impels to
unity; the divisive spirit of conspiracy manifested by the
holding back of goods can only come from another, inimical
spirit: Ἀνανία διὰ τί ἐπλήρωσεν ὁ Σατανᾶς τὴν καρδίαν σου;[1]
the same force at work in Judas was at work in Ananias.[2] The
phrase ψεύσασθαί σε τὸ πνεῦμα τὸ ἅγιον should be especially
noted. Ananias has not yet lied verbally to Peter (that is
left to Sapphira, 5:8); here the lying is linked directly to
the action of holding back the money: καὶ νοσφίσασθαι ἀπὸ τῆς
τιμῆς τοῦ χωρίου (5:3). By the action of conspiracy itself, in
other words, the couple has lied to the Holy Spirit. What is
strange about this phrase is that τὸ πνεῦμα τὸ ἅγιον stands as
the direct object of ψεύσασθαι, when we would have expected
either a preposition (e.g., κατά) or the use of the dative (as
in 5:4). We could interpret this as meaning that the Holy
Spirit was the one injured by the conspiracy. This is a daring
enough statement to be made by Luke. It is not just the unity
of a human assembly which is threatened by conspiracy, but the
Spirit of God Himself who creates that unity. An offense
against the unity is therefore an offense against God. Perhaps
we could also render the verse in this way (admittedly conjectural, but not without precedent):[3] "Why have you falsified

---

[1]The mss evidence for ἐπλήρωσεν is overwhelming, and
against A. D'Ales, "Actes V,3," RSR 24 (1934) 199-200, must be
taken as the original reading, particularly in the light of Lk
22:3. Cf. also Ropes, 46.

[2]Cf. Brown, Apostasy and Perseverence, 106.

[3]Cf. the references in Liddell-Scott, Greek-English
Lexicon, under ψεύδω, B II.

the Holy Spirit by holding back from the price of the field?"
In this translation the full force of the direct object is left
intact as well as the critical counterfeiting nature of the
couple's action. The sharing of all things was a direct sign
of the unity generated by the Spirit; it was a Spirit-filled
gesture. To falsify the sign is to falsify the Spirit itself.
Even without this conjectural translation, it is clear that
Luke identifies the gesture of conspiracy manifested by the
holding back of possessions as a sign of sinning against the
Spirit of God.

V. 4 emphasizes the gratuitousness of the couple's action.
The implication appears to be that they were not obliged to
hand over their goods, and if they did not, they had ἐξουσία
over the use of them.[1] But by making the gesture of laying the
possessions at the feet of the Apostles, they were symbolizing
the handing over of that ἐξουσία to them, and therefore could
no longer hold back anything for themselves. Peter is saying
that this deliberate πρᾶγμα on their part is a direct challenge
to the authority of the Apostles. This is made clear by the
next words: οὐκ ἐψεύσω ἀνθρώποις ἀλλὰ τῷ θεῷ. The Apostles as
the authority over the community were not just men; they were
filled with the Spirit of God, they were prophets. Just as
Luke sees the rejection of their witness as a rejection of
God's Spirit (cf. 5:32), so lying to them is lying to God.[2]
By having Peter perceive the hidden conspiracy, of course, Luke

---

[1]F. Schneidweiler, "Zu Act 5:4," ZNW 49 (1958) 136-137,
suggests an emendation of οὐχὶ to οὐχ ὅ, so that the verse
would read: "In no way does that which when unsold remained
at your disposal, still fall under your disposition once it has
been sold." But this does not help us much.

[2]W. Mundle, "Das Apostelbild der Apostelgeschichte," ZNW
27 (1928) 42, notes, "Die Lüge gegen dem Apostel ist Lüge gegen
Gott, eine Versuchung des Geistes des Herrn." Brown, Apostasy
and Perseverence, correctly sees the relation of this passage
to the saying on blasphemy against the Holy Spirit in Lk 12:10,
but distinguishes too carefully between "lie" and "blasphemy";
in Acts, both responses are in effect rejections of the prophetic authority of God's witnesses. Brown further notes (109)
that, "Here the Apostles appear not as preachers of the Word
but as administrators who have charge of disposing of the goods
of the community." This is correct, but it should be noted
that Luke uses this authority over possessions to express
precisely the Apostles' prophetic authority.

shows that the challenge to his prophetic authority has been
met. By not recognizing that authority for what it was,
Ananias has rejected the Prophet and is therefore now himself
rejected. Simply on hearing the words of Peter, he falls
dead.[1]

In recounting Peter's confrontation with Sapphira (5:7-10),
Luke again uses distinct touches of irony. The setting now is
juridical. Sapphira comes into Peter's presence as if for
judgment. By having the couple confronted separately, of
course, Luke shows that the conspiracy is already broken.
This is the first irony: the woman who had conspired with
her husband (συνειδυίης) now knew nothing of his fate (μὴ
εἰδυῖα τὸ γέγονος). She thought the conspiracy was still on.
But the reader knows differently. In her answer to Peter,
Sapphira compounds the sin of conspiracy by a verbal lie and
seals her own fate as an active member of the conspiracy. Luke
here uses still a third expression for their offense. They
have conspired (συνεφωνήθη ὑμῖν) to test (πειράσαι) the Spirit
of the Lord (5:9). Now Peter's prophetic word is even more
active. Peter states that Sapphira will die. The second
irony: she had joined her husband in conspiracy against the
community; she will join him in the grave (cf. 5:10). The
third irony: Ananias and Sapphira had tested the prophetic
authority of Peter when they laid a fraudulent gift "at the
feet of the Apostles"; his prophetic authority is vindicated
when they fall dead "at his feet" (5:10).

This episode reminds us again of the prophecy of Jesus
(Lk 22:32) that Satan would seek to sift the disciples like
wheat, but that Peter would turn and strengthen his brothers.
As a result of this occurrence, great fear came upon the whole
ἐκκλησία and over all who heard of it. This is Luke's first
use of the term ἐκκλησία, and together with 4:32, it fixes the
setting of these passages within the community. The great fear
that came over all who heard of it leads directly into the
recital of the great power of the Apostles in 5:12ff. We have
shown that these passages have served the function of showing

---

[1] ἐκψύχω is used also for the death of Sapphira in 5:10,
and of Herod in 12:23, who also died by Divine punishment
because οὐκ ἔδωκεν τὴν δόξαν τῷ θεῷ.

the authority of the Twelve over the people, the faithful
Israel, within the broader lines of the story in which that
authority was being challenged by the erstwhile leaders of the
people.

   h) We are now able to draw together some conclusions
concerning the way Luke has used possessions in these passages.
He has used them to symbolize four concerns pertinent to this
part of his story.

   i.   What is the nature of the believing Israel?
It is a people responsive to the word of the Prophet, which
means in effect responsive to the witness of the Apostles. It
is a people filled with the Spirit of God and drawn into a
perfect unity of mind and heart, enjoying the blessings promised to Abraham. The negative side is presented by Ananias
and Sapphira. They were not filled with the Spirit of God,
but by Satan; they were not united heart and mind with the
community, but conspired against it. They did not heed the
voice of the prophet, but mocked it. The role of possessions?
The spiritual unity of the believers is directly expressed by
their sharing all goods in common and calling nothing their
own. The spiritual divisiveness of Ananias and Sapphira is
directly expressed by their holding back something of their
possessions to call their own.

   ii.   Who belongs to the people, or how can
inclusion in the people be expressed? Luke attaches this
question, as we have seen throughout Luke-Acts, to the acceptance or rejection of the Prophet. Acceptance of God's Prophet
means inclusion in the faithful Israel; rejection of Him means
exclusion from the people. The role of possessions? The
believers express their acceptance of the prophetic authority
of the Apostles and therefore their inclusion in the people by
laying their possessions at the feet of the Apostles. By
counterfeiting that gesture, Ananias and Sapphira showed that
they mistook that prophetic authority as the administration of
men, did not recognize the Apostles as prophets, and were
thereby excluded from the people.

   iii.   Who possesses authority over God's people?
This is clearly the obverse of the previous question. By
placing the Apostles over the community of goods, Luke expresses

symbolically their spiritual authority over Israel. By having
Peter sit in judgment over those who challenged that authority
only heightens the same reality.

iv. How will the authority of the Twelve over
Israel be extended to the believing Gentile community? We will
explore this more explicitly in the next passages, but we have
seen Luke take the first step in symbolizing the transfer of
the mission to the Gentiles and the submission of this mission
to the authority of the Twelve by having Barnabas named by the
Apostles and laying his possessions at their feet.

E. The Appointment of the Seven (6:1-7).

By the end of chapter five Luke has successfully established a believing Israel and the authority of the Twelve over
it. In chapter six he prepares for the second stage of Jesus'
prophecy in Acts 1:8, that the Gospel would move out from
Jerusalem to Judea and Samaria and the ends of the earth. He
does this, typically, by establishing a continuity of ministry.
He shows that the ministers who carried the Gospel beyond
Jerusalem received their authority from the Twelve. He uses
possessions to symbolize this transfer of spiritual authority.

The basic lines of the account appear very simple, but as
repeated attempts to get to the historical reality which may
underlie the account have shown,[1] the simplicity is deceptive.
The account simply does not hold together very well. Our
understanding of the way in which Luke uses possessions
symbolically, however, enables us to make sense of the account,
if not at the historical level, at the level of Luke's purpose
in the story.

---

[1]In addition to the works cited above, p. 51, cf. H. J.
Cadbury, "The Hellenists," Beginnings V, 59-74; E. Blackman,
"The Hellenists of Acts VI.1," ExpT 48 (1936-7) 524-525; C. F.
D. Moule, "Once more, who were the Hellenists," ExpT 70 (1958-
9) 100-102; Trocmé, "Livre des Actes," 188-191; Reicke, Glaube
und Leben, 115-128; K. Lake, "The Communism of Acts II and
IV-VI and the Appointment of the Seven," Beginnings V, 140-151;
W. Grundmann, "Das Problem des hellenistischen Christentums
innerhalb der Jerusalemer Urgemeinde," ZNW 38 (1939) 45-73,
and "Die Apostel zwischen Jerusalem und Antiochia," ZNW 39
(1940) 110-137; Haenchen, 258-269; H. Windisch, "ἕλλην," TDNT
2 (1964) 504-516; J. Lienhard, "Acts 6:1-6: A Redactional View,"
CBQ 37 (1975) 228-236.

There are several very puzzling features of the account. The decision of the Apostles is presented as a solution to a crisis which had arisen concerning the distribution of the community goods. The "Hellenists" complained against the "Hebrews" that their widows were being neglected in the daily distribution (6:1).[1] But it is not at all clear how the Apostles' abandonment of the service of the tables solves the problem. How are seven men better able to handle the business than twelve? Or if we are to conclude from the hellenistic names of the seven that they were to minister to the hellenistic widows,[2] who would take care of the Hebrew widows once the Apostles left the job? The reason the Apostles give for abandoning the task was that it caused them to neglect the service of the Word (6:2). Yet the whole course of the narrative from 4:31 to 5:42 has stressed the impressive success of their preaching and the power of their prayer (4:23ff).

The final and most puzzling aspect also provides the clue to interpretation. The seven men were ostensibly chosen to carry out the work of distributing the community goods (οὓς καταστήσομεν[3] ἐπὶ τῆς χρείας ταύτης, 6:3). Yet although the whole of the narrative from this point till the end of chapter eight is devoted to two of these seven (Stephen and Philip), we nowhere find that they had anything to do with the διακονία τῆς τραπέζης. Instead, as we showed in chapter one of this study, they carry out the same work as the Apostles. They are prophetic witnesses to Jesus, preaching God's Word, working

---

[1]We should note that Luke has carefully placed this incident within the framework of the expansion of the community. Thus 6:1 πληθυνόντων τῶν μαθητῶν and 6:7 ἐπληθύνετο ὁ ἀριθμὸς τῶν μαθητῶν. The locus of this growth is Jerusalem (6:7), but by stressing the growth in number, Luke prepares the reader not only for the internal tensions which this growth occasions, but also for the spread of the mission beyond Jerusalem which the next chapters will recount.

[2]Trocmé's suggestion ("Livre des Actes," 191) that the ἐξ ὑμῶν (6:3) refers to the members of the Hellenist party, and that the action of the Twelve and community established them as an autonomous group with control over their own goods appears doubtful.

[3]The same expression, we should note, as that used in the saying on the faithful householder in Lk 12:42.

signs and wonders, experiencing acceptance and rejection. In
a word, they carry on the spiritual ministry of the Twelve,
with the sole difference being their sphere of activity.
Stephen disputes with the hellenists in Jerusalem, and, because
of the persecution his death causes, the other hellenists are
scattered beyond Jerusalem; Philip carries the Gospel to
Samaria.

The problem of this passage in brief is this: there seems
to be no connection at all between the purported role of the
Seven and their actual role. They were supposed to be placed
over possessions, but they actually are ministers of the Word.
Not only that, there seems to be only the most tenuous connection between the account of their placement over the community
possessions and the account of their actual ministry.

This discrepancy disappears when we are aware that Luke
uses authority over possessions as a symbol of spiritual
authority. If we see Luke operating here in the same way as
he has in 4:32ff, the passage becomes clear. He wants to
express a bestowal of authority on hellenistic missionaries.
He wants to show two things: that the hellenistic missionaries
are fully prophetic figures, like the Twelve, and yet that
their authority is less than, and dependent on, the Twelve.
The primary symbol for expressing the authority of the Twelve
over the people has been their place over the community of
goods. He therefore expresses the bestowal of spiritual
authority on the Seven by having them placed over the disposition of goods. What Luke is really talking about is the
transferral of power. The symbol he uses is power over
possessions. It is awkward; once the image is established,
he forgets it and talks about the reality of spiritual power.
But the establishing of the image in the first place is so
consistent with what we have seen in the previous chapters that
the possibility is real that Luke has used the dispute and its
resolution in order to symbolize through possessions the transfer of spiritual power to the hellenistic missionaries.

F. The Story of Simon Magus (8:9-24).

We have shown in chapter one of this study that Philip,
one of those ostensibly appointed to oversee the distribution

of goods, actually functions as a minister of the Gospel in
Samaria (8:4), performing great signs and wonders just as the
Apostles had (8:6-7, 13), and converting many of the Samaritans.
That Luke has the Apostles in Jerusalem send down Peter and
John for the laying on of hands, and delays till then the
Samaritans' reception of the Spirit, even though they had been
baptized (8:14-16), presents certain problems for understanding
Luke's view of the relationship between baptism and the
Spirit;[1] but in terms of the story and Luke's major concerns,
the action is perfectly consistent. The appearance of the
Apostles sets Jerusalem's seal of approval on this first
success of the Gospel outside Jerusalem, and the reception of
the Spirit at the hands of the Apostles creates the strongest
possible bond between the mission and the mother community,
since the believers in Jerusalem and Samaria received the same
Spirit and at the hands of the same men.[2] Luke has also
thereby placed Peter on the scene to resolve still another
crisis regarding the apostolic authority, in which possessions
again play an interesting role.

Simon was a figure of considerable importance in Samaria.[3]
His mission had preceded that of Philip, and by his wonderworking he was able to proclaim himself to be τινα μέγαν (8:9).
The credulous multitude in turn was eager to recognize him as
ἡ δύναμις τοῦ θεοῦ ἡ καλουμένη μεγάλη (8:10). Having worked
the area for a considerable period of time (8:11), he had
reason to consider his prestige well secured.

Philips' preaching could not but be a threat to Simon's
position. Simon's followers, men and women, believed the
preaching of Philip and were baptized (8:12). Indeed, so
impressed was Simon himself by the wonders worked by Philip

---

[1]Cf. J. Oulton, "The Holy Spirit, Baptism and Laying on
of Hands in Acts," ExpT 66 (1954-5) 236-240.

[2]Cf. Brown, Apostasy and Perseverence, 110-111.

[3]For the discussion of the historical figure Simon and
his relationship to Gnosticism, cf. R. Casey, "Simon Magus,"
Beginnings V, 151-163; E. Haenchen, "Gab es eine vorchristlichen Gnosis?" Gott und Mensch (Tübingen: J. C. B. Mohr,
1965) 265-298; R. Mc. Wilson, The Gnostic Problem (London:
A. R. Mowbray, 1958) 97-115; Cerfaux, Recueil 1, 191-262.

that he too became a believer and was baptized (8:13). To this
point, the story might well have appeared as an example of the
great power of the Gospel, sweeping all before it, conquering
even the wonderworking magician. But we may also wonder
whether a man who called himself the "Great Power of God"
could be satisfied as a simple believer.

The crisis was stimulated by the power exercised by Peter
and John. By the laying on of their hands, the believers were
filled with the Holy Spirit.[1] Philip had been wonderful, but
the Apostles were overwhelming. Simon clearly thought that
this was the sort of exercise of power he was fitted for, so
προσήνεγκεν αὐτοῖς χρήματα, λέγων: Δότε κἀμοὶ τὴν ἐξουσίαν
ταύτην ἵνα ᾧ ἐὰν ἐπιθῶ τὰς χεῖρας λαμβάνῃ πνεῦμα ἅγιον (8:19).
His gesture itself is strikingly similar to that of the
believers in 4:35, 37, who laid their possessions at the feet
of the Apostles. But whereas that gesture signified a participation in the unity of heart and mind created by the Spirit
and a submission to the authority of the Apostles, Simon's act
meant something else altogether. As in the story of Ananias
and Sapphira, the handing over of possessions was a counterfeit.
Simon was really looking for a quid pro quo. His offer of
money is not an expression of his desire to be among those who
call nothing their own, but a payment precisely to get something for himself. It is not an acknowledgement of the
authority of the Twelve, but an attempt to buy for himself a
position equal to theirs, to be again in this new community
τις μέγας.

Simon makes clear what the money is for: ἐξουσία.
Peter's response also brings the issue into the open. Simon
thought he could buy the δωρεὰν τοῦ θεοῦ, the gift of God
meaning clearly not the gift of the Spirit itself, but the
power to bestow the Spirit. By calling the apostolic authority
the "gift of God" Peter indicates at once its derivation, its
exalted character, and its utter inaccessibility to the manipu-
lations of men. Thus the depth of Simon's misunderstanding is

---

[1]That the gift was manifested in this instance by
glossolalia (so Wendt, Die Apostelgeschichte, 159; Haenchen,
304; Brown, Apostasy and Perseverence, 110) is simply a guess,
and not found in the text.

revealed. Like Ananias and Sapphira he saw the Apostles as
powerful men, but nothing more; he thought theirs was a position of human prestige that could be purchased. He did not
know that he was dealing with the real "Great Power of God."

As Simon's intention was expressed by his use of money,
so is his peril. Peter tells him: τὸ ἀργύριόν σου σὺν σοὶ
εἴη εἰς ἀπώλειαν (8:20). This reminds us of the Luke of the
Gospel, and the way he associated there the loss of the self
and the loss of possessions (cf. Lk 12:20; 17:27-33; 15:17).
Simon has expressed by his use of money his self-aggrandizing
drive, his desire to secure his "self"; the money can also
express the loss of his "self" as it joins him in perdition.
Again, as in the case of Judas and Ananias, the use of
possessions has revealed the state of a man's heart: ἡ γὰρ
καρδία σου οὐκ ἔστιν εὐθεῖα ἔναντι τοῦ θεοῦ (8:21).[1] Simon is
therefore utterly rejected from any participation in the
apostolic office: οὐκ ἔστιν σοι μερὶς οὐδὲ κλῆρος ἐν τῷ λόγῳ
τούτῳ (8:21).[2] We have seen repeatedly (as in 6:2, 4; 8:4)
that the apostolic ministry is one of "the Word," and the use
of κλῆρος here reminds us of the language found in the election
of Matthias (1:17, 26).

Peter's response to Simon is considerably less severe than
to Ananias and Sapphira. By his attempt to buy his way into
the apostleship he had shown himself to be "poisoned with gall
and caught in the trap of sin" (8:23), but his heart is not
possessed by Satan, and there is still hope of repentance; the
Lord may yet forgive the evil inclination of his heart (8:22-
23). The pericope ends with Simon's prayer that these evils

---

[1] Brown, Apostasy and Perseverence, 112-113, distinguishes
the case of Simon from that of Judas and Ananias and Sapphira
by stressing that Simon was not yet a believer in the full
sense (that is a disciple who had received the Holy Spirit),
and therefore could not apostasize in the same way they did.
But the text does not really tell us whether or not Simon
received the Spirit. It is true that Luke does not deal as
harshly with Simon, and that his heart is only said to be
crooked, and not possessed by Satan, but we cannot learn much
about Simon's ecclesial status from this.

[2] In agreement with Brown, Apostasy and Perseverence, 111,
and against Haenchen, 305, who sees the λόγος here as meaning
Christianity. The use of κλῆρος and ἐξουσία appears to make
certain the identification of the λόγος with the apostolic

not befall him (8:24).

The resemblance of this story to the Judas account provides us with the opportunity to reflect a little further on Luke's use of the motif of possessions in both cases. We have seen already how the community of possessions is a symbol for spiritual unity in the community. We have also seen how Luke describes the Men of the Spirit in identical terms. We have suggested that by this means he is able to express the continuity of spiritual power, and this is so. But is there a still deeper reason for these stereotyped descriptions of spiritual power which so diminish the individuality of the ministers?

Luke has stated emphatically that the Spirit at work in these ministers is not their own, but is the Spirit of God, the Spirit of the Prophet Jesus. Does Luke see the power at work in each of the ministers as a sharing in the power of the one Spirit? If he does, this may be why he finds the language of possessions congenial for expressing inclusion and exclusion in regard to the apostolic office. Judas before his betrayal had a share in this commonality; but his self-seeking in betrayal (expressed by buying a place of "his own") lost him that share. Matthias was then given a share in the apostolic office. Similarly, the attempt of Simon to seek a place for himself in the apostolic circle is represented as the "buying of a share," which is refused him by Peter. In each case the self-aggrandizement manifested by the use of possessions revealed a perversion of the apostolic ministry. The "sharing" of spiritual power which was the essence of the apostolic ministry, therefore, lent itself to description by the language of possessions, just as the spiritual sharing of the believers was appropriately symbolized by holding all goods in common.

G. The Collection for Jerusalem (11:27-30; 12:25).

After Luke secured the validity of the Gentile mission in principle by having Peter convert Cornelius, his narrative turns to the first real preaching to non-Jews which takes place in Antioch (11:19ff). Like the first mission to Samaria, this

---

ministry.

218

one too is ratified by the Church in Jerusalem. When the
church there heard of the successful preaching to the Gentiles,
they sent Barnabas to investigate (11:22).[1] This is Barnabas'
third appearance in the story. We have already seen in the
first appearance that he received a new name from the Apostles
and expressed his submission to them by his gift of property
laid at their feet (4:36-37). In his second appearance,
Barnabas reveals his real role in the story of Acts, that is,
to be the link between the Jerusalem church and Paul. In 9:27,
he appears as a mediator, championing Paul after his conversion
when the believers in Jerusalem would have nothing to do with
him. Barnabas took Paul to the Apostles and related to them
Paul's conversion and work. When Paul got into further
trouble in his preaching to the hellenists, however, he was
shipped out to Tarsus (9:30). Luke has already made Barnabas
the go-between of Paul and the Apostles and had him earn his
sobriquet of υἱὸς παρακλήσεως. Now in this third appearance
we recognize the significance of Luke's noting Barnabas' birth-
place in 4:36, for the first preachers to the Greeks were men
from Cyrene and Cyprus (11:20).[2] When Barnabas sees the
results of their work, ἐχάρη καὶ παρεκάλει πάντας, again
fulfilling the interpretation of his name (11:23). He is also
here identified for the first time as a prophetic figure:
ἀνὴρ ἀγαθὸς καὶ πλήρης πνεύματος ἁγίου καὶ πίστεως (11:24).

Now Barnabas sends to Tarsus for Paul and introduces him
for a second time to the mission; together they preach in
Antioch (11:25-26). Barnabas' relation to the church in
Jerusalem has already been symbolized by means of possessions;
Paul's has not.

When the disciples in Antioch hear of the famine that will
affect the needy in Jerusalem, they take up a collection and
send it to the elders (πρεσβυτέρους) in Jerusalem διὰ χειρὸς
Βαρναβᾶ καὶ Σαύλου (11:30).[3] Luke does not let the matter drop

---

[1]Cf. J. Sanders, "Peter and Paul in Acts," NTS 2 (1955-6)
134.

[2]Cf. Haenchen, 232, 365.

[3]Among the many attempts to relate this trip of Paul to
the pauline letters and chronology, cf. Sanders, "Peter and

with this one reference. After recounting events which
occurred in Jerusalem, he is careful to note in 12:25 that the
mission has been carried out (πληρώσαντες τὴν διακονίαν) when
Paul and Barnabas return to Antioch.[1] And when is this?
Immediately before Paul and Barnabas are commissioned by the
Holy Spirit and the church of Antioch to begin that missionary
labor which will dominate the rest of the story of Acts.

Having already seen how Luke has used possessions both to
symbolize the authority of the Twelve and the transmission of
authority to the Seven, it is difficult to avoid the impression
that he is doing the same thing here in regard to Paul. From
the very beginning of his ministry, the Paul of Acts is linked
to the authority of the Jerusalem church. First he is recruit-
ed and championed by the man whom we have already seen described as doubly submissive to the authority of the Twelve.
Second, together with that man, he himself brings possessions
to the leaders of the Jerusalem community.

When we analyzed Paul's final trip to Jerusalem in the
first chapter of this study, we wondered why Luke omitted there
any mention of the collection. We may now have found the
answer. In Paul's own view, his act of διακονία was not a
gesture of submission to the Jerusalem authority, but an act

Paul," 133-143; Dupont, Etudes, 173-184; O. Holtzmann, "Die
Jerusalemreisen des Paulus und die Kollekte," ZNW 6 (1905)
102-104; P. Benoit, "La deuxième visite de Saint Paul à
Jerusalem," Bib 40 (1959) 778-792; R. Funk, "The Enigma of
the Famine Visit," JBL 75 (1956) 130-136.

[1]Dupont, Etudes, 217-241, has devoted a long and careful
study to the textual and literary problems of this verse,
12:25. Simply stated, the problem is this: in spite of considerable mss evidence for the reading from Jerusalem (either
by ἐξ or ἀπό), the best witnesses have the harder reading εἰς
Ἰερουσαλήμ. On the grounds of textual analysis alone, this
reading would appear to be the preferred one (221). But in
literary terms, that reading makes little sense; Luke is
wrapping up old business before turning to the new mission,
not disposing of a wholly different visit with one verse (221-
227). Dupont seeks to resolve the problem by retaining the
harder reading, but interpreting it in a manner that will
square with the obvious literary function of the verse. He
does this (237-241) by reading εἰς Ἰερουσαλήμ as the object
of πληρώσαντες τὴν διακονίαν. The verse would then read,
"Having fulfilled their service to Jerusalem, they returned."

220

of fellowship from an Apostle appointed not by men but by God
and from his independent churches. In the light of Luke's
concern to show the continuity of the spread of the Gospel and
the derivation of all authority over the people from the Twelve,
it would make sense that he should see Paul's bringing the
collection from Antioch as a sign of his recognition of the
authority of Jerusalem, and therefore from the very beginning
he has his mission validated.

H. Conclusions to Chapter Four

The exegetical conclusions reached in the course of this
chapter have been stated clearly enough that we need not repeat
them here. It may be appropriate, however, to summarize the
course of this study as a whole. We began with a series of
exegetical questions concerning a particular passage, finding
that studies concerning its language and structure did not
really tell us much about what the passage meant in the course
of the narrative. As we sought an answer to those questions,
it quickly became evident that to understand the part, we must
have some grasp of the whole. For better or worse, this exercise in exegesis has grown into a somewhat full-blown literary
analysis of Luke-Acts. To discover why Luke used the language
he did when speaking about possessions, why he used it where he
did, and why he did not use it elsewhere, we were required to
understand the significance and structure of the Jerusalem
narrative within Luke-Acts.

Two major questions therefore shaped the course of the
study, and from the search for the answer to those questions
emerged the two theses advanced by the study. The questions:
what is the literary pattern of the story Luke is telling, and
how do possessions figure within that literary pattern? The
theses: a literary analysis of Luke-Acts at the level of story
reveals a dominant dramatic pattern which structures the work
as a whole; we have called this pattern the story of the
Prophet and the People. Within the telling of that story,
Luke uses the language of possessions symbolically.

We have tried to note in the course of the study the
limits to each thesis. We do not suggest that the literary
pattern we have discerned is the only significant pattern in

Luke-Acts, nor that the significance of the possessions
material within the work are exhausted by their symbolic
literary function. But we have found that the pattern of the
Prophet and the People provides a literary framework within
which not only Acts 4:32ff, but the larger part of Luke's
language about possessions finds an intelligible and convincing
literary role. We have also found that by analyzing possessions within that framework, the pattern of the Prophet and the
People emerges with greater sharpness.

Our method of reaching these conclusions has been original
only in the sense that it has been independent. We have tried
to respect the shape of the text and to impose as few historical or theological preconceptions as possible on the lines of
the story. We have been motivated by the traditional conviction that a passage can only be understood if its context is
understood.

There remain fascinating questions concerning Luke's view
of possessions which we cannot pursue. The first question
concerns the shape of Luke's metaphoric appreciation of
possessions. We have only been able to suggest from time to
time in the course of exegesis various aspects of that structure. It seems clear, for example, that Luke sees possessions
as a primary symbol of human existence, an immediate exteriori-
zation of and manifestation of the self. But the nuances are
many. Possessions do not merely express the inner condition of
a man's heart; they are also capable of expressing relations
between persons and the play of power between persons. Indeed,
when all the aspects are brought together, power appears as
reality which underpins them all. Possessions are a sign of
power. From this central and compelling view of possessions
comes their protean metaphoric potential.

Another question which we cannot pursue here concerns the
origins of this understanding. Where did Luke get it? We know
that he was a student of the Scripture, and that he was indebted to the prophetic critique of the rich and the promise of
God to the poor. Yet Luke is more radical than the prophets.
We know that Luke had assimilated in the most profound manner
the Greek ideal of shared life and the role of possessions in
expressing that inner unity called friendship. We can point to

these influences, perhaps even weigh here and there the contribution of each. Yet we understand that the mysterious mix of
these influences within the mind and imagination of Luke,
whoever he was, are available to us only in the words he has
written. In the end, it is not this background or that which
speaks to us, but the unique and personal vision of a man.

About the ultimate shape of the metaphor within Luke's
imagination, we can only surmise. About the roots of that
metaphor in his education, culture, experience, we can only
guess. What is available to us is the most important thing,
and that is the story.

BIBLIOGRAPHY

A. Texts and Tools

Aland, K., Black, M., Metzger, B., Wikgren, A. (eds). The
Greek New Testament. Stuttgart: Würtemberg Bible Society,
1966.

Aland, K. Synopsis Quattuor Evangeliorum, locis parallelis
evangeliorum apocryphorum et Patrum adhibitis edita.
Stuttgart: Würtembergische Bibelanstalt, 1964.

Bauer, W. A Greek-English Lexicon of the New Testament and
Other Early Christian Literature. Trans. and adapted by
W. F. Arndt and F. W. Gingrich. Chicago: University
Press, 1957.

Blass, F. and Debrunner, A. A Greek Grammar of the New Testament and Other Early Christian Literature. Trans. and
rev. of German ed. by R. W. Funk incorporating supplemen-
tary notes of A. Debrunner. Chicago: University Press,
1961.

Hatch, E. and Redpath, A. A Concordance to the Septuagint and
Other Greek versions of the Old Testament. 2 vols.
Austria: Akademische Druck-u.Verlaganstalt, 1954.

Kittel, G. and Friedrich, G. (eds). Theological Dictionary of
the New Testament. Trans. and ed. by G. Bromiley. 9
vols. Grand Rapids: Wm. B. Eerdmans, 1964-1974.

Liddell, H. G. and Scott, R. A Greek-English Lexicon. Oxford:
Clarendon Press, 1925-1940.

Moulton, W. F. and Geden, A. S. A Concordance to the Greek
Testament. 4th rev. ed. Edinburgh: T. & T. Clark, 1963.

Nestle, E. and Aland, K. (eds). Novum Testamentum Graece.
25th ed. London: United Bible Societies, 1969.

Rahlfs, A. (ed). Septuaginta: id est vetus testamentum graece
juxta LXX interpretes. 8th ed. Stuttgart: Würtembergische Bibelanstalt, 1905.

Strack, H. and Billerbeck, P. Kommentar zum Neuen Testament
aus Talmud und Midrasch. 6 vols. Munich: Beck, 1922-1961

Wettstein, J. J. Novum Testamentum Graecum. 2 vols.
Amsterdam: Domerian, 1752.

Zerwick, M. Analysis Philologica Novi Testamenti Graeci.
Edition altera emendata. Rome: Pontifical Biblical
Institute, 1960.

223

224

B. Commentaries on the Gospel

Creed, J. M. The Gospel according to St. Luke. London: Macmillan and Co., 1930.

Easton, B. S. The Gospel according to St. Luke. New York: Charles Scribner's Sons, 1926.

Ellis, E. The Gospel of Luke. The Century Bible. London: Nelson, 1966.

Grundmann, W. Das Evangelium nach Lukas. Theologischer Handkommentar zum Neuen Testament III. Berlin: Evangelische Verlaganstalt, 1963.

Klostermann, E. Das Lukasevangelium. Handbuck zum Neuen Testament II,1. Tübingen: J. C. B. Mohr (Paul Siebeck), 1919.

Lagrange, M.-J. Evangile selon Saint Luc. Etudes Bibliques. Paris: J. Gabalda, 1948.

Loisy, A. L'Evangile selon Luc. Paris: 1924.

Plummer, A. A Critical and Exegetical Commentary on the Gospel according to St. Luke. 9th ed. International Critical Commentary. New York: Charles Scribner's Sons, 1910.

Schürmann, H. Das Lukasevangelium. Herders Theologischer Kommentar zum Neuen Testament III. Erster Teil. Freiburg: Herder, 1969.

Taylor, V. The Gospel according to St. Mark. 2nd ed. London: Macmillan, 1966.

C. Commentaries on Acts

Bauernfeind, O. Die Apostelgeschichte. Theologischer Handkommentar zum Neuen Testament V. Leipzig: A. Deichertsche, 1939.

Bruce, F. The Acts of the Apostles. London: Tyndale Press, 1951.

Clark, A. C. The Acts of the Apostles. Oxford: Clarendon Press, 1933.

Conzelmann, H. Die Apostelgeschichte. 2nd ed. Handbuch zum Neuen Testament 7. Tübingen: J. C. B. Mohr (Paul Siebeck), 1972.

Foakes-Jackson, F. J. and Lake, K. (eds). The Beginnings of Christianity: Part I. The Acts of the Apostles. 5 vols. London: Macmillan and Co., 1920-1933. (Cf. Table of Abbreviations for listing of individual volumes.)

Haenchen, E. The Acts of the Apostles. Trans. by B. Noble,
et al. from Die Apostelgeschichte, 14th ed. (H. A. W.
Meyer, Kritischexegetischer Kommentar über das Neue
Testament; Göttingen: Vandenhoeck and Ruprecht, 1965).
Philadelphia: Westminster, 1971.

Harnack, A. Die Apostelgeschichte. Beiträge zur Einleitung
in das N.T. III. Leipzig: J. C. Hinrichs'sche, 1908.

Knox, W. L. The Acts of the Apostles. Cambridge: University
Press, 1948.

Loisy, A. Les Actes des Apôtres. Paris: Emile Nourry, 1920.

Spitta, F. Die Apostelgeschichte, ihre Quellen und deren
geschichtlicher Wert. Halle: Waisenhause, 1891.

Weiss, J. Die Apostelgeschichte. Leipzig: J. C. Hinrichs'sche,
1893.

Wendt, H. Die Apostelgeschichte. H. A. W. Meyer, Kritischexegetischer Kommentar über das Neue Testament.
Göttingen: Vandenhoeck und Ruprecht, 1913.

Wikenhauser, A. Die Apostelgeschichte. Regensburger Neues
Testament 5. Regensburg: Friedrich Pustet, 1961.

D. Studies

Anderson, H. "The Rejection at Nazareth Pericope of Luke
4:16-30 in Light of Recent Critical Trends." Interpretation 18 (1964) 259-275.

Bacon, B. W. "Stephen's Speech: Its Argument and Doctrinal
Relationship." Biblical and Semitic Studies. Yale
Bicentennial Publications. New York: Charles Scribner's
Sons, 1901.

Baer, H. Von. Der Heilige Geist in den Lukasschriften.
Beiträge zur Wissenschaft vom Alten und Neuen Testament
39. Stuttgart: W. Kohlhammer, 1926.

Bajard, J. "La Structure de la Pericope de Nazareth en Lc. iv
16-30." Ephemerides theologicae lovanienses 45 (1969)
165-171.

Barrett, C. K. Luke the Historian in Recent Study. London:
Epworth Press, 1961.

_____. The Holy Spirit in the Gospel Tradition. London:
S.P.C.K., 1947.

Bauernfeind, O. "Tradition und Komposition in dem
Apokatastasisspruch Apostelgeschichte,3:20." Abraham
Unser Vater. Ed. by O. Betz. Arbeiten zur Geschichte
des Spätjudentums und Urchristentums V. Leiden: E. J.
Brill, 1963.

226

Beardslee, W. A. <u>Literary Criticism of the New Testament</u>.
Philadelphia: Fortress Press, 1970.

_____. "The Casting of Lots at Qumran and in the Book of
Acts." <u>Novum Testamentum</u> 4 (1960) 245-252.

Bengel, J. <u>Gnomon Novi Testamenti</u>. 3rd ed. Berlin: Gustav
Schlawitz, 1855.

Benoit, P. "L'Enfance de Jean-Baptiste selon Luc 1." <u>New
Testament Studies</u> 3 (1956-7) 169-194.

_____. "La deuxième visite de Saint Paul à Jerusalem."
<u>Biblica</u> 40 (1959) 778-792.

_____. "La Mort de Judas." <u>Synoptische Studien</u>. Ed. by
J. Schmid and A. Vögtle. München: Karl Zink Verlag, 1953,
1-19.

_____. "Qumran et le Nouveau Testament." <u>New Testament
Studies</u> 7 (1967) 276-296.

_____. "Remarques sûr les 'Sommaires' de Actes 2:42 à 5."
<u>Aux Sources de la Tradition Chrétienne</u>. Biblioteque
Théologique. Mélanges Maurice Goguel. Neuchatel:
Delachaux et Niestle, 1950, 1-10.

Bietenhard, H. "ὄνομα." <u>Theological Dictionary of the New
Testament</u> 5 (1967) 242-283.

Bihler, J. <u>Die Stephanusgeschichte</u>. Münchener Theologische
Studien I. Historische Abteilung 30. München: Max
Hueber, 1963.

Blackman, E. "The Hellenists of Acts VI.1." <u>Expository Times</u>
48 (1936-7) 524-525.

Blinzler, J. "Die literarische Eigenart des sogennanten
Reiseberichts im Lukasevangelium." <u>Synoptische Studien</u>.
Ed. by J. Schmid and A. Vögtle. München: Karl Zink
Verlag, 1953, 20-52.

Bohnenblust, G. <u>Beiträge zum Topos περὶ φιλίας</u>. Berlin:
Universitäts-Buchdruckerei von Gustav Schade, 1905.

Bornhäuser, K. <u>Studien zum Sondergut des Lukas</u>. Gütersloh:
C. Bertelsmann, 1934.

Braun, H. <u>Qumran und das Neue Testament</u> I. Tübingen: J. C.
B. Mohr (Paul Siebeck), 1966.

Brown, S. <u>Apostasy and Perseverence in the Theology of Luke</u>.
Analecta Biblica 36. Rome: Pontifical Biblical Institute,
1969.

Bultmann, R. <u>The History of the Synoptic Tradition</u>. rev. ed.
Trans. by J. Marsh. New York: Harper and Row, 1968.

227

_____. "Zur Frage nach den Quellen der Apostelgeschichte."
New Testament Essays. Ed. by A. J. B. Higgins.
Manchester: University Press, 1959, 68-80.

Cadbury, H. J. "Dust and Garments." Beginnings V, 269-277.

_____. "Four Features of Lukan Style." Studies in Luke-
Acts, 87-102.

_____. "Luke--Translator or Author?" American Journal of
Theology 24 (1924) 436-455.

_____. "Some Personal Names in Luke-Acts." Amicitiae
Corolla. Ed. by H. Wood. London: University of London
Press, 1933, 45-56.

_____. The Book of Acts in History. New York: Harper and
Brothers, 1955.

_____. "The Hellenists," Beginnings V, 59-74.

_____. The Making of Luke-Acts. New York: The Macmillan
Co., 1927.

_____. "The Speeches of Acts." Beginnings V, 402-427.

_____. The Style and Literary Method of Luke. Harvard
Theological Studies VI. Cambridge: Harvard University
Press, 1920.

_____. "The Summaries of Acts." Beginnings V, 392-402.

Campbell, C. Critical Studies in St. Luke's Gospel.
Edinburgh: Blackwood and Sons, 1891.

Campbell, J. "κοινωνία and its cognates in the New Testament."
Journal of Biblical Literature 51 (1932) 352-380.

Casey, R. "Simon Magus." Beginnings V, 151-163.

Cerfaux, L. Recueil Lucien Cerfaux. 2 vols. Biblioteca
Ephemeridum Theologicarum Lovaniensium VI-VII. Gembloux:
J. Duculot, 1954.

Childs, B. S. Biblical Theology in Crisis. Philadelphia:
Westminster, 1970.

_____. Exodus. The Old Testament Library. Philadelphia:
Westminster, 1974.

Comblin, J. "La Paix dans la Théologie de Saint Luc."
Ephemerides theologicae lovanienses 32 (1956) 439-460.

Conzelmann, H. The Theology of St. Luke. Trans. by G.
Buswell. New York: Harper and Row, 1961.

_____. "Zur Lukasanalyze." Zeitschrift für Theologie und
Kirche 49 (1952) 16-33.

228

Cullmann, O. "The Significance of the Qumran Texts for
    Research into the Beginnings of Christianity." Journal
    of Biblical Literature 74 (1955) 213-226.

Dabeck, P. "Siehe es erschienen Moses und Elias." Biblica 23
    (1942) 175-189.

Dahl, N. A. "'A People for His Name' (Acts 15:14)." New
    Testament Studies 4 (1957-8) 319-327.

_____. "The Story of Abraham in Luke-Acts." Studies in
    Luke-Acts, 139-158.

D'Ales, A. "Actes V,3." Recherches de science religieuse 24
    (1934) 199-200.

Danker, F. "Luke 16:16--An Opposition Logion." Journal of
    Biblical Literature 77 (1958) 231-243.

Davies, J. "The Purpose of the Central Section of St. Luke's
    Gospel." Studia Evangelica II. Texte und Untersuchungen
    87, Part 1. Berlin: Akademie-Verlag, 1964, 164-169.

Degenhardt, H.-J. Lukas Evangelist der Armen. Stuttgart:
    Katholisches Bibelwerk, 1965.

Deissmann, A. "Barnabas." Zeitschrift für die neutestament-
    liche Wissenschaft 7 (1906) 91-92.

_____. Bible Studies. Trans. by A. Grieve. Edinburgh:
    T. & T. Clark, 1901.

Denaux, A. "L'hypocrisie des Pharisiens et le dessein de Dieu;
    Analyse de Lc.XIII 31-33." L'Evangile de Luc. Ed. by F.
    Neirynck. Bibliotheca Ephemeridum Theologicarum
    Lovaniensium XXXII. Gembloux: J. Duculot, 1973, 245-285.

Derrett, J. "Ananias, Sapphira, and the Right of Property."
    Downside Review 89 (1971) 225-232.

_____. "Fresh Light on Luke XVI. II. Dives and Lazarus and
    the Preceding Sayings." New Testament Studies 7 (1960-1)
    364-380.

_____. "Fresh Light on St. Luke XVI. I. The Parable of the
    Unjust Steward." New Testament Studies 7 (1960-1) 198-
    219.

_____. Law in the New Testament. London: Darton, Longman
    and Todd, 1970.

_____. "The Parable of the Prodigal Son." New Testament
    Studies 14 (1967) 56-74.

Descamps, A. "La composition littéraire de Luc XVI 9-13."
    Novum Testamentum 1 (1956) 47-53.

_____. Les Justes et la Justice dans les evangiles et le christianisme primitive hormis la doctrine proprement paulinienne. Gambloux: J. Duculot, 1950.

Dibelius, M. Studies in the Acts of the Apostles. Trans. by M. Ling. London: SCM, 1956.

Dieu, L. "Marc, source des Actes? ch. I-XV." Revue Biblique 29 (1920) 555-569, and 30 (1921) 86-96.

Dodd, C. H. "The Appearance of the Risen Christ: An Essay in Form-Criticism of the Gospels." Studies in the Gospels. Ed. by D. E. Nineham. Oxford: Basil Blackwood, 1955, 9-35.

_____. The Apostolic Preaching and its Development. London: Hodder and Stoughton, 1936.

_____. The Parables of the Kingdom. London: Nisbet, 1935.

Dombrowski, B. "ḥyḥd in 1QS and τὸ κοινόν: An Instance of early Greek and Jewish Synthesis." Harvard Theological Review 59 (1966) 293-307.

Dowd, W. "Breaking Bread, Acts 2:46." Catholic Biblical Quarterly 1 (1939) 358-362.

Dubois, J.-D. "La Figure d'Elie dans la Perspective Lucanienne." Revue d'histoire et de philosophie religieuses 53 (1973) 155-176.

Dugas, L. L'Amitié Antique. Paris: Félix Alcan, 1914.

Dupont, J. Etudes sur les Actes des Apotres. Lectio Divina 45. Paris: Editions du Cerf, 1967.

_____. "La Parabole des Talents (Mat.25:14-30) ou des Mines (Luc 19:12-27)." Revue de théologie et de philosophie ser.3 19 (1969) 376-391.

_____. Le Discours de Milet: Testament Pastoral de Saint Paul. Lectio Divina 32. Paris: Editions du Cerf, 1962.

_____. "Le Logion des douze Trônes (Mt. 19:28, Lk. 22:28-30)." Biblica 45 (1964) 355-392.

_____. Les Béatitudes. 3 vols. I. Le problème littéraire--les deux versions du Sermon sur la montagne et des Béatitudes. 2nd ed. Louvain: E. Nauwelaerts, 1958. II. La Bonne Nouvelle. Paris: J. Gabalda, 1969. III. Les Evangelistes. Paris: J. Gabalda, 1973.

_____. "Les Discours de Pierre dans les Actes et le chapitre XXIV de l'évangile de Luc." L'Evangile de Luc. Ed. by F. Neirynck. Bibliotheca Ephemeridum Theologicarum Lovaniensium XXXII. Gembloux: J. Duculot, 1973.

230

_____. "L'Union entre les prèmieres Chrétiens dans les Actes des Apôtres." La nouvelle revue théologique 91 (1969) 898-915.

_____. The Sources of the Acts. Trans. by K. Pond. New York: Herder and Herder, 1964.

Easton, B. S. The Purpose of Acts. London: S.P.C.K., 1936.

Eglinger, R. Der Begriff der Freundschaft in der Philosophie. Basel: Inaugural Dissertation, 1916.

Ehrhardt, A. The Acts of the Apostles. Manchester: University Press, 1969.

_____. "The Construction and Purpose of the Acts of the Apostles." Studia Theologica 12 (1958) 44-79.

_____. "The Disciples of Emmaus." New Testament Studies 10 (1963) 182-201.

Ellis, E. "The Role of the Christian Prophet in Acts." Apostolic History and the Gospel. Ed. by W. Gasque and R. Martin. Exeter: Paternoster Press, 1970, 55-67.

Epp, E. J. The Theological Tendency of Codex Bezae Cantabrigiensis in Acts. New Testament Studies Monograph Series 3. Cambridge: University Press, 1966.

Evans, C. "The Central Section of St. Luke's Gospel." Studies in the Gospels. Ed. by D. E. Nineham. Oxford: Basil Blackwood, 1955, 37-53.

_____. "Uncomfortable Words--V." Expository Times 81 (1969-70) 260-264.

Fascher, E. "Theologische Beobachtungen zu δεῖ." Neutestamentliche Studien für Rudolf Bultmann. Beihefte zur Zeitschrift für die neutestamentliche Wissenschaft 21. Berlin: A. Töpelmann, 1954, 228-254.

Feuillet, A. "Les Riches intendents du Christ." Recherches de science religieuse 34 (1947) 30-54.

Fitzmyer, J. "Jewish Christianity in Acts in Light of the Qumran Scrolls." Studies in Luke-Acts, 233-257.

_____. "4Q Testimonia and the New Testament." Theological Studies 18 (1957) 513-537.

Flender, H. St. Luke, Theologian of Redemptive History. Trans. by R. and I. Fuller. London: S.P.C.K., 1967.

Flusser, D. "Blessed are the Poor in Spirit." Israel Exploration Journal 10 (1960) 1-13.

Foerster, W. "βδελύσσομαι κτλ." Theological Dictionary of the New Testament 1 (1964) 598-600.

Franklin, W. Die Kollekte des Paulus. Scottsdale: Mennonite Publishing House, 1938.

Funk, R. "The Enigma of the Famine Visit." Journal of Biblical Literature 75 (1956) 130-136.

Gächter, P. "The Parable of the Dishonest Steward after Oriental Conceptions." Catholic Biblical Quarterly 12 (1950) 121-131.

Gasse, W. "Zum Reisebericht des Lukas." Zeitschrift für die neutestamentliche Wissenschaft 34 (1935) 293-299.

Gaston, L. No Stone on Another: Studies in the Significance of the Fall of Jerusalem in the Synoptic Gospels. Novum Testamentum Supplements, 23. Leiden: E. J. Brill, 1970.

Gelin, A. Les Pauvres de Yahvé. Paris: Editions du Cerf, 1953.

George, A. "Israël dans l'Oeuvre de Luc." Revue biblique 75 (1968) 481-525.

Gerhardsson, B. "Einige Bemerkungen zu Apg. 4:32." Studia Theologica 24 (1970) 142-149.

Gill, D. "Observations on the Lukan Travel Narrative and some related Passages." Harvard Theological Review 63 (1970) 199-221.

Gils, F. Jésus Prophète d'après les Evangiles Synoptiques. Orientalia et Biblica Lovaniensia II. Louvain: Publications Universitaires, 1957.

Glombitza, O. "Das Grosse Abendmahl: Lk. XIV 12-24." Novum Testamentum 5 (1962) 10-16.

Goguel, M. "Quelque Observations sur l'Oeuvre de Luc." Revue d'histoire et de philosophie religieuses 33 (1953) 37-51.

Goodenough, E. "The Perspective of Acts." Studies in Luke-Acts, 51-59.

Goudoever, J. "The Place of Israel in Luke's Gospel." Placita Pleiadia. Leiden: E. J. Brill, 1966.

Goulder, M. D. "The Chiastic Structure of the Lucan Journey." Studia Evangelica II. Texte und Untersuchungen 87, Part 1. Berlin: Akademie-Verlag, 1964, 195-202.

_____. Type and History in Acts. London: S.P.C.K., 1964.

Grundmann, W. "Das Problem des hellenistischen Christentums innerhalb der Jerusalemer Urgemeinde." Zeitschrift für die neutestamentliche Wissenschaft 38 (1939) 45-73.

_____. "δεῖ." _Theological Dictionary of the New Testament_ 2 (1964) 21-25.

_____. "δύναμαι, κτλ." _Theological Dictionary of the New Testament_ 2 (1964) 284-317.

_____. "Die Apostel zwischen Jerusalem und Antiochia." _Zeitschrift für die neutestamentliche Wissenschaft_ 39 (1940) 110-137.

_____. "Fragen der Komposition des lukanischen 'Reiseberichte'." _Zeitschrift für die neutestamentliche Wissenschaft_ 50 (1959) 252-271.

_____. "ἰσχύω." _Theological Dictionary of the New Testament_ 3 (1965) 397-402.

_____. "ταπεινός, κτλ." _Theological Dictionary of the New Testament_ 8 (1972) 1-26.

Haenchen, E. "Gab es eine vorchristlichen Gnosis?" _Gott und Mensch._ Tübingen: J. C. B. Mohr, 1965.

_____. "Judentum und Christentum in der Apostelgeschichte." _Zeitschrift für die neutestamentliche Wissenschaft_ 54 (1963) 155-187.

_____. "Schriftzitate und Textüberlieferung in der Apostelgeschichte." _Zeitschrift für Theologie und Kirche_ 51 (1954) 153-167.

_____. "The Book of Acts as Source-Material for the History of Early Christianity." _Studies in Luke-Acts_, 258-278.

_____. "Tradition und Komposition in der Apostelgeschichte." _Zeitschrift für Theologie und Kirche_ 52 (1955) 205-225.

Hahn, F. _Christologische Hoheitstitel._ Forschungen zur Religion und Literatur des Alten und Neuen Testaments 83. Göttingen: Vandenhoeck and Ruprecht, 1963.

Hauck, F. "κοινός, κτλ." _Theological Dictionary of the New Testament_ 3 (1965) 789-809.

Holtz, T. _Untersuchungen über die Alttestamentliche Zitate bei Lukas._ Texte und Untersuchungen 104. Berlin: Akademie-Verlag, 1968.

Holtzmann, O. "Die Jerusalemreisen des Paulus und die Kollekte." _Zeitschrift für die neutestamentliche Wissenschaft_ 6 (1905) 102-104.

Jeremias, J. _Die Abendmahlsworte Jesu._ 3rd ed. Göttingen: Vandenhoeck and Ruprecht, 1960.

_____. _Jerusalem in the Time of Jesus._ 3rd rev. ed. Trans. by F. H. and C. H. Cave. Philadelphia: Fortress Press, 1967.

_____. "Paarweise Sendung im Neuen Testament." New Testament Essays. Ed. by A. J. B. Higgins. Manchester: University Press, 1959, 136-144.

_____. The Parables of Jesus. 6th ed. Trans. by S. Hooke. New York: Charles Scribner's Sons, 1963.

_____. "Untersuchungen zum Quellenproblem der Apostelgeschichte." Zeitschrift für die neutestamentliche Wissenschaft 36 (1937) 205-221.

_____. "Zum Gleichnis vom verlorenen Sohn." Theologische Zeitschrift 5 (1949) 228-231.

Jervell, J. Luke and the People of God. Minneapolis: Augsburg Publishing House, 1972.

Johnson, S. "A proposed Form-Critical Treatment of Acts." Anglican Theological Review 21 (1939) 22-31.

Jonsson, J. Humor and Irony in the New Testament. Reykjavik: Bokaútgáfa Menningarsjóds, 1965.

Kandler, H. "Die Bedeutung der Armut im Schriften von Chirbet Qumran." Judaica 13 (1957) 193-209.

Keck, L. and Martyn, J. L. (eds). Studies in Luke-Acts. Nashville: Abingdon, 1966.

_____. "The Poor among the Saints in Jewish Christianity and Qumran." Zeitschrift für die neutestamentliche Wissenschaft 57 (1966) 54-78.

_____. "The Poor among the Saints in the New Testament." Zeitschrift für die neutestamentliche Wissenschaft 56 (1965) 109-129.

Kilpatrick, G. "An Eclectic Study of the Text of Acts." Biblical and Patristic Studies. Ed. by J. Birdsall and R. Thomson. New York: Herder, 1973.

_____. "A Theme of the Lucan Passion Story and Luke XXIII.47." Journal of Theological Studies 43 (1942) 34-36.

_____. "λαοί at Lk.2:31 and Acts 4:25,27." Journal of Theological Studies 16 (1965) 127.

Klijn, A. "In Search of the Original Text of Acts." Studies in Luke-Acts, 103-110.

_____. "Stephen's Speech--Acts VII 2-53." New Testament Studies 4 (1957-8) 25-31.

Knox, A. "The Death of Judas." Journal of Theological Studies 25 (1923-4) 289-290.

Knox, J. Chapters in a Life of Paul. New York: Abingdon, 1950.

234

Koch, R. "Die Wertung des Besitzes im Lukasevangelium." *Biblica* 38 (1957) 151-169.

Kodell, J. "Luke's use of Laos, 'People', especially in the Jerusalem Narrative." *Catholic Biblical Quarterly* 31 (1969) 327-343.

Krüger, G. "Die geistesgeschichtlichen Grundlagen des Gleichnisses vom ungerechten Verwalter." *Biblische Zeitschrift* 21 (1933) 170-181.

Lake, K. "The Communism of Acts II and IV-VI and the Appointment of the Seven." *Beginnings* V, 140-151.

_____. "The Death of Judas." *Beginnings* V, 22-30.

Lampe, G. W. H. "The Holy Spirit in the Writings of St. Luke." *Studies in the Gospels*. Ed. by D. E. Nineham. Oxford: Basil Blackwell, 1955, 159-200.

_____. "The Lucan Portrait of Christ." *New Testament Studies* 2 (1955-6) 160-175.

Laurentin, R. *Structure et Théologie de Luc I-II*. Etudes Bibliques. Paris: J. Gabalda, 1957.

Leaney, R. "The Resurrection Narratives in Luke (xxiv 12-53)." *New Testament Studies* 2 (1955-6) 110-114.

Legasse, S. "'L'Homme Fort' de Luc XI 21-22." *Novum Testamentum* 5 (1962) 5-9.

Leon-Dufour, X. *Etudes d'Evangiles*. Paris: Editions du Seuil, 1965.

Lienhard, J. "Acts 6:1-6: A Redactional View." *Catholic Biblical Quarterly* 37 (1975) 228-236.

Lightfoot, R. H. *History and Interpretation in the Gospels*. London: Hodder and Stoughton, 1935.

_____. *Locality and Doctrine in the Gospels*. New York: Harper and Brothers, 1937.

Lindars, B. *New Testament Apologetic: The Doctrinal Significance of Old Testament Quotations*. Philadelphia: Westminster Press, 1961.

Lohse, E. "Lukas als Theologe der Heilsgeschichte." *Evangelische Theologie* 14 (1954) 256-275.

_____. "Missionarisches Handeln Jesu nach dem Evangelium des Lukas." *Theologische Zeitschrift* 10 (1954) 1-13.

Lüthi, K. "Das Problem des Judas Iskariot -- neu untersucht." *Evangelische Theologie* 16 (1956) 98-114.

Malherbe, A. J. "The Corinthian Contribution." *Restoration Quarterly* 3 (1959) 221-233.

Mánek, J. "The New Exodus in the Books of Luke." Novum
Testamentum 2 (1958) 8-23.

Marshall, I. H. Luke: Historian and Theologian. Exeter:
Paternoster Press, 1970.

_____. "Recent Study of the Acts of the Apostles."
Expository Times 80 (1968-9) 292-296.

Masson, C. "La Reconstitution du Collège des Douze." Revue
de théologie et de philosophie ser.3 5 (1955) 193-201.

Meeks, W. A. The Prophet King. Novum Testamentum Supplements
14. Leiden: E. J. Brill, 1967.

Menoud, Ph.-H. "La Mort d'Ananias et de Saphira (Actes 5:1-
11)." Aux Sources de la Tradition Chrétienne. Biblioteque Théologique. Mélanges Maurice Goguel. Neuchatel:
Delachaux et Niestle, 1950, 146-154.

_____. "Le Plan des Actes des Apôtres." New Testament
Studies 1 (1954-5) 44-51.

_____. "Les Actes des Apôtres et l'Eucharistie." Revue
d'histoire et de philosophie religieuses 33 (1953) 21-36.

_____. "Les Additions au Groupe des douze Apôtres d'apres
le Livre des Actes." Revue d'histoire et de philosophie
religieuses 37 (1957) 71-80.

Metzger, B. "Seventy or Seventy-Two Disciples?" New Testament
Studies 5 (1958-9) 299-306.

Minear, P. "A Note on Luke 22:36." Novum Testamentum 7
(1964-5), 128-134.

_____. "Luke's Use of the Birth Stories." Studies in
Luke-Acts, 111-130.

Miyoshi, M. Der Anfang des Reiseberichts. Analecta Biblica
60. Rome: Biblical Institute Press, 1974.

Moore, G. F. Judaism in the First Centuries of the Christian
Era. 3 vols. Cambridge: Harvard University Press, 1927-
1930.

Morgenthaler, R. Die lukanische Geschichtsschreibung als
Zeugnis. 2 vols. Zürich: Zwingli-Verlag, 1949.

Morton, A. Q. and Macgregor, G. H. The Structure of Luke and
Acts. New York: Harper and Row, 1964.

Mosely, A. "Jesus' Audiences in the Gospels of St. Mark and
St. Luke." New Testament Studies 10 (1963) 139-149.

Moule, C. F. D. "Once more, who were the Hellenists."
Expository Times 70 (1958-9) 100-102.

236

_____. "The Christology of Acts." _Studies in Luke-Acts_, 159-185.

Munck, J. "Discours d'adieu dans le Nouveau Testament et dans la littérature biblique." _Aux Sources de la Tradition Chrétienne_. Biblioteque Théologique. Mélanges Maurice Goguel. Neuchatel: Delachaux et Niestle, 1950, 155-170.

Mundle, W. "Das Apostelbild der Apostelgeschichte." _Zeitschrift für die neutestamentliche Wissenschaft_ 27 (1928) 36-54.

_____. "Die Stephanusrede Apg.7: Eine Martyrerapologie." _Zeitschrift für die neutestamentliche Wissenschaft_ 20 (1921) 133-146.

Mussner, F. "Die Idee der Apokatastasis in der Apostelgeschichte." _Praesentia Salutis_. Düsseldorf: Patmos-Verlag, 1967, 223-234.

_____. "Die Una Sancta nach Apg. 2,42." _Praesentia Salutis_. Düsseldorf: Patmos-Verlag, 1967.

_____. "In den letzten Tagem." _Biblische Zeitschrift_ n.f. 5 (1961) 263-265.

Neusner, J. "The Fellowship (ʻbwrh) in the Second Jewish Commonwealth." _Harvard Theological Review_ 53 (1960) 125-142.

Nickle, K. _The Collection: A Study in Paul's Strategy_. Studies in Biblical Theology 48. Naperville: Alec R. Allenson, 1966.

Noack, B. _Das Gottesreich bei Lukas_. Symbolae biblicae upsalienses, 10. Uppsala: C. W. K. Gleerup, 1948.

Ogg, G. "The Central Section of the Gospel according to St. Luke." _New Testament Studies_ 18 (1971-2) 39-53.

Oliver, H. "The Lukan Birth Stories and the Purpose of Luke-Acts." _New Testament Studies_ 10 (1963) 202-226.

O'Neill, J. C. _The Theology of Luke in its Historical Setting_. 2nd ed. London: S.P.C.K., 1970.

Oulton, J. "The Holy Spirit, Baptism and Laying on of Hands in Acts." _Expository Times_ 66 (1954-5) 236-240.

Paley, W. _Horae Paulinae_. London: J. Davis, 1790.

Payne, D. "Semitisms in the Book of Acts." _Apostolic History and the Gospel_. Ed. by W. Gasque and R. Martin. Exeter: Paternoster Press, 1970, 134-150.

Percy, E. _Die Botschaft Jesu_. Lunds Universitets Arsskrift, n.f. Avd.1, Bd.49, Nr.5. Lund: C. W. K. Gleerup, 1953.

Plümacher, E. Lukas als hellenistischer Schriftsteller. Studien zur Umwelt des Neuen Testaments 9. Göttingen: Vandenhoeck and Ruprecht, 1972.

Potterie, I. de la. "L'Onction du Christ." Nouvelle revue théologique 80 (1958) 225-252.

Rabin, C. Qumran Studies. London: Oxford University Press, 1957.

Ramsay, W. St. Paul the Traveller and the Roman Citizen. New York: Putnam, 1904.

Rau, G. "Das Volk in der lukanischen Passionsgeschichte: Eine Konjekture zu Lk. 23:13." Zeitschrift für die neutestamentliche Wissenschaft 56 (1965) 41-51.

Reicke, B. Glaube und Leben der Urgemeinde. Abhandlungen zur Theologie des Alten und Neuen Testaments 32. Zürich: Zwingli-Verlag, 1957.

_____. "Instruction and Discussion in the Travel Narrative." Studia Evangelica I. Ed. by K. Aland, F. Cross, et al. Texte und Untersuchungen 73. Berlin: Akademie-Verlag, 1959, 206-216.

Rengstorf, K. Die Re-Investitur des Verlorenen Sohnes in der Gleichniserzählung Jesu Luk. 15, 11-32. Arbeitsgemein-schaft für Forschung des Landes Nordrheim-Westfalen. Geisteswissenschaften 137. Köln: Westdeutscher Verlag, 1967.

_____. "Die Zuwahl des Matthias." Studia Theologica 15 (1961) 35-67.

_____. "γελάω, κτλ." Theological Dictionary of the New Testament 1 (1964) 658-662.

_____. "σημεῖον, κτλ." Theological Dictionary of the New Testament 7 (1971) 200-269.

Renie, J. "L'Election de Matthias (Actes 1, 15-26); Authenticité du Récit." Revue biblique 55 (1948) 43-53.

Rese, M. Alttestamentliche Motive in der Christologie des Lukas. Studien zum Neuen Testament 1. Gütersloh: Gerd Mohn, 1969.

Retif, A. "Témoignage et Prédication Missionaire dans les Actes des Apôtres." Nouvelle revue theologique 73 (1951) 152-165.

Roberts, C. "The Kingdom of Heaven (Lk XVII,21)." Harvard Theological Review 41 (1948) 1-8.

Robinson, J. A. T. "The Most Primitive Christology of All?" Journal of Theological Studies n.s. 7 (1956) 177-189.

238

Robinson, W. "The Theological Context for Interpreting Luke's Travel Narrative (9:51ff)." <u>Journal of Biblical Literature</u> 79 (1960) 20-31.

Sanders, J. "Peter and Paul in the Acts." <u>New Testament Studies</u> 2 (1955-6) 133-143.

Scharlemann, M. <u>Stephen: A Singular Saint</u>. Analecta Biblica 34. Rome: Pontifical Biblical Institute, 1968.

Schlier, H. "δείκνυμι." <u>Theological Dictionary of the New Testament</u> 2 (1964) 25-33.

_____. "παρρησία." <u>Theological Dictionary of the New Testament</u> 5 (1967) 871-886.

Schmidt, K. "καλέω, κτλ." <u>Theological Dictionary of the New Testament</u> 3 (1965) 487-536.

Schmitt, J. "L'église de Jerusalem, ou la 'restauration' d'Israel." <u>Revue de sciences religieuses</u> 27 (1953) 209-218.

Schnackenburg, R. "Die Erwartung des 'Propheten' nach dem Neuen Testament und den Qumran-Texten." <u>Studia Evangelica</u> I. Ed. by K. Aland, F. Cross, <u>et al</u>. Texte und Untersuchungen 73. Berlin: Akademie-Verlag, 1959, 622-639.

_____. <u>The Moral Teaching of the New Testament</u>. 2nd rev. ed. Trans. by J. Holland-Smith and W. O'Hare. New York: Herder and Herder, 1965.

Schneider, J. "Zur Analyze des lukanischen Reiseberichtes." <u>Synoptische Studien</u>. Ed. by J. Schmid and A. Vögtle. München: Karl Zink Verlag, 1953, 207-229.

Schneidweiler, F. "Zu Act 5:4." <u>Zeitschrift für die neutestamentliche Wissenschaft</u> 49 (1958) 136-137.

Schrenk, G. "διαλέγομαι." <u>Theological Dictionary of the New Testament</u> 2 (1964) 93-98.

Schubert, H. von. <u>Der Kommunismus der Wiedertäufer im Münster und seine Quellen</u>. Sitzungsberichte der Heidelberger Akademie der Wissenschaften; Phil. Hist. Klasse. 11, 1919.

Schubert, P. "The Structure and Significance of Luke 24." <u>Neutestamentliche Studien für Rudolf Bultmann</u>. Beihefte zur Zeitschrift für die neutestamentliche Wissenschaft 21. Berlin: A. Töpelmann, 1954, 165-186.

Schürmann, H. "Das Testament des Paulus für die Kirche." <u>Traditionsgeschichtliche Untersuchungen zu synoptischen Evangelien</u>. Düsseldorf: Patmos-Verlag, 1967, 310-340.

Schweizer, E. "Zur Frage der Lukasquellen, Analyze von Luk. 15,11-32." <u>Theologische Zeitschrift</u> 4 (1948) 460-471.

Scott, C. A. "The 'Fellowship' or κοινωνία." Expository Times 36 (1923-4) 567.

Seesemann, H. Der Begriff KOINΩNIA im Neuen Testament. Beihefte zur Zeitschrift für die neutestamentliche Wissenschaft 14. Giessen: Alfred Töpelmann, 1933.

Sickenberger, J. "Judas als Stifter des Blutackers; Apg.1, 18f." Biblische Zeitschrift 18 (1929) 69-71.

Simon, M. St. Stephen and the Hellenists in the Primitive Church. London: Longmans, Green and Co., 1958.

Sparks, H. F. D. "The Semitisms of Acts." Journal of Theological Studies n.s. 1 (1950) 16-28.

_____. "The Semitisms of St. Luke's Gospel." Journal of Theological Studies 43 (1942) 129-138.

Stählin, G. "ἴσος, κτλ." Theological Dictionary of the New Testament 3 (1965) 343-355.

Stauffer, E. "Jüdisches Erbe im urchristlichen Kirchenrecht." Theologische Literaturzeitung 77 (1952) 201-206.

Strathmann, H. "μάρτυς, κτλ." Theological Dictionary of the New Testament 4 (1967) 474-514.

Talbert, C. H. Literary Patterns, Theological Themes and the Genre of Luke-Acts. Society of Biblical Literature Monograph Series 20. Missoula: Scholar's Press, 1974.

Tatum, W. B. "The Epoch of Israel: Luke i-ii and the Theological Plan of Luke-Acts." New Testament Studies 13 (1966-7) 184-195.

Teeple, H. The Mosaic Eschatological Prophet. Society of Biblical Literature Monograph Series 10. Philadelphia: Society of Biblical Literature, 1957.

Thornton, L. "The Choice of Matthias." Journal of Theological Studies 46 (1945) 51-59.

_____. The Common Life in the Body of Christ. London: Dacre Press, 1941.

Topel, J. "On the Injustice of the Unjust Steward." Catholic Biblical Quarterly 37 (1975) 216-227.

Torrey, C. The Composition and Date of Acts. Harvard Theological Studies I. Cambridge: Harvard University Press, 1916.

Tricot, A. "Sur Actes 1,15 et 25." Recherches de science religieuse 15 (1925) 166-167.

Trocmé, E. Le "Livre des Actes" et l'Histoire. Paris: Presses Universitaires de France, 1957.

Trompf, G. "La Section Médiane de l'Evangile de Luc: l'Organisation des Documents." Revue d'histoire et de religieuses 53 (1973) 141-154.

Turner, N. "The Relation of Luke I and II to Hebraic Sources and to the Rest of Luke-Acts." New Testament Studies 2 (1955-6) 100-109.

Unnik, W. C. Van. "Elements artistiques dans l'Evangile de Luc." L'Evangile de Luc. Ed. by F. Neirynck. Bibliotheca Ephemeridum Theologicarum Lovaniensium XXXII. Gembloux: J. Duculot, 1973.

_____. "Luke-Acts, a Storm Center in Contemporary Scholarship." Studies in Luke-Acts, 15-32.

_____. "The 'Book of Acts' the Confirmation of the Gospel." Novum Testamentum 4 (1960) 26-59.

Vermes, G. "Essenes--Qumran--Therapeutae." Revue de Qumran 2 (1960) 427-433.

Vielhauer, Ph. "Zum 'Paulinismus' der Apostelgeschichte." Evangelische Theologie 10 (1950-1) 1-15.

Waard, J. de. A Comparative Study of the Old Testament Text in the Dead Sea Scrolls and in the New Testament. Studies in the texts of the desert of Judah 4. Leiden: E. J. Brill, 1966.

Wanke, J. Die Emmauserzählung. Erfurter Theologische Studien 31. Leipzig: St. Benno-Verlag, 1973.

Wilckens, U. Die Missionsreden der Apostelgeschichte. Wissenschaftliche Monographien zum Alten und Neuen Testament 5. Neukirchen: Neukirchener Verlag, 1961.

_____. "Interpreting Luke-Acts in a Period of Existentialist Theology." Studies in Luke-Acts, 60-83.

Wilcox, M. The Semitisms of Acts. Oxford: Clarendon Press, 1965.

Wilder, A. "Variant Traditions of the Resurrection in Acts." Journal of Biblical Literature 62 (1943) 308-318.

Wilkin, R. "Collegia, Philosophical Schools, and Theology." The Catacombs and the Colosseum. Ed. by S. Benko and J. O'Rourke. Valley Forge: Judson Press, 1971.

Wilson, R. Mc. "Some Recent Studies in the Lucan Infancy Narratives." Studia Evangelica I. Ed. by K. Aland, F. Cross, et al. Texte und Untersuchungen 73. Berlin: Akademie-Verlag, 1959, 235-253.

_____. The Gnostic Problem. London: A. R. Mowbray, 1958.

Wilson, S. G. The Gentiles and the Gentile Mission in Luke-
    Acts. New Testament Studies Monograph Series 23.
    Cambridge: University Press, 1973.

Windisch, H. "ἕλλην." Theological Dictionary of the New
    Testament 2 (1964) 504-516.

Winter, P. "On Luke and Lukan Sources." Zeitschrift für die
    neutestamentliche Wissenschaft 47 (1956) 217-242.

_____. "Some Observations on the Language in the Birth and
    Infancy Narratives of the Third Gospel." New Testament
    Studies 1 (1954-5) 111-121.

_____. "The Proto-Source of Luke I." Novum Testamentum 1
    (1956) 184-199.

_____. "The Treatment of his Sources by the Third Evange-
    list." Studia Theologica 8 (1955) 138-172.

Zehnle, R. Peter's Pentecost Discourse. Society of Biblical
    Literature Monograph Series 15. Nashville: Abingdon,
    1971.

Zimmermann, H. "Die Sammelberichte der Apostelgeschichte."
    Biblische Zeitschrift n.f. 5 (1961) 71-82.

_____. Neutestamentliche Methodenlehre. Stuttgart:
    Katholisches Bibelwerk, 1968.